Yosano Akiko and *The Tale of Genji*

"Akiko on a Certain Day," from the early years of the Taishō period. Courtesy of Chikuma Shobō Publishing Co., Ltd.

Yosano Akiko and *The Tale of Genji*

G. G. Rowley

University of Michigan Press
Ann Arbor

Material for chapter three draws upon an article "Literary Canon and National Identity: *The Tale of Genji* in Meiji Japan," *Japan Forum* 9.1 (1997): 1-15 and is reprinted here with permission of the British Association for Japanese Studies and Routledge.

Material for chapter six first appeared in an article "Textual Malfeasance in Yosano Akiko's *Shiny aku Genji monogatari*" *Harvard Journal of Asiatic Studies* 58.1 (June 1998): 201-19 and is reprinted here with permission of the editors.

For questions or permissions, please contact um.press.perms@umich.edu

Michigan Monograph Series in Japanese Studies, Number 28

Published in the United States of America by the
University of Michigan Press
Manufactured in the United States of America
Printed on acid-free paper
First published December 2022

A CIP catalog record for this book is available from the British Library.

Library of Congress Cataloging-in-Publication Data

    Rowley, Gillian Gaye, 1960-
      Yosano Akiko and the Tale of Genji / G.G. Rowley.
        p. cm. — (Michigan monograph series in Japanese studies no. 28)
      Includes bibliographical references and index.
      ISBN 0-939512-98-X (cloth: alk. paper)
        1. Yosano, Akiko, 1878-1942—Criticism and interpretation.
      2. Murasaki Shikibu, b. 978? Genji monogatari. I. Murasaki Shikibu,
      b. 978? Genji monogatari. II. Title. III. Series.

      PL819.O8R68 2000
      895.6'144—dc21

                        99-089978

ISBN 978-0-472-03918-0 (paper : alk. paper)
ISBN 978-0-472-90307-8 (open access ebook)

https://doi.org/10.3998/mpub.12314698

Open access edition funded by the National Endowment for the Humanities/Andrew W. Mellon Foundation Humanities Open Book Program.

The University of Michigan Press's open access publishing program is made possible thanks to additional funding from the University of Michigan Office of the Provost and the generous support of contributing libraries.

To my parents

Kenneth and Nancy Rowley

"Akiko at about Age Sixty." Courtesy of Chikuma Shobō Publishing Co., Ltd.

Contents

Digital materials related to this title can be found on the
Fulcrum platform via the following citable URL:
https://doi.org/10.3998/mpub.12314698

Acknowledgements

I have been helped by many friends and scholars, in some cases for many years, in the preparation of this study. It is a pleasure, at long last, to be able to thank them. My first debt is to the Cambridge Commonwealth Trust for the scholarship that enabled me to spend three years studying at Newnham College and in the Faculty of Oriental Studies of the University of Cambridge. A Japan Foundation Dissertation Fellowship made possible a period of research in Tokyo. At that time Professor Kumasaka Atsuko, who had supervised my work on Akiko when I was an M.A. student at Japan Women's University, welcomed me back to her seminar. Professor Itsumi Kumi graciously invited me to attend her classes on Akiko at Aoyama Gakuin Women's Junior College. Professor Itsumi's dauntless energy, of a sort that invites comparison with Akiko's own, continues to be both infectious and inspiring. My debt to her many publications on Akiko will be evident in the footnotes to this study. Professor Ichikawa Chihiro has for many years been an unstinting source of learned guidance, fruitful discussion, and practical assistance. Without her generous gift of textually reliable editions of Akiko's *Shin'yaku Genji monogatari* and *Shin-shin'yaku Genji monogatari,* chapters five, six, and eight could not have been written. Professor Ichikawa also introduced me to the group of scholars who used to meet monthly to read *The Tale of Genji* under the guidance of the late Professor Teramoto Naohiko. It was a privilege to attend these meetings, and I am greatly indebted to Professor Teramoto for his patient advice on a number of difficult points.

I am grateful to Professor Edwin A. Cranston of the Department of East Asian Languages and Civilizations at Harvard University, who has encouraged me from the outset of my study of Akiko. I would also like to thank Professor Ken K. Ito of the University of Michigan and Professor Janet A. Walker of Rutgers University for their support at different stages of this project. In Cambridge, the learning and counsel of Dr. Carmen Blacker, Professor Richard Bowring, Dr. Peter Kornicki, Mr. Koyama Noboru, Dr. Stephen Large, and Dr. Mark Morris were invaluable. I am also grateful to Dr. James McMullen and Dr. Brian Powell of the University of Oxford for their careful reading of an earlier version of this study.

For warm hospitality during many visits over the years I am indebted to Professor W J. Boot and the other members of the Centre for Japanese and Korean Studies at the University of Leiden. Professor Adriana Boscaro of the Department of East Asian Studies, University Ca' Foscari, Venice, looked after me during three months of writing in the autumn of 1991, and I am grateful for her continued encouragement. Friends Julia Borossa, Charlotte Klonk, Nicola Liscutin, Gail Marshall, and Margaret Mehl have been unstinting in their support and I thank them for their generosity. Thanks also to Douglas Anthony, Janet Richards, Rosemary Smith, Mark Teeuwen, and my other colleagues in the Japanese Studies Centre of the University of Wales, Cardiff, for enabling me to take a semester of study leave in 1995, and for their consideration during the final months of writing. Charles Boyle gave me much needed help with Japanese word processing technology, for which I am most grateful.

Mrs. Kawai Noriyo and the late Dr. Kawai Tashiro of Gifu first looked after me in Japan with rare sympathy and forbearance. This book is also for them. All the mistakes and infelicities of thought and style are, of course, my own.

Abbreviations

The following abbreviations are used for multivolume series:

MBZ   *Meiji bungaku zenshū.* 100 vols. Chikuma Shobō, 1966–89.
NKBD   *Nihon koten bungaku daijiten.* 6 vols. Iwanami Shoten, 1983–85.
NKBT   *Nihon koten bungaku taikei.* 102 vols. Iwanami Shoten, 1957–68.
NKBZ   *Nihon koten bungaku zenshū.* 51 vols. Shōgakukan, 1970–76.
TYAZ   *Teihon Yosano Akiko zenshū.* 20 vols. Kōdansha, 1979–81.

References in the text:

The text of *The Tale of Genji* cited is the six-volume *Genji monogatari,* edited by Abe Akio, Akiyama Ken, and Imai Gen'e, vols. 12–17 of *Nihon koten bungaku zenshū (NKBZ),* published by Shōgakukan, 1970–76. Each quotation is identified by volume and page number, followed by the corresponding page number of the English translation by Edward G. Seidensticker, *The Tale of Genji,* 2 vols. (New York: Alfred A. Knopf, 1976). They are given in the following form: (4:345; S 662). Unless otherwise identified, however, all translations are my own.

References to the collected works of Yosano Akiko are to *Teihon Yosano Akiko zenshū (TYAZ),* ed. Kimata Osamu, 20 vols. (Kōdansha, 1979–81). They are given by volume and page number in the following form: (1:299).

Unless otherwise noted, the place of publication of Japanese works is Tokyo.

Preface to the Open Access Edition

Yosano Akiko and The Tale of Genji was first published in 2000. I remain indebted to Bruce Willoughby, then Executive Editor of the Center for Japanese Studies Publications Program at the University of Michigan, for his expert guidance through the process of turning an accepted manuscript into a published book; and to Seiko Semones for her beautiful jacket design. I should also like to thank reviewers Janine Beichman (*Journal of Asian Studies*), Maria-Teresa Orsi (*Asiatica Venetiana*), Donald Richie (*The Japan Times*), Laurel Rasplica Rodd (*Monumenta Nipponica*), and Anne Walthall (*Bulletin of the School of Oriental and African Studies*) for their forbearance and generosity.

To those readers who politely took issue with what I wrote—most notably Janine Beichman—I really am grateful. It is infinitely better to be disagreed with than ignored. Janine's creative and satisfying solutions to the difficulty of translating Akiko's poems have convinced me that she was right to suggest that I had pushed my argument too far and that Akiko was, as Janine put it, "someone who understood how it is possible to wholly love more than one thing."

Nonetheless, in this open access edition I have refrained from any significant rewriting. Errors and omissions kindly pointed out by reviewers and colleagues have been corrected, and I have also taken the opportunity to include some bibliographical references that I failed to mention in the footnotes to the original publication. During the twelve years I spent researching and writing *Akiko and Genji*, it was my good fortune to live for extended periods in half a dozen countries and more than a dozen different rooms in dormitories, flats, and other people's houses. Occasionally losing track of things I'd read was the price of such a peripatetic life.

A wealth of new research on the nineteenth- and twentieth-century reception of *The Tale of Genji* has been published since 2000 and I cannot claim to have kept up with it all. In English, Michael Emmerich's *The Tale of Genji: Translation, Canonization, and World Literature* is a wide-ranging and stimulating guide. Midorikawa Machiko's "Coming to Terms with the Alien" is the most incisive analysis of translations of *Genji* from Akiko's *Shin'yaku* (1912–13) through Royall Tyler's English version (2001.) In Japanese, I should particularly like to direct interested readers to the work of Kannotō Akio, Emeritus Professor of Atomi University. Since 2001, Professor Kannotō has published a series of research notes and essays on the subject of Akiko and *Genji* that provide a vastly more detailed account of the material covered in my book. All of his essays to date are listed in the revised bibliography.

References to Akiko's collected works are to the *Teihon Yosano Akiko zenshū* listed in the bibliography. Most recently, Akiko's writings have been published with those of her husband, Yosano Hiroshi, in *Tekkan Akiko zenshū*, edited by a team led by the indefatigable Itsumi Kumi. This new collected works runs to 32 volumes plus 7 supplementary volumes and was published by Benseisha, 2001–19.

Tokyo
September 2020

Introduction: *The Tale of Genji* in the Life and Work of Yosano Akiko

露しけき葎か宿の琴の音に秋を添へたる鈴むしのこゑ

Tsuyu shigeki mugura ga yado no koto no ne ni
  aki o soetaru suzumushi no koe. (1:299)

To strains of the koto from a house amid dew-drenched vines
  the cry of the bell cricket adds its autumnal plaint.

源氏をば一人となりて後に書く紫女年若くわれは然らず

Genji oba hitori to narite nochi ni kaku
  Shijo toshi wakaku ware wa shikarazu. (7:156)

Writing Genji alone, left behind
  Murasaki was young; I am not.

Some people are one-book people; their lives and their work are dominated, usually with conscious complicity, by a single book. William Pitt, first Earl of Chatham (1708–78), seems to have found a "politician's *vade-mecum*" in Spenser's *Faerie Queene*.[1] Umberto Eco, despite the vast range of reference apparent in all that he wrote, insisted that the guiding star of it all was Gérard de Nerval's *Sylvie* (1853).[2] Kujō Tanemichi (1507–94), when asked by Satomura Jōha (1527–1602) what he was currently reading, what he regarded as the most valuable

1. Geoffrey Shepherd, introduction to *An Apology for Poetry,* by Sir Philip Sidney (Manchester: Manchester University Press, 1973), 1.
2. Remarks in the seminar following his 1990 Tanner lectures, Robinson College, University of Cambridge, 9 March 1990. The point is not so firmly stressed in the printed version of Eco's remarks, *Interpretation and Overinterpretation,* ed. Stefan Collini (Cambridge: Cambridge University Press, 1992), 147–48. In his 1993 Charles Eliot Norton lectures, however, Eco returns to the subject:

   I read *[Sylvie]* at the age of twenty and still keep rereading it.... By now I know every comma and every secret mechanism of that novella.... Every time I pick up *Sylvie* ... I fall in love with it again, as if I were reading it for the first time.

   Six Walks in the Fictional Woods (Cambridge: Harvard University Press, 1994), 11–12. Gérard de Nerval was the pseudonym of the French writer Gerard Labrunie (1808–55).

reference for poets, and whom he would most welcome as a companion of his leisure hours, answered *"Genji, Genji,* Genji."[3]

Yosano Akiko (1878–1942), had she ever been asked a similar set of questions, could with equal sincerity and accuracy simply have repeated Tanemichi's reply. The poems cited above, from the beginning and the end of Akiko's literary life, bracket the career of this author, another one-book person. Her book, too, was *The Tale of Genji.*

The first poem is Akiko's earliest known published poem. When it appeared in the September 1895 issue of the literary journal *Bungei kurabu,* she was seventeen years old. One commentator suggests that the poem has much in common with a poem from the *Murasaki Shikibu shū,*[4] a "reply to someone who wished to borrow a koto for a while, asking if [she] might come and learn from me":

露しげきよもぎが中の虫の音をおぼろけにてや人の尋ねむ

Tsuyu shigeki yomogi ga naka no mushi no ne o
oboroke nite ya hito no tazunemu.[5]
Would you seek out the sound, so ordinary,
    of the insect amid dew-drenched wormwood?

---

3. The anecdote is recorded by Matsunaga Teitoku (1571–1653), a disciple of Tanemichi, in his *Taionki:*

> Always after meals he would be leaning over his desk, morning and night reading *Genji.* Time and again he said, "There is nothing so fascinating as this *monogatari.* Even after more than sixty years I do not tire of it. Reading it, I feel as if I were living in the Engi (901-23) era." Once [Satomura] Jōha Hokkyō called upon him and said, "What are you reading?"
> *"Genji."*
> Then he asked, "What is the most valuable reference for poets?"
> *"Genji."*
> And then again, "Whom would you most welcome as a companion of your leisure hours?"
> *"Genji."*
> Three times he gave the same answer.

Taionki, ed. Odaka Toshio, NKBT95:44.

4. Itsumi Kumi, "Hiroshi, Akiko no tegami kara mita Akiko *Genji,*" *Komabano,* no. 33 (Tōkyō to Kindai Bungaku Hakubutsukan, 1982): 3; and "Yosano Akiko no *Genji monogatari* kōgoyaku ni tsuite," *Kokugakuin zasshi* 94.1 January 1993): 15.

5. *Murasaki Shikibu shū,* poem no. 3, in Murasaki Shikibu, *Murasaki Shikibu nikki Murasaki Shikibu shū,* ed. Yamamoto Ritatsu, Shinchō Nihon koten shūsei (Shinchōsha, 1980), 200.

Striking though the resemblances are, however, it seems more likely that Akiko's poem is an allusive variation on a poem that appears in the 'Yokobue' (The Flute) chapter of *Genji*. One autumn evening, Yūgiri visits Kashiwagi's widow, the Second Princess. He is received by the Princess's mother Miyasudokoro. Yūgiri plays on the koto a strain that he had often heard Kashiwagi play, and he suggests that the Princess play something too, but her response is reluctant and brief. As he prepares to leave, Miyasudokoro presents him with a flute that had been a favorite of Kashiwagi and he sounds a few notes on the instrument. Miyasudokoro replies with the following poem:

露しげきむぐらの宿にいにしへの秋にかはらぬ虫の声かな

Tsuyu shigeki mugura no yado ni inishie no
aki ni kawaranu mushi no koe kana. (4:345; S 662)
In the house covered in dew-drenched vines
the cry of insects is unchanged from autumns past.

The "house covered in dew-drenched vines;" the season, autumn; the cry of the insects—in all these respects Akiko's poem is identical to the poem from 'Yokobue.' Whereas Miyasudokoro's poem is a specific response to the notes Yūgiri plays on Kashiwagi's flute, Akiko's poem epitomizes the events of that evening and adds a conceit of her own, that the cry of the bell cricket/the notes sounded on the flute "add" autumn, which is to say a feeling of sadness and loss. No "Sumagaeri" reader Akiko: even in her late teens she was sufficiently well versed in the classics to enrich this first of her published poems with a sophisticated allusion to a scene from the latter half of *Genji*.[6]

The second of the two poems was written forty years later in 1935 when Akiko was fifty-seven years old. The meaning is fairly straightforward: "Shijo," that is, Murasaki Shikibu, "was young when she wrote *Genji*, but I am not." In describing Murasaki as a widow like herself, Akiko draws upon one of the legends, or theories, concerning the composition of *The Tale of Genji*, according to which Murasaki began work on *Genji* after losing her husband Fujiwara no Nobutaka (born 947?) in 1001. More recently, Gotō Shōko has estimated that

6. A *Suma-gaeri* reader gets as far as 'Suma,' the twelfth chapter of *Genji*, and then gives up.

Murasaki was just over thirty years old, which is to say that by the standards of life expectancy of her day, she was entering middle age when she became a widow.[7] In Akiko's own estimation, gleaned from her 1928 essay "Murasaki Shikibu shinkō" (A New Study of Murasaki Shikibu, 12:478–5 08), Murasaki would have been no more than twenty-three or -four in 1001. In that same essay, Akiko writes that she believes Murasaki may have begun writing *Genji* even before her marriage to Nobutaka. For the purposes of the 1935 poem, however, she accepts the notion that Murasaki began writing *Genji* to console herself following the loss of her husband.

In this poem the speaker explicitly compares herself to Murasaki. The subject of *kaku* is deliberately left vague, allowing the reader to infer that both *Shijo* and *ware* are "writing" *Genji*. The identity of the act is total; the only difference is that *Shijo* is young, whereas *ware* is not. No longer young, in her own estimation at least, Akiko had begun her final attempt at a modern Japanese translation of *The Tale of Genji* in 1932. Devastated by the death of her husband in 1935, she thought of giving up the project, but, never one to shirk work, she persevered, and the final volume was published in 1939, less than a year before she had the cerebral hemorrhage that left her an invalid for the rest of her life. In this poem, Akiko reveals how thoroughly she had come to see her work on *Genji* as a major and vital part of her life.

These two poems, one from the very beginning and the other written towards the end of Akiko's career, are, I think, emblematic of the life that was lived in between. My reason for making this point is that she is so often described in other terms. To most readers, as well as to many scholars, Akiko is known principally as a "poetess of passion" (*jōnetsu no joryū kajin*), a "new woman" (*atarashii onna*),[8] or even a

---

7. Gotō Shōko, "Murasaki Shikibu jiten," in *Genji monogatari jiten,* ed. Akiyama Ken, Bessatsu kokubungaku series, no. 36 (Gakutosha, 1989), 304–5.
8. An example of this view is Nishio Yoshihito, *Akiko, Tomiko, Meiji no atarashii onna— ai to bungaku—*(Yūhikaku, 1986). On the origin of the epithet "new woman" and for an account of Akiko's participation in contemporary discussions concerning women's roles, see Laurel Rasplica Rodd, "Yosano Akiko and the Taishō Debate over the 'New Woman'," in *Recreating Japanese Women, 1600–194:;,* ed. Gail Lee Bernstein (Berkeley and Los Angeles: University of California Press, 1991), 175–98.

suffragette.[9] In June of 1901, she ran away from her home in Sakai and traveled alone to Tokyo to be with her mentor, later her husband, Yosano Hiroshi (1873–1935), then known by his pen name Tekkan. Later that year she published what has remained her most celebrated work, a collection of 399 *tanka* entitled *Midaregami* (Tangled Hair). It might almost be said that this collection dogged her for the rest of her life and continues, long after her death, to overwhelm her reputation. That it does contain poems of passion can hardly be denied:

> くろ髪の千すぢの髪のみだれ髪かつおもひみだれおもひみだるる
> *Kurokami no chisuji no kami no midaregami*
>   *katsu omoimidare omoimidaruru.* (1:43)
> A thousand strands of black hair, tangled hair
>   like them my thoughts, tangling and entangled.

> いとせめてもゆるがままにもえしめよ斯くぞ覚ゆる暮れて行く春
> *Ito semete moyuru ga mama ni moeshimeyo*
>   *kaku zo oboyuru kurete yuku haru.* (1:53)
> Pressed relentlessly, this burning shall burn me up!
>   Such at least is how I feel as spring approaches its end.

> みだれごこちまどひごこちぞ頻なる百合ふむ神に乳おほひあへず
> *Midaregokochi madoigokochi zo shikiri naru*
>   *yuri fumu kami ni chichi ōiaezu.* (1:8)
>   Tangled desires,
> Blind, errant desires
>   Ever upon me:
> From the god who tramples lilies
> I cannot cover my breasts.[10]

As even this meager sampling suggests, some of the *Midaregami* poems are vivid, sensitive, and evocative, while others, such as "the god who tramples lilies," are heavy-handed and suffer from an excess

9. For the first All Japan Women's Suffrage Conference, held 27 April 1930, Akiko composed the "Women's Suffrage Song" *(Fusen no uta)* that is apparently still sung today. See Ichikawa Fusae, "Yosano Akiko-shi no omoide," *Teihon Yosano Akiko zenshū geppō,* no. 8 Only 1980): 3–6; and Yamamoto Chie, *Yama no ugoku hi kitaru—hyōden Yosano Akiko* (Ōtsuki Shoten, 1986), especially 211–13, for an account of Akiko's involvement with the women's suffrage movement in Japan.
10. Translation by Edwin A. Cranston, "Young Akiko: The Literary Debut of Yosano Akiko," *Literature East and West* 18.1 (March 1974): 39. A slightly revised version of "Young

of (no doubt sincerely felt) passion. In later years Akiko was deeply embarrassed by her early poetry. As early as 1915 she admitted that *Midaregami* contained "many juvenile poems and I cannot but blush" (13:37). A selection of 2,963 of her poems that she made in 1938 contains only fourteen from that collection.[11] Nonetheless, *Midaregami* remains easily the most famous of the thirty-some collections of poetry that were published during her lifetime.[12] Whatever other qualities the *Midaregami* poems might possess, it was their passion that was to establish and distinguish Akiko's reputation for most of her readers most of the time.

No less so for scholars of modern Japanese literature is Akiko the great "poetess of passion." Exegesis of Akiko's *tanka*, is heavily biographical. Masatomi Ōyō's *Akiko no koi to shi:jissetsu Midaregami*, which might be translated as *Akiko: her passion and her poetry—the real story behind Midaregami* is a type-title.[13] The view of literature that informs such works is that a single, correct reading of a poem can be found if only one has access to sufficient biographical detail and preferably some romantic escapade. Hence, for example, debate raged for years as to whether or not Akiko managed to slip away from

---

Akiko" appears in Edwin A. Cranston's collection *The Secret Island and the Enticing Flame: Worlds of Memory, Discovery, and Loss in Japanese Poetry* (Ithaca: Cornell East Asia Series, 2008), 19–49.

11. Yosano Akiko, *Yosano Akiko kashū* (1938; rev. ed., Iwanami Shoten, 1985). See Akiko's "Atogaki" (361–62) to this selection for more disparaging remarks about her own early poetry.

12. A comprehensive list can be found in Irie Haruyuki, *Yosano Akiko no bungaku* (Ōfūsha, 1983), 136–90.

13. Masatomi Ōyō, *Akiko no koi to shi: jissetsu Midaregami* (San'ō Shobō, 1967). Masatomi Ōyō (1881–1967) was connected to the Yosano ménage by his marriage to Hayashi Takino (1878–1966), who had been Tekkan's common-law wife for a brief period. In 1889 Tekkan took a job teaching Japanese language and classical Chinese at a school for girls run by his brother in Tokuyama. There he formed a relationship with Asada Sada, who bore him a daughter in August 1899. The child died a month after birth and the two separated soon after. Two months later, in October 1899, Tekkan left Tokuyama for Tokyo with Takino, who had been a student of his at the school. Takino had a son by Tekkan in September 1900 but early in June 1901 she took the boy with her and returned to her parents' home. Akiko arrived at Tekkan's house in Tokyo shortly thereafter, but their marriage was not formally registered until 13 January 1902.

her family for an illicit few days alone with Tekkan at an inn on the outskirts of Kyoto before they were married. Various interpretations of Akiko's early poems, such as the following, were cited as "evidence" for one view or the other:

春寒のふた日を京の山ごもり梅にふさはぬわが髪の乱れ

Harusamu no futahi o kyō no yamagomori
　　　ume ni fusawanu waga kami no midare. (1:56)
　　In the cold of spring
Two days we spent secluded
　　In the hills of Kyō
Plum blossoms were poorly matched
With the wild tangle of my hair.[14]

The debate was brought to an end only with the publication of a number of Akiko's letters from the period in question, demonstrating in convincing detail that the meeting had indeed taken place.[15]

Questions of this sort—whether or not she had been trysting premaritally and "adulterously" with Tekkan; whether her relationship with Arishima Takeo (1878–1923)—subject of a book[16] and the 1988 film *Hana no ran* (Flowers in Riot)—was more than platonic or not; who the "young preacher" of the following poem might really have been:

やは肌のあつき血汐にふれも見でさびしからずや道を説く君

Yawahada no atsuki chishio ni fure mo mide
　　　sabishikarazu ya michi o toku kimi. (1:6)
　　Beneath my soft skin
Pulses the hot tide of blood
　　You have never tried
To touch; aren't you lonely
O young preacher of the Way?[17]

14. Cranston, "Young Akiko," 35.
15. See Shinma Shin'ichi, *Yosano Akiko* (Ōfūsha, 1981), 39; and Itsumi Kumi, "*Midaregami—Awatayama teisetsu to Saga no hitoyo—*," *Kokubungaku: kaishaku to kanshō* 59.2 (February 1994): 49–52. The full text of the letters appears in Satō Ryōyū, *Midaregami kō* (1956; reprint, *Kindai sakka kenkyū sōsho*, vol. 104, Nihon Tosho Sentaa, 1990), 245–80. As Itsumi notes, excerpts had been published earlier, in 1948 and 1949.
16. Nagahata Michiko, *Yume no kakehashi—Akiko to Takeo yūjō* (Shinhyōron, 1985). See also Itsumi Kumi's review of the book, "Jisshō no teiji o," *Tanka shinbun*, 10 August 1985, 6.
17. Cranston, "Young Akiko," 25.

—all of these are questions of but secondary importance. Yet at times it seems that to practitioners of this biographical mode of criticism, the sole purpose of analyzing Akiko's poems is to document every feeling, passion, and event in her love life. Evidence other than biographical, one suspects, is not only overlooked, but unwelcome.

The standard edition of Akiko's complete works fills twenty volumes and includes free-verse poetry *(shintaishi),* children's stories, a novel, her experiments in drama and her essays, as well as seven volumes of *tanka* amounting to some 25,000 poems. Of this vast oeuvre, only five collections of her poetry have received more than cursory attention;[18] overwhelmingly, it is *Midaregami* to which scholars have returned again and again.[19] The great bulk of writing about Akiko,

---

18. They are: *Midaregami;* her second collection, *Koōgi* (Little Fan, 1904): Itsumi Kumi, *Koōgi zenshaku* (Yagi Shoten, 1988); her fifth, *Maihime* (Dancing Girl, 1906): Satō Kazuo, *Yosano Akiko Maihime hyōshaku* (Meiji Shain, 1978); Itsumi Kumi, *Maihime zenshaku* (Tanka Shinbunsha, 1999); and her sixth, *Yume no hana* (Dream Flowers, 1906): Satō Kazuo, *Yume no hana kanshō* (Sōbunsha, 1988); Itsumi Kumi, *Yume no hana zenshaku* (Yagi Shoten, 1994).

19. The major postwar monographs are: Satō, *Midaregami kō;* Satake Kazuhiko, *Zenshaku Midaregami kenkyū* (Yūhōdō, 1957); Matsuda Yoshio, *Midaregami kenkyū* (Isshōdō Shoten, 1952); Satō Haruo, *Midaregami o yomu* (Kūdansha, 1959); Itsumi Kumi, *Midaregami zenshaku* (Ōfūsha, 1978; rev. ed. 1986); Itsumi Kumi, *Shin Midaregami zenshaku* (Yagi Shoten, 1996).

   The most detailed and scholarly account of *Midaregami* in a Western language is Janine Beichman's *Embracing the Firebird: Yosano Akiko and the Birth of the Female Voice in Modern Japanese Poetry* (Honolulu: University of Hawai'i Press, 2002), which covers Akiko's provincial childhood and adolescence, her meeting with Yosano Tekkan, and their ensuing amour. The final one hundred pages of Beichman's book brilliantly elucidate how the *Midaregami* collection was edited and structured. Other studies include Cranston, "Young Akiko"; Noriko Takeda, "The Japanese Reformation of Poetic Language: Yosano Akiko's *Tangled Hair* as Avant-Garde Centrality," *A Flowering Word: The Modernist Expression in Stéphane Mallarmé, T. S. Eliot, and Yosano Akiko* (New York: Peter Lang, 2000), 25–55; Leith Morton, "The Canonization of Yosano Akiko's *Midaregami,*" *Japanese Studies* 20.3 (2000): 237–54, and "Naturalizing the Alien: Yosano Akiko's Revolution in Verse," *The Alien Within: Representations of the Exotic in Twentieth-Century Japanese Literature* (Honolulu: University of Hawai'i Press, 2009), 43–72; and Nicholas Albertson, "Tangled *Kami:* Yosano Akiko's Supernatural Symbolism," *U.S.-Japan Women's Journal,* no. 47 (2014): 28–44. In German, see Katharina May, *Die Erneuerung der Tanka-Poesie in der Meiji-Zeit und die Lyrik Yosano Akikos* (Wiesbaden: Otto Harrassowitz, 1975), 110–245; in Dutch, Henri Kerlen, *De talloze treden naar mijn hart* (Soest: Kairos, 1987); and in French, Claire Dodane, *Yosano Akiko: Poète de la passion et figure de proue du féminisme japonais* (Paris: Publications Orientalistes de France, 2000), 68–133.

both scholarly and popular, still concerns itself with the details of her love affair with Tekkan; the "real story" behind the *Midaregami* collection; and a few years of the Yosanos strained life together, usually up until their trip to Europe in 1912.[20] An otherwise serious bibliography of Akiko studies even lists an article entitled "You too could be Yosano Akiko—why not give burning passion a try?"[21] Not until 1986 was a book published about Akiko that was based on a reading of her essays and journalism.[22] And among the popular accounts of Akiko's life published since then has been the three-volume comic book *Koi murasaki* (Deep Purple Passion).[23] Best-selling *tanka* poet Tawara Machi (1962–) has published a modern Japanese translation of *Midaregami*.[24] A companion volume, consisting of fifty-five of these poems accompanied by an equivalent number of photographs of nude women, takes as its title Tawara's extraordinarily free rendition of the *Midaregami* poem cited above: *Moeru hada o daku koto mo*

Partial English translations of *Midaregami* include: Shio Sakanishi, *Tangled Hair* (Boston: Marshall Jones, 1935); Sanford Goldstein and Seishi Shinoda, *Tangled Hair: Selected Tanka from Midaregami* (1971; rpt. Rutland, Vermont & Tokyo: Charles E. Tuttle, 1987); Hiroaki Sato and Burton Watson, ed., *From the Country of Eight Islands* (Garden City: Anchor Press/Doubleday, 1981), 431–35; Dennis Maloney and Hide Oshiro, *Tangled Hair: Love Poems of Yosano Akiko* (Fredonia: White Pine Press, 1987); Edwin A. Cranston, "Carmine-Purple: A Translation of 'Enji-Murasaki,' the First Ninety-Eight Poems of Yosano Akiko's *Midaregami*," *Journal of the Association of Teachers of Japanese* 25.1 (1991): 91–111; and Sam Hamill and Keiko Matsui Gibson, *River of Stars: Selected Poems of Yosano Akiko* (Boston and London: Shambala, 1996), 3–101.

20. This is the extent of the acclaimed biographical novels by Satō Haruo, *Akiko mandara* (Kōdansha, 1954) and Tanabe Seiko, *Chisuji no kurokami: Waga ai no Yosano Akiko* (Bungei Shunjū, 1972), the latter translated by Meredith McKinney as *A Thousand Strands of Black Hair* (London: Thames River Press, 2012); as well as Phyllis Hyland Larson's *Yosano Akiko: The Early Years*, Ph.D. diss. University of Minnesota 1985.

21. Irie Haruyuki, "Saikin no Akiko kenkyū ni tsuite," *Tanka kenkyū geppō*, no. 20 (November 1981): 6. The article in question is "Anata mo Yosano Akiko ni … 'moeru yō na koi' shite minai?" and is to be found in *Yangu redei* 15.5 (8 March 1977): 98–100.

22. Yamamoto, *Yama no ugoku hi kitaru*. See also Ōgi Motoko, "Yosano Akiko to Taishō jaanari-zumu," in *Kindai Nihon ni okeru jaanarizumu no seijiteki kinō*, ed. Tanaka Hiroshi (Ochanomizu Shobō, 1982), 155–72; and Ichikawa Chihiro, "*Yokohama bōeki shinpō* to Akiko," *Namiki no sato*, no. 42 (June 1995): 35–41.

23. Kurahashi Yōko and Takahashi Chizuru, *Koi murasaki—Yosano Akiko monogatari*, 3 vols. (Kōdansha, 1991). The strip originally appeared in *mimi* magazine and was later published in novel form: Kurahashi Yōko, *Koi murasaki: shōsetsu Yosano Akiko* (Kōdansha, 1992).

24. Tawara Machi, *Chokoreeto-go yaku Midaregami*, 2 vols. (Kawade Shobō Shinsha, 1998).

naku jinsei o kataritsuzukete sabishikunai no (Never even making love to skin burning with desire, just talking on and on about life, aren't you missing something?)[25]

Another closely related view of Akiko's early poetry, and of *Midaregami* in particular, is that it represents a radical departure from tradition and is the work of a literary revolutionary. This is a view that has appealed particularly to Western commentators. Atsumi Ikuko and Graeme Wilson, for example, maintain that both the "diction and vocabulary [of the *Midaregami* poems] were revolutionary."[26] Janine Beichman writes, "[a]s the young Akiko had broken the taboo on speaking about passionate love, so now the middle-aged Akiko broke the taboo on speaking in public of the act of birth."[27] It is of course true that the subject matter of her compositions and some of the vocabulary with which her concerns are articulated both shocked and excited the poetry reading public of the time. A review of *Midaregami* in the September 1901 issue of *Kokoro no hana* thundered:

> Morality is the foundation of a society; if there is a decline in morality, on what basis can the state be preserved, even briefly? In the first place, this book depicts many instances of obscene behavior and shameful conduct; moreover it is damaging to human decency. I have no hesitation in adjudging it a poison to public morality.[28]

Today, more than a hundred years after *Midaregami* was first published, modern admirers still romanticize what they see as Akiko's disregard for the poetic and moral conventions of the time. To wit, this brief excerpt from Tanikawa Shuntarō's paean to Akiko:

> *Karada no oku fukaku kakusareta sei no himitsu o*
> *shichigochō ga tokihanatsu*
> *koi yue ni anata wa furui ishō o nugisuteta*
> *mabushisugiru sono rashin wa*

25. Tawara Machi and Nomura Sakiko, *Moeru hada o daku koto mo nakujinsei o kataritsu-zukete sabishikunai no* (Kawade Shobō Shinsha, 1998).
26. Atsumi Ikuko and Graeme Wilson, "The Poetry of Yosano Akiko," *Japan Quarterly* 21.2 (April–June 1974): 182.
27. Janine Beichman, "Yosano Akiko: Return to the Female," *Japan Quarterly* 36.2 (April–June 1990): 224.
28. "Kashū sōmakuri," review of *Midaregami,* in *Kokoro no hana* 4.9 (September 1901): 77.

toki o hedatete ima mo kagayaite iru.[29]
The secrets of life hidden deep within your body
were set free by seven-five rhythms;
for love you threw off old raiment;
too blindingly bright, that naked body
shines still, through time now long past.

Of course there is much that is new in Akiko's poetry. The *Midaregami* poems could not be slipped unnoticed into a court anthology. Yet Akiko's most memorable images of passion—those of tangled hair, *midaregami*, and of besetting love, *ito semete*—have a history that is routinely overlooked, and this oversight continues to distort our view of Akiko and her work. The following poem of Izumi Shikibu (born 977?) is a famous example of similarly tangled hair:

黒髪のみだれもしらずうちふせばまづかきやりし人ぞこひしき
Kurokami no midare mo shirazu uchifuseba
    mazu kakiyarishi hito zo koishiki.[30]
I fling myself down,
Heedless of the wild disorder
    Of my long black hair,
And soon I'm yearning once again
For him who used to stroke it smooth.[31]

And Ono no Komachi (fl. ca. 850) employed the *ito semete* image to stunning effect in one of her best-known poems:

いとせめて恋しきときはうばたまの夜の衣を返してぞ着る
Ito semete koishiki toki wa ubatama no
    yoru no koromo o kaeshite zo kiru.[32]
When love presses me,
Relentless in the glistening night,
    I take off my robe,
Then lie down to sleep again,
Wearing it inside out.[33]

29. Tanikawa Shuntarō, untitled poem in *Meiji no shiika* (Gakken, 1981), 12.
30. *Izumi Shikibu shū*, poem no. 27, in Izumi Shikibu, *Izumi Shikibu nikki Izumi Shikibu shū*, ed. Nomura Seiichi, Shinchō Nihon koten shūsei (Shinchōsha, 1981), 98.
31. Translation by Edwin A. Cranston, "The Dark Path: Images of Longing in Japanese Love Poetry," *Harvard Journal of Asiatic Studies* 5 (1975): 81.
32. Poem no. 554, in *Kokinwakashū*, ed. Ozawa Masao, *NKBZ* 7:236.
33. Cranston, "The Dark Path," 75.

However nakedly new Akiko's poems may be, they are at the same time unmistakable allusive variations on these much older models. My point is not merely that her allusions are sometimes missed, but that there are vital forces at work in Akiko's poetry that have been ignored in the desire to see her *tanka,* and her life, as new, radical, taboo-breaking. As with the biographical interpretations, the important is passed over in favor of the insignificant; for as Helen Vendler has written, "[t]aboo-breaking is not in itself a poetic task. No poem is improved by having a shattered taboo in it.... . The poet does well by perception in vesting it in language, or does not. The poem finds a language for its experience, or it does not."[34]

This characterization of Akiko as a totem figure of modernity, whether as "poetess of passion" or trailblazer of the New, distorts our view of her life and work in two major ways. In the first place, as is clear even from the few poems already cited, it fosters the misreading of that portion of her oeuvre for which she is best known, her poetry. And second, it diverts attention from an equally important part of her career, that part devoted not to poetry but to work on the Japanese classics, in particular *The Tale of Genji.*

Fortunately, the first of these biases is slowly but steadily being set straight through the painstaking work of Professor Ichikawa Chihiro. Ichikawa, whose training as a *Genji* scholar uniquely qualifies her for the task, has methodically scrutinized the vast corpus of Akiko's poetry, identifying her sources in *Genji* and revising the interpretations of commentators who were unaware of these sources.[35] One example of Ichikawa's approach must suffice here. In her first article, Ichikawa argues that a number of poems in the *Midaregami* collection have an interesting parallel in the portrait of Ukifune in the Uji chapters of *Genji.* Ichikawa recalls that the beauty of Ukifune's hair is stressed at many points during the

---

34. Helen Vendler, *The Music of What Happens* (Cambridge: Harvard University Press, 1988), 301.
35. See the essays collected in Ichikawa Chihiro, *Yosano Akiko to Genji monogatari* (Ryūgasaki: Kokuken Shuppan, 1998), 3–194. In English, Ichikawa Chihiro, trans. G. G. Rowley, "Yosano Akiko and *The Tale of Genji*: Ukifune and *Midaregami*," *Journal of the Association of Teachers of Japanese* 28.2 (1994): 27–43.

account of her life in *Genji:* when she is found by the Uji river she is described as someone with "hair that was long and lustrous" (6:270; S 1044). Some months later, one of the nuns who has taken her in combs out her hair. "Although it had been tied back so unbecomingly and left that way, it was not so very tangled, and when combed right to the ends, it was lustrous and bright" (6:287; S 1051), and so on. As its very title suggests, *Midaregami* contains many poems about women's hair. But the classical antecedents of Akiko's metaphors of hair have gone unnoticed. With Ukifune's tale in mind, Ichikawa suggests that a different interpretation of the following *Midaregami* poem-one which has consistently been seen as a display of youthful egotism-is possible:

その子二十櫛にながるる黒髪のおごりの春のうつくしきかな
Sono ko hatachi kushi ni nagaruru kurokami no
   ogori no haru no utsukushiki kana. (1:4)
Twenty that girl; the black hair flowing through her comb
   the beauty of her proud and glorious spring.

Ichikawa cites Kimata Osamu's comment: "Although one might assume that *sono ko* here refers to someone else, [Akiko] in fact writes of herself."[36] Haga Tōru takes a similar view: "Referring to herself, *sono ko hatachi* ... proudly applauds the gorgeousness of her own youth, head held so high as to be arrogant... ."[37] For Ichikawa the *Genji* scholar, however, *sono ko* clearly indicates "the existence in Akiko's mind of an object other than herself":

If we interpret Akiko's *sono ko hatachi* broadly and refrain from insisting on a strictly biographical reading, Ukifune might well be included in the field of reference of this expression. The poem then becomes one which provides a gentle lesson in life, a rich, reso-nant, delightful poem in praise of youth. "That girl is twenty. The black hair loosened by her comb is thick and shines with youthful beauty. This very moment is life's glorious spring!"[38]

36. Kirnata Osarnu, *Kindai tanka no kanshō to hihyō* (Meiji Shoin, 1964), 147.
37. Haga Tōru, *Midaregami no keifu* (Bijutsu Koronsha, 1981), 20.
38. Ichikawa Chihiro, "*Midaregami* to 'Ukifune,'" 109.

Ichikawa's work has been received with respect in the world of *Genji* scholarship.[39] Her discoveries have, however, been greeted with resounding silence by scholars of modern literature in Japan. The part played by classical literature, especially *The Tale of Genji*, in the formation of Akiko's poetic voice is acknowledged at best with remarks such as "[her] poetic style, especially in her early works from *Midaregami* to *Yume no hana* is, on the whole, vaguely reminiscent of the tone of the *Shinkokinshū*."[40] Although much remains to be done, Ichikawa has observed that *Genji* was an ever present part of Akiko's mental landscape, that an awareness of the depth and magnitude of Akiko's attachment to *Genji* demands reinterpretation of a considerable portion of her massive poetic output.[41]

The aim of this book is not so much to contribute to Ichikawa's project as to elaborate the perspective that underlies it, to bring into clearer view those aspects of Akiko's life and work that still remain in the shadow of her reputation as a poet. I shall attempt to delineate the full range of her involvement with *Genji*, and I shall argue that this involvement was the bedrock upon which her literary career was built. As Akiko herself recalls, "From the age of eleven or twelve, Murasaki Shikibu has been my teacher, and I feel that I have had *The Tale of Genji* from [her] very mouth" (19:258). By 1909, in her thirty first year, she already knew that translating and explicating *Genji* would be her "whole life's work."[42] Indeed, the very idea that a woman could live by her writing was suggested to her, she says, by her reading of the Heian classics (14:440).

One looks at a chronology of Akiko's life and sees a steady increase in the amount of work she did on *Genji* and other classics. There are the translations, of course, most of them multivolume works in their original form; as well as several volumes of texts in the *Nihon koten zenshū* series that she edited; and her introductions to some of these volumes; and enough learned articles on Murasaki Shikibu and

---

39. See, for example, the review by Murai Toshihiko, *Tekkan to Akiko*, no. 5 (1999): 143–46.
40. Shinma, *Yosano Akiko*, 130.
41. Ichikawa Chihiro, "*Midaregami* to 'Ukifune,'" 105, 112.
42. Letter to Kobayashi Tenmin, 18 September 1909, in Ueda Ayako and Itsumi Kumi, eds., *Yosano Hiroshi Akiko shokanshū: Tenmin bunko zō* (Yagi Shoten, 1983), 21.

other Heian authors to form a separate volume; and a commentary on *Genji* that went up in flames.[43] It is of course impossible to calculate the amount of time these activities, presented with such misleading concision in the chronologies, must have consumed; nonetheless, one is tempted to conclude that in the latter half of her career, Akiko must have devoted far more of her working hours to *Genji* and the classics than to poetry. One looks in vain, however, in works of Akiko criticism for anything like proportional representation of this shift. The familiar poet is everywhere in evidence, jotting down the outpourings of passion, while the scholar (and mother of eleven), bent over her desk in projects of research, translation, and editing-the "core of my work," as she herself once put it[44]—that consumed months and years of her time, is hardly to be glimpsed. Thus it was that the more I studied Akiko, the stronger became the sense of the astonishing speed with which the lived texture of a person's life—even the life of some one deemed a major literary figure—can disappear from the record; and the more important it seemed to retrieve now what remains to be retrieved, before a cornerstone of her life is reduced to a few items in her bibliography, ultimately to be buried under a myth.

It must be admitted, of course, that the fault is not entirely that of her biographers and admirers. Akiko herself is reticent about her work with *Genji* and other classics. On the nature of poetry and the craft of composition she has written volumes.[45] Of her work on *Genji*,

---

43. A list of Akiko's publications on *Genji* and other works from the classical canon may be found in Appendix A.

44. Yosano Akiko, "Shin'yaku Genji monogatari no nochi ni," in *Shin'yaku Genji monogatari* (Kanao Bun'endō, 1912–13), 4:2. The afterword is numbered separately from the text at the end of the volume. A complete translation of the afterword may be found in Appendix B.

45. Yosano Akiko, *Uta no tsukuriyō* (How to Compose Poetry, 1915); *Tanka sanbyakkō* (Lectures on Three Hundred Tanka, 1916); *Akiko utabanashi* (Akiko's Talks on Poetry, 1919); "Tanka no kanshō to tsukurikata," (The Appreciation and Composition of Tanka, 1929–30). See *TYAZ* 13 for all these works. In English, see Makoto Ueda, *Modern Japanese Poets and the Nature of Literature* (Stanford: Stanford University Press, 1983), 53–94; and two articles by Laurel Rasplica Rodd, " 'On Poetry,' by Yosano Akiko, with a Selection of Her Poems," in *New Leaves: Studies and Translations of Japanese Literature in Honor of Edward Seidensticker,* ed. Aileen Gatten and Anthony Hood Chambers, Michigan Monograph Series in Japanese Studies, no. 11 (Ann Arbor: Center

she has virtually nothing to say—with the result that much of the information that she might so easily have recorded died with her. For this reason, much of the work that has gone into this study has consisted of scrutinizing her translations, studying her scholarship, and searching the works of those who have written about her for snippets of information or leads to other possible sources.

With what I have retrieved, I have attempted to situate Akiko's formative childhood reading of *Genji* within a history of other readers and responses; and in order that Akiko's work on *Genji* be seen as something other than the automatic outpourings of a singular genius, I have tried to sketch the web of relationships through which she was connected to the literary milieu of her day. And finally, I have tried to demonstrate the importance that *The Tale of Genji* held in Akiko's own conception of herself and her work, throughout her entire working lifetime.

The result, I hope, will be to demonstrate that *The Tale of Genji* provided Akiko with her conception of herself as a writer and inspired many of her most significant literary projects, and that facile descriptions of Akiko as "poetess of passion" and "new woman" will no longer suffice as assessments of her life and work.

Chapter One:
The Tale of Genji:
Women's Romance, Men's Classic

春曙抄に伊勢をかさねてかさ足らぬ枕はやがてくづれけるかな

Shunjoshō ni Ise o kasanete kasataranu
   makura wa yagate kuzurekeru kana. (1: 127)[1]
Piled the *Ise* on *The Pillow Book* but it wasn't pile enough;
   no sooner I lay down than my pillow collapsed!

美を愛ずる女にしかず源氏をば男作らず法師の書かず

Bi o mezuru onna ni shikazu Genji oba
   otoko tsukurazu hōshi no kakazu. (5:562)
Genji: made not by man; written not by monk;
   neither can equal a woman enamored of beauty.

The first of the two poems above evokes a woman's world of *monogatari* reading reminiscent of that described centuries earlier by Murasaki Shikibu in the 'Hotaru' (Fireflies) chapter of *Genji:* a young woman spends the day alternately reading and dozing, her books spread about the room, some of them piled up as a makeshift pillow (3:202; S 436–37). It is a world in which *The Tale of Genji* might be said to exist, as it had for nearly a millennium, as a "romance."

In the second poem-in words and inflections that almost carica-ture the heavily sinified style of monks and men—Akiko is concerned to defend *Genji* from men who would claim it as their own work.[2]

---

1. The *Shunshoshō* (c. 1674) is an edition of Sei Shōnagon's *Makura no sōshi,* with com-mentary, compiled by Kitamura Kigin (1624–1705). The most widely circulated text of *Makura no sōshi* during the Edo period, its interpretations were considered "definitive" (*NKBD* 5:515). An unvoiced second syllable *(Shunshoshō)* is the preferred pronunciation today; *furigana* in Akiko's *Koigoromo* (Love's Raiment, 1905; *TYAZ* 1:127) collection, where this poem first appeared, indicate a voiced sound and so I have transcribed it as *Shunjoshō.*
2. For example, the theories that Murasaki's patron Fujiwara no Michinaga (966–1027), or her father Fujiwara no Tametoki (fl. c. 1000), wrote or assisted her in the writing of *Genji.*

In so doing, she limns a realm in which *Genji* is something other than a "romance" for women, the realm of *Genji* as a "classic," or, as it would come to be seen in her day, *Genji* as *koten*.[3]

An awareness of the history and vicissitudes of these two worlds that Akiko briefly illuminates, the worlds of *Genji* as women's romance and men's classic, is crucial to an understanding of the nature of the role played by *Genji* in Akiko's own life and work. In order to grasp the significance that *Genji* had for Akiko throughout her career, it is important to note that the *"Genji-world"* that she inhabited in her youth was by no means the same as that of her old age. The changes this conceptual world underwent in her lifetime can be seen clearly only against a background of earlier *Genji-worlds,* and the upheavals of the Meiji era that made possible many of the changes in Akiko's own *Genji-world.* These latter changes will be discussed in chapter three. In this chapter I will attempt a brief sketch of earlier *Genji-*worlds with the principal aim of suggesting something of the variety of readers' interactions with *Genji.*

Monogatari seem always to have been regarded as reading for women that was dangerous for women. In the preface to the *Sanbōe* (984), a collection of Buddhist tales compiled as a spiritual guide for an imperial princess in her new life as a nun, Minamoto Tamenori (941?–1011) describes *monogatari* reading as a dangerous distraction from the imperative task of attaining the tranquillity of mind that leads to enlightenment:

> To pass the time of day at a game of go may be diverting, but how fruitless to waste one's thoughts in striving and contention. The koto, too, can be a pleasant companion of an evening; but one is

---

See Ii Haruki, *Genji monogatari no densetsu* (Shōwa Shuppan, 1976), 69–90, for a careful rebuttal of these views.

3. On the history of the word *koten* in Japan, see Melanie Trede, "Terminology and Ideology: Coming to Terms with 'Classicism' in Japanese Art-Historical Writing," in *Critical Perspectives on Classicism in Japanese Painting, 1600–1700,* ed. Elizabeth Lillehoj (Honolulu: University of Hawai'i Press, 2004), 28–30; and the discussion in chapter three.

apt to grow over-fond of its music. And *monogatari*—*these* are but for the amusement of women. They flourish in greater profusion than the weeds upon the wooded graves of old, they are as numerous as the grains of sand upon the rocky strand. To creatures that lack the gift of speech they give words; to insentient objects they impart feelings—even to the trees and grasses, mountains and rivers, birds and beasts, fishes and insects. Their words flow forth unchecked, as flotsam upon the sea; unlike reeds at the river's edge, they have no root in truth. *The Old Trickster (Iga no taome), The Tosa Minister (Tosa no otodo), The Fashionable Captain (Imameki no chūjō), The Lady of the Inner Chamber (Nakai no jijū)*—these and all of their ilk describe the affairs of men and women as if they were possessed of all the beauty of flowers and butterflies. They are the very root of sin. They amount to not so much as a drop of dew in the Grove of Letters.[4]

By the latter half of the tenth century, the *monogatari* was clearly identified as a women's plaything. Murasaki Shikibu seems not to have taken issue with the designation of the genre as reading matter for women, but only with its evaluation. When Genji says that *monogatari* "have set down and preserved happenings from the age of the gods to our own" (Seidensticker's translation, 3:204; S 437),]; his comparison is with historical writing. But *monogatari* are much more than mere historical record. Genji continues:

> "*The Chronicles of Japan* are really very one-sided. But these must give you all the choice little details," he said with a smile. "At any rate, they do not simply relate the events of some person's life exactly as they happened. Rather I think that some things seen and heard of people's lives, be they good or evil, so intrigue one that they

4. Translation after T. J. Harper, "Motoori Norinaga's Criticism of the *Genji monogatari:* A Study of the Background and Critical Content of his *Genji monogatari Tama no Ogushi*" (Ph.D. diss., University of Michigan, 1971), 27; amended with reference to Minamoto Tamenori, *Sanbōe*, ed. Mabuchi Kazuo and Koizumi Hiroshi, in *Sanbōe, Chūkōsen*, ed. Mabuchi Kazuo, Koizumi Hiroshi, and Konno Tōru, vol. 31 of *Shin Nihon koten bungaku taikei*, (Iwanami Shoten, 1997), 5–6. For a complete translation, see Edward Kamens, *The Three Jewels: A Study and Translation of Minamoto Tamenori's Sanbōe*, Michigan Monograph Series in Japanese Studies, no. 2 (Ann Arbor: Center for Japanese Studies, The University of Michigan, 1988). None of the *monogatari* mentioned in this passage are extant.

cannot be shut away in the heart but make one wish to pass them on
to generations to come—and so one sets out to tell the story."[5]

And, as if in answer to Tamenori:

"Even in the Holy Law which the Buddha in his righteousness has
expounded to us, there are what we call the Partial Truths *(hōben)*
which, owing to the occasional contradictions they contain, the
unenlightened doubtless view with suspicion. In the Vaipulya
sutras these are numerous, but in the final analysis, they all share
a single aim. And this disparity between enlightenment and delu-
sion, you see, is of the same order as that between the good and
evil in these characters. Given their fair due, then, none of them are
utterly bereft of benefit." So saying, he deftly described *monogatari* as indispensable. (3:205; S 438)[6]

Although Fujiwara no Kintō (966–1041) revealed a certain familiarity with *Genji* when he asked the author whether "little
Murasaki" was in attendance,[7] and although we also know that
Michinaga made off with sections of *Genji* from Murasaki's room
while she was serving his daughter, Empress Shōshi (988–1074),[8] the
only explicit contemporary response to *Genji* that we have came from
the Ichijō emperor (r. 986–1011):

His Majesty was listening to someone reading the *Tale of Genji*
aloud. "She must have read the Chronicles of Japan!" he said.
"She seems very learned."[9]

Murasaki's account of Ichijō's exclamation serves subtly to under-
score the claims she has made for the *monogatari* genre in the 'Hotaru'
chapter: this *monogatari*, my *Genji*, justifies them.

5. Harper, "Motoori Norinaga's Criticism," 172, slightly adapted.
6. Ibid., 180–82, slightly adapted.
7. Murasaki Shikibu, *Murasaki Shikibu nikki Murasaki Shikibu shū*, ed. Yamamoto Ritatsu,
    Shinchō Nihon koten shūsei (Shinchōsha, 1980), 52. For a translation, see Richard
    Bowring, *Murasaki Shikibu: Her Diary and Poetic Memoirs* (Princeton: Princeton
    University Press, 1982), 91.
8. *Murasaki Shikibu nikki*, 55. Bowring, *Murasaki Shikibu*, 95.
9. Bowring, *Murasaki Shikibu*, 137. *Murasaki Shikibu nikki*, 96.

Despite Ichijō's amazed—or perhaps merely amused— recognition of the author's learning, there remains something cautious about the attitude to *monogatari* of both Genji and Michinaga as they are depicted by Murasaki Shikibu. Genji admits only to standing by and listening as tales are read to his daughter (3:203; S 437). Later he will "spend a great deal of time selecting romances he thought suitable, and order[ing] them copied and illustrated" (Seidensticker's translation, 3:208; S 439). He does not admit to reading them himself. As for Michinaga, he must slip into the author's unguarded room and make off with her chapter drafts if he is to read the whole of the *Genji*. In any case, Murasaki's own interpretation of the theft is that it was for the benefit of Michinaga's second daughter Kenshi (994–1027).

In one sense this male/female division was a total fiction. It is clear even from the meager evidence just examined that men *did* read *monogatari*. Yet tradition may as readily take root in fantasy as in fact. Whatever the facts of the matter, the fiction that *monogatari* were only for women proved a hardy notion. In Murasaki's day, defend the worth of the genre though she may, refer obliquely to her own erudition as well, *The Tale of Genji* was decidedly a women's book—in Tamagami Takuya's pithy formulation, *Genji* was "a story by a woman, for women, of a woman's world."[10] For a man to be able to admit to more than standing by and listening as his womenfolk read aloud; for a man to ask unabashed about the possibility of obtaining a complete manuscript to read and have copied, as Fujiwara Teika (1162–1241) records doing in his diary entry for the sixteenth day of the second month of Gennin 2 (1225)[11]—the first mention of any *monogatari* in a man's diary[12]—Genji had to become something other than a "story for

---

10. Tamagami Takuya, "Onna ni yoru onna no tame no onna no sekai no monogatari," *Kokubungaku: kaishaku to kanshō* 26.6 (1961). Reprinted as "Onna no tame ni onna ga kaita onna no sekai no monogatari," in *Genji monogatari kenkyū* (Kadokawa Shoten, 1966), 432–40.
11. Fujiwara Teika, *Meigetsuki,* ed. Hayakawa Junzaburō (Kōbundō, 1911), 2:411.
12. Ikeda Toshio, "Kaisetsu," in *Kōgai Genji monogatari,* by Yosano Akiko (Yokohama: Tsurumi Daigaku, 1993), 1–2. Ikeda attaches considerable importance to this statistic: "Michinaga's diary *Midō kanpaku ki,* as well as [Fujiwara no Sanesuke's diary] *Shōyūki* and [Fujiwara no Yukinari's diary] *Gonki,* by court nobles who lived in the same age as Murasaki Shikibu, transmit to the present age a vast body of fact concerning court

women." The Ichijō emperor's wonder at the author's learning showed the way. If the *Genji* were to become an object of study—a classic—as works in Chinese had long been, then it might become openly the province of male as well as female readers.

By the late twelfth century, the first known commentary on *Genji* had been compiled.[13] *Genji* had become the object of scholarly enquiry by men and therefore might be said to have entered the realm of the classic. It is not that *Genji* ceased to be read as a romance; but that by and large, men's concern with *Genji* has necessarily been of a different order from the ecstatic reading described by Sugawara no Takasue no Musume (1008–?) in her *Sarashina nikki*.[14]

The study of *Genji* the classic took many different forms. As political power shifted from the court aristocracy to a succession of military clans, *Genji* became a vital source of information about the correct conduct of court ceremony.[15] *Genji* was mined by those who believed that such fiction was sinful, salacious, or simply frivolous, and, for different reasons, by those who did not.[16] An ability to understand and make allusions to *Genji* became *de rigueur* for poets after

---

society; yet not a single mention survives in any of them, either of *Genji monogatari* or of any other work that bears the name *monogatari*. Examination of the corpus of the best known records of later times reveals the same. The first appearance of *Genji monogatari* in the diary of a male aristocrat is in fact not to be found until the Kamakura period, in the *Meigetsuki* of Fujiwara Teika. However much men may have discussed them in conversation, *monogatari* seem to have existed in a separate sphere that was kept at a considerable remove from the province of male diaries of the Heian period, which were recorded in a succession of *kanji*."

13. The first extant commentary on *The Tale of Genji* is *Genji shaku* by Fujiwara no Koreyuki (?–1175). See Ikeda Kikan, *Genji monogatari jiten* (Tōkyōdō Shuppan, 1960), 2:65.

14. For English translations see Ivan Morris, *As I Crossed the Bridge of Dreams* (New York: Dial Press, 1971), 55–57; Thomas Harper and Haruo Shirane, *Reading The Tale of Genji: Sources From the First Millennium* (New York: Columbia University Press, 2015), 32–35; and Sonja Arntzen and Moriyuki Itō, *The Sarashina Diary: A Woman's Life in Eleventh-Century Japan, Reader's Edition* (New York: Columbia University Press, 2018), 12–14.

15. A commentary concerned exclusively with court dress, for example, compiled by *renga* poet Sōseki (1474–1533) and entitled *Genji nannyo shōzokushō* (completed c. 1516; first woodblock edition 1685) was printed at least seven times during the Edo period.

16. Buddhist apologies for *Genji* are discussed in Harper, "Motoori Norinaga's Criticism," 48–58; for Confucian defenses of *Genji*, see 80–88.

Fujiwara Shunzei's (1114–1204) famous declaration, at a poetry contest held in 1193, that "to compose poetry without having read *Genji* is deplorable *(Genji mizaru utayomi wa ikon no koto nari)*."[17]

By the time we reach the end of the Muromachi period, this accumulation of scholarship, lore, and the products of its application had grown so vast that it could only be mastered by those willing and able to devote their lives to the study of *Genji*. For the poet and would be classicist with somewhat less than a lifetime to devote to the pursuit, Kitamura Kigin compiled a selection from the best of the multivolume commentaries, which he published in combination with a complete text of *Genji*. This work, the *Kogetsushō* (The Moonlit Lake Commentary, completed 1673), was to become the most widely circulated edition of *The Tale of Genji* throughout the Edo period and well into the present century.

With the development of a commercial publishing industry in the early years of the Pax Tokugawa, together with the new market for books that it built and the new literacy that it fed, there came greater changes in the readership of *Genji* than at any time during the previous six centuries.[18] What then became of the traditional male/female division within this vastly larger and more varied readership? We must recall first of all the shift in the custodianship of the classics in which the study of *Genji* passed from the hands of the court nobility to a line of nonaristocratic scholars who practiced what Hagiwara Hiromichi (1815–63) termed the "New Criticism" *(shinchū)—Keichū.* (1640–1701), Kamo no Mabuchi (1697–1769), Motoori Norinaga (1730–1801), and of course Hiromichi himself.[19] Revolutionary though the

17. Fujiwara Shunzei, in *Kenkyū yonen roppyakuban uta-awase*, ed. Taniyama Shigeru, *NKBT* 74:442.

18. See Peter Kornicki, *The Book in Japan: A Cultural History from the Beginnings to the Nineteenth Century* (Leiden, Boston, Köln: Brill, 1998), esp. 136–43 on the development of commercial publishing, 169–222 on the book trade, and 258–69 on readers and reading practices after 1600.

19. This shift in custodianship is discussed by Thomas J. Harper, *"The Tale of Genji* in the Eighteenth Century: Keichū, Mabuchi and Norinaga," in *18th Century Japan: Culture and Society,* ed. C. Andrew Gerstle (Sydney: Allen and Unwin, 1989), 106–23. Keichū is the author of *Genchūshūi* (manuscript completed 1698; first published 1834); Mabuchi of *Genji monogatari shinshaku* (c. 1758, first published 1816); Norinaga of *Genji*

interpretations of these scholars were, however, we must also note that the nature of their activities remained commentarial and the practitioners exclusively male. There was to be no crossing the male/female divide in the world of the classics.

More surprisingly, in the larger world of book publishing, we find that according to the most comprehensive modern catalogues, not a single new edition of a complete text of *The Tale of Genji* appeared between 1706 and 1890, a period of almost two centuries.[20] This is not to say that the text was unobtainable during these years. Andrew Markus suggests that the numerous extant copies of the 1675 printing of the *Kogetsushō* indicate a large initial issue, many of which would have remained in circulation.[21] It is also likely that reprints were made

---

monogatari Tama no ogushi (1799); and Hiromichi of *Genji monogatari hyōshaku* (1861). On Hiromichi, see Patrick W. Caddeau, *Appraising Genji: Literary Criticism and Cultural Anxiety in the Age of the Last Samurai* (Albany: State University of New York Press, 2006).

20. 1706 is the date of a reprint of the *Shusho Genji monogatari* (first published 1673), one of the first editions of *Genji* to print the complete text within a frame that divided it from the commentary. Extant printed editions of *Genji* are listed in *Kokusho sōmokuroku: hoteiban* (Iwanami Shoten, 1989–90), 3:124. For listings of Meiji period publications, I have relied on the National Diet Library (Kokuritsu Kokkai Toshokan) catalogue *Meiji-ki kankō tosho mokuroku: Kokuritsu Kokkai Toshokan shozō*, vol. 4 (Kokkai Toshokan, 1973).

   The Kan'en 2 (1749) "edition" of *Genji* listed in *Kokusho sōmokuroku* is in fact a set of *mamehon* or miniature books. Each of the twenty-eight volumes contains just five leaves of paper, the first of which is an illustration. The first volume consists of an outline *(tai'i)* and table of contents; into each subsequent volume are squeezed explanations of the origin of two chapter titles. There is a photograph of what appears to be a very similar set of *Genji mamehon* in two Tsurumi University Library catalogues: *Tsurumi Daigaku Toshokan zō kichō shoten mokuroku* (Yokohama: Tsurumi Daigaku, 1989), 30; and *Geirinshūha: Tsurumi Daigaku Toshokan shinchiku kichōsho toroku* (Yokohama: Tsurumi Daigaku, 1986), 36, and commentary 82–83. The Tsurumi set, however, includes a large sheet of heavy paper divided into numbered rectangles, complete with instructions for its use. This sheet is the "board" on which the tiny volumes are moved in place of the pieces customarily used in the game of *sugoroku* or backgammon, of which this is apparently a version. Although the Tsurumi set is slightly smaller than the set held by the National Diet Library, given the other similarities of form and presentation, it is probably safe to assume that the National Diet Library set was also originally intended to be used in a version of *sugoroku*.

21. Andrew L. Markus, "Representations of *Genji monogatari* in Edo Period Fiction" (paper presented at the 8th conference on Oriental-Western Literary and Cultural Relations, Indiana University, August 1982), 6. The 1675 printing of the *Kogetsushō* is the only one listed in *Kokusho sōmokuroku*, 3:389.

from old blocks without altering the colophons, even though evidence of such printings cannot be gleaned from catalogues. Be that as it may, demand for printed editions of other works in the classical canon, particularly *Kokinshū, Ise monogatari,* and *Tsurezuregusa,* seems to have been far greater than demand for *Genji.*

The immense cost of a complete text of *Genji* is surely one reason for the apparent lack of demand for the work. As Richard Bowring points out, "[I]n 1696 a copy [of the *Kogetsushō]* was selling for well over twenty times what it cost to buy a work of contemporary fiction, well beyond the reach of the average reading public."[22] Indeed, the long hiatus in the publication of new editions of *Genji* lends further support to Bowring's assertion that "[t]he work was so long and so difficult, the language now so remote, that it remained one of the great 'unreads.'"[23]

This does not mean, however, that *Genji* passed out of the consciousness of generations of readers. For those without the money to buy or borrow a copy, or for those who lacked the time, the desire, or simply the linguistic ability to read the complete text, there were digests that could be used to acquire a passing acquaintance with the work. Originally compiled for use by poets as a "shortcut" to *Genji,* several had been in circulation since the first half of the fifteenth century. As the *renga* master Sōchō (1448–1532) said when asked, "People nowadays say that if you do not know *Genji* thoroughly you should not use it when the preceding link happens to allude to something from the past. Is this indeed so?"

> Of course it is best to have been through the entire work and know it well, but it would be hard to find one person in a thousand who has. A scrap of brocade, small though it be, can still make a talisman or an ornament. And likewise with *The Tale of Genji.* Even if you know only one passage, why shouldn't you make a link of it if an appropriate occasion arises?[24]

22. Richard Bowring, *Landmarks of World Literature: Murasaki Shikibu: The Tale of Genji* (Cambridge: Cambridge University Press, 1988), 92–93. Bowring's information is from Markus, "Representations of *Genji monogatari,*" 6.
23. Bowring, *Landmarks,* 92.
24. Sōchō, "Renga hikyō shū," in *Renga ronshū ge,* ed. Ijichi Tetsuo (Iwanami Shoten, 1956), 174–75.

The longevity of Sōchō's attitude is attested in the variety of digest versions of *Genji*, and their rapid proliferation during the Edo period.[25] The titles of these works are revealing. The most popular, for example, was *Genji kokagami*, "A Little *Genji* Mirror."[26] In 1661, the *haikai* poet Nonoguchi Ryūho (1595–1669) published an illustrated digest called *Fūjō Genji*, "A *Genji* in Ten Chapters;" and in 1665 he brought out a simplified version of the same work to which he gave the title *Osana Genji*, "A Young Person's *Genji*."[27] Of course such titles need not be taken entirely at face value, for they are likely to have been read by anyone, male or female, who was content to have their dose of the classic in popular, abbreviated, or simplified form.

Another "shortcut" to *Genji* open to both sexes was vernacular translation (*zokugoyaku*). These were part of a growing interest in and demand for translations of the classics, apparently among those who read for pleasure as well as for academic or artistic ends.[28] The most complete list of Edo period vernacular versions of *Genji* was compiled

25. See the list in Teramoto Naohiko, *Genji monogatari juyōshi ronkō (seihen)* (Kazama Shobō, 1970), 595–96. An account in English is provided by Markus, "Representations of *Genji monogatari*," 7–8.
26. Although the date of the compilation of *Genji kokagami* is unknown, Shimizu Fukuko, "Kaisetsu," in *Shusho Genji monogatari Eawase Matsukaze* (Izumi Shoin, 1989), 141, firmly dates the first printed edition as Keichō 15 (1610).
27. Information from Ikeda, *Genji monogatarijiten* 2:40 *(Osana Genji);* 2:107–8 *(Fūjō Genji);* and *NKBD* 1:487 *(Osana Genjz);* 3:277 *(Fūjō Genji).* For facsimile editions of these works see *Genji monogatari shiryō eiin shūsei*, ed. Nakano Kōichi (Waseda Daigaku Shuppanbu, 1989–90), vol. 10 *(Osana Genji)* and vols. 11–12 *(Fūjō Genjz).* The discussion *of Fūjō Genji* in Markus, "Representations of *Genji monogatari*," 8–9, contains two errors that should be corrected: the work *was* illustrated, with over a hundred woodcuts by the author; and it was printed more than once, though the dates of subsequent printings have not been established.
28. I am grateful to Joshua Mostow of the University of British Columbia for informing me that the first complete translation of a classical text into modern Japanese was *Ise monogatari hirakotoba* (Tales of Ise in Plain Words, 1678) by Ki no Zankei (dates unknown), illustrated by Hishikawa Moronobu (1618–94). In this work, the prose of *Ise monogatari* is translated into the seventeenth-century vernacular, while the poems are given in their original form and provided instead with an extended paraphrase. For a printed edition, see *Tsūzoku Ise monogatari*, ed. Imanishi Yūichirō, (Heibonsha, 1991), pp. 2–142. More than a century later, both Motoori Norinaga and Ozaki Masayoshi (1755–1827) published versions of the *Kokinshū* in eighteenth-century vernacular. Masayoshi's version was entitled *Kokinshū hinakotoba* (A Rustic Kokinshū, 1796). Norinaga called his

by Fujita Tokutarō (1901–45) in 1932.[29] His chapter of "translations and versions" *(yakubun hon'an)* lists more than a dozen attempts to render *Genji* in the contemporary language. Given that these items in Fujita's bibliography constitute but a small subgenre of a large branch of the publishing industry devoted to the translation of all manner of works originally written in classical Japanese (not to mention Chinese), it seems no exaggeration to say that vernacular translation was to become almost as important in the Edo period as it is today.[30]

Not only were there what might be called "pure" translations; the translation of classical Japanese into the vernacular might at times verge upon parody[31] and even pornography. *Fūryū Genji monogatari* (A Fashionable Tale of Genji, 1703), for example, is described by Noguchi Takehiko as a "decidedly pornographic, in reality parodic" version of *Genji*.[32] One might also mention *Kōshoku ichidai otoko* (The Life of an Amorous Man, 1682) by Ihara Saikaku (1642–93) and *Nise murasaki inaka Genji* (An Imposter Murasaki and a Rustic Genji, 1829–42) by Ryūtei Tanehiko (1783–1842) as works which, while principally parody, also contain elements of translation.[33]

---

version *Kokinshū tōkagami* (A Kokinshū Telescope, 1797); it may be found in *Motoori Norinaga zenshū*, ed. Ōkubo Tadashi (Chikuma Shobō, 1969), 3:1–291. For a translation of Norinaga's preface to *Kokinshū tōkagami*, see T. J. Harper, "Norinaga on the Translation of *Waka*: His Preface to *A Kokinshū Telescope*," in *The Distant Isle: Studies and Translations of Japanese Literature in Honor of Robert H. Brower*, ed. Thomas Hare, Robert Borgen, and Sharalyn Orbaugh, Michigan Monograph Series in Japanese Studies, no. 15 (Ann Arbor: Center for Japanese Studies, The University of Michigan, 1996), 205–30.

29. Fujita Tokutarō, *Genji monogatari kenkyū shomoku yōran* (Rokubunkan, 1932).
30. On this subject, the most comprehensive study is Rebekah Clements, *A Cultural History of Translation in Early Modern Japan* (Cambridge: Cambridge University Press, 2015.)
31. Reuben A. Brower acknowledges the connection between the two activities in the "Translation as Parody" chapter of his *Mirror on Mirror: Translation, Imitation, Parody* (Cambridge: Harvard University Press, 1974), 1–16.
32. Noguchi Takehiko, *Genji monogatari o Eda kara yomu* (Kōdansha, 1985), 85.
33. See Noguchi's chapter "Takai bungaku toshite no Inaka Genji," in ibid., 81–106, for a much more subtle and detailed discussion of these points. In English, see Andrew L. Markus, *The Willow in Autumn: Ryūtei Tanehiko, 1783–1842*, Harvard-Yenching Institute Monograph Series, no. 35 (Cambridge and London: Council on East Asian Studies, Harvard University, 1992) and Michael Emmerich, *The Tale of Genji: Translation, Canonization, and World Literature* (New York: Columbia University Press, 2013).

The popularity of these new "shortcuts" to *Genji*—*digests,* vernacular translations, and parodies-signals not the disappearance of the
old polarity of men's classic/women's romance but rather the development of a multitude of hybrid responses that lay somewhere between
the two extremes. Near one end of the continuum, a digest, originally
written for *renga/haikai* poets in a hurry, might just as well serve the
needs of a woman wishing to acquire a quick veneer of courtly refinement: hence the woodblock print showing a prostitute writing a letter
to one of her clients with a *Genji* digest on her desk at the ready.[34] Near
the opposite end is a work such as the *Amayo monogatari damikotoba*
(The Rainy Night Tale in Eastern Dialect). Completed in 1769 and
first published c. 1777, it is a commentary on the famous "Rainy Night
Ranking" of women section of the 'Hahakigi' (The Broom Tree) chapter. Although prepared by the bakufu official and scholar of National
Learning *(kokugakusha)* Katō Umaki (1721–77), *Amayo monogatari
damikotoba* was ostensibly not intended for use by (male) classicists,
but was commissioned by "a person who had many daughters" as a
version of *Genji* suitable for them to read.[35]

Evidence of specifically female readership of *The Tale of Genji*
is unfortunately scanty: we know of only one or two women who were
reading *Genji,* and not because they have left accounts of their reading, but because that reading left its traces in their writing. Ōgimachi
Machiko (1679?–1724), a consort of Yanagisawa Yoshiyasu (1658–
1714), Chief Adjutant to the fifth shogun Tokugawa Tsunayoshi

34. See the colored reproduction of the woodblock print in the collection of the Riccar Art
    Museum, Tokyo, by Chōbunsai Eishi (1756–1829) entitled "Fūryū ryaku rokkasen mitate
    Kisen," in *Ukiyo-e sanbyakunen meisakuten* (Nihon Keizai Shinbunsha, 1979), unnum-
    bered pages before page 1. The print is item no. 152, discussed on p. 9. The woman
    depicted is probably a Fukagawa prostitute, since Kisen's poem, *(Kokinshū,* no. 983,
    NKBZ 7:365) which appears in the top right-hand corner of the print, begins "Waga io
    wa miyako no tatsumi," and Fukagawa was to the southeast of Edo and hence referred to
    obliquely as "tatsumi." The whole conception of the print is heavily ironic: the prostitute
    instead of the monk, the brothel instead of the hermitage, and of course Kisen himself
    was long dead by the time *Genji* was written.
35. Information from Ikeda, *Genji monogatari jiten,* 2:36 and *NKBD* 1:660–61. Despite
    Katō's protestations of the modesty of his aims, Motoori Norinaga pays *Damikotoba* the
    compliment of frequent criticism in his commentary on the 'Hahakigi' chapter.

(1646–1709; r. 1680–1709), was one such reader. Her *Matsukage nikki* (*In the Shelter of the Pine*, 1710–12) is resonant with echoes of *The Tale of Genji*. For example, an account of a visit by Tsunayoshi to Yanagisawa's residence recalls the 'Otome' chapter, and a description of Yanagisawa's villa on the then outskirts of Edo at Komagome calls to mind Genji's Rokujō-in.[36] The *Matsukage nikki* provides clear evidence that Machiko had access to a copy of *Genji* and was intimately familiar with the work.

Markus maintains that "it is a certainty that *[Genji]* was read and did retain a devoted female following in the latter Edo period."[37] He cites several *senryū* about women who read *Genji;* and a satirical passage from *Ukiyoburo* (1809–13) by Shikitei Sanba (1776–1822) in which two women (named after two species of duck whose names happen to coincide with two verb endings commonly found in classical poetry: one is "Kamoko," the other "Keriko") encounter each other at a bathhouse and chat about their recent reading: one has begun to reread *Utsuho monogatari;* the other is "annotating" her copy of *Genji* with the help of Mabuchi's *Shinshaku* and Norinaga's *Tama no ogushi*. Markus's translation of the scene, unfortunately only available in typescript, is given here in full:

> Keriko: "Kamoko-san. What are you perusing these days?"
> Kamoko: "Well now, just as I was thinking that I might reread *Utsuho*, I was lucky enough to find an edition in movable type and so I am collating the texts. But I have been interrupted by this and that since last year and so I put it aside having got as far as the latter half of the 'Toshikage' chapter [the first chapter of *Utsuho*]."
> Keriko: "You have got your hands on something nice."
> Kamoko: "Keriko-san. I expect you're still with *Genji?*"
> Keriko: "Yes indeed. With the Venerable Kamo's *Shinshaku* and the Great Motoori's *Tama no ogushi* as my guides, I had just begun

36. The most reliable edition of *Matsukage nikki* is Miyakawa Yoko, *Yanagisawa-ke no kotengaku (jō): Matsukage nikki* (Shintensha, 2007). Miyakawa's edition also includes copious annotation and a modern Japanese translation. In English, see G. G. Rowley, trans., *In the Shelter of the Pine: A Memoir of Yanagisawa Yoshiyasu and Tokugawa Japan* (New York: Columbia University Press, 2021).
37. Markus, "Representations of *Genji monogatari*," 28–29.

annotating it, but what with all the distractions of the mundane world, I have hardly had time to pick up my brush."[38]

Although "Kamoko" and "Keriko" could be "figments of Sanba's fantasy" as much as "the exaggeration of observable stereotypes," Markus concludes that "there were women of leisure and education who at least attempted the study of classics on their own, and made use of major commentaries in their pursuit of a cultivated understanding of the texts."[39]

One such woman was Kanzawa Tami, the daughter of Kanzawa Tokō (1710–95), a deputy *(yoriki)* in the office of the Kyoto City Magistrate *(Kyōto machi bugyō)*. Tokō also wrote *haikai* and was a prolific essayist. Tami was the youngest of his five children, and, as she was the only one to survive childhood, he made her his heir. In his 200–volume miscellany *Okinagusa* (published in part 1784), Tokō describes how he copied the entire *Mingō nisso*[40]—a total of 3,333 pages—by getting up early in the morning and working by lamplight in the evening. He then explains his decision to pass the finished work on to his daughter:

> My heir Tamiko has from childhood adored *[Genji]* and always had it by her side. Often Tamiko would enlighten me about things which I was unclear about, or could not remember at all. Therefore, rather than keep [the copy of the *Mingō nisso]* for myself, though not without some reluctance, I decided to pass it on to Tamiko as something to remember me by. When I gave it to her, box and all, she was as delighted as ever I could have hoped. Moreover, taking the poetry index, she wrote in it a preface of her own.[41]

38. Ibid., 29–30, slightly adapted. Original in Shikitei Sanba, *Ukiyoburo,* ed. Nakamura Michio, *NKBT* 63:220. See also Maruya Saiichi's humorous comments on these *onna kokugakusha* in Ōno Susumu and Maruya Saiichi, "Kamoko to Keriko no koto kara hanashi wa hajimaru," in *Nihongo de ichiban daiji na mono* (Chūō Kōronsha, 1990), 7.
39. Markus, "Representations of *Genji monogatari,*" 30.
40. A commentary on *Genji* by Nakanoin Michikatsu (1556–1610), completed in 1598.
41. Kanzawa Tokō, "Mingō nisso," in *Okinagusa* book 141, *Nihon zuihitsu taisei,* 3rd ser. (Nihon Zuihitsu Taisei Kankōkai, 1931), 13:131that since last year and so I put it aside having got as far as the latter half of the 32.

Tami's preface, in which the imagery of conventional Buddhist sentiment acts as a veil of modesty for her passion for *Genji,* reads as follows:

> Surely this has been said any number of times by poets from ages past: when one does not comprehend the nuances of a text, to what can one turn for help? But the moon shines with equal brilliance upon the eaves of the poor; how then can it pass by unheeding the humble hut of the saltmaker? I have for many years steeped myself deeply in this *monogatari.* Brushing away the mists of dawn, dampened by the dews of evening, I have pored over these fiftyfour chapters, time and again, scroll after scroll, a thousand upon thousands of times; all the while persisting in my delusion in this ephemeral mundane world where one knows not which will be the first to fall, the dewdrop upon the tip of the branch or the droplet upon the stem, where just as the hailstone upon the leaf of the scrub bamboo *(tamasasa)* vanishes no sooner than it is taken up, time passes not as one would wish; and so it is with those unfathomable thousand-league depths [of *Genji*] that I failed to understand no matter how often I read. Shallow as I am, how am I to abandon these ties of fondness and affection [for *Genji*], to cross the floating bridge of dreams from this life to a world of words free of frivolity? Such is the excess of my pride.
>
> ことの葉をかきあつめたるもしほ草よむともつきじみるにまさりて
> *Koto no ha o kakiatsumetaru moshiogusa*
>   *yomu tomo tsukiji miru ni masarite.*
> Words raked together as seaweed: however much read, inexhaustible;
>   better than actual experience.[42]

Another woman who made use of a major commentary to deepen her understanding of *Genji* was Matsuo Taseko (1811–94), a peasant from the Ina Valley of Shinano Province in central Japan. Aged about 40, she invested in a copy of Kigin's *Kogetsushō* so that she could better incorporate allusions to the tale in her poetry.[43]

42. Ibid. The interpretation suggested here depends upon taking *miru* in its sense of "to experience," though it was probably chosen by the author more for its service as an *engo* than for its denotational meaning. Even specialists in Japanese poetry with whom I have discussed possible interpretations of the poem find it mystifying.

43. See Anne Walthall, *The Weak Body of a Useless Woman: Matsuo Taseko and the Meiji Revolution* (Chicago: Chicago University Press, 1998), esp. pp. 35–37, 103.

Further evidence, though less direct, of female readership is to be found in the ongoing debate over the moral advisability of women reading *The Tale of Genji*—and even in the demimonde.[44] The Confucian scholars Kumazawa Banzan (1619–91) and Andō Tameakira (1659–1716) maintained that the female characters in *Genji* were exemplars of the various virtues women ought to cultivate.[45] Such a view explains, perhaps, *Genji's* suitability as *yome-iri dōgu,* an item in a bride's trousseau, exquisitely bound and arranged (in more expensive versions) in a set of black and gold lacquered drawers.[46] Kanzawa Tami's father certainly approved of his daughter's knowledge of *Genji* and the same may well have been true for Ōgimachi Machiko, since in her *Matsukage nikki* she recalls receiving her education at her father's side.

Others, however, seem to have felt that reading *Genji* was not merely a threat to morality but positively unhealthy. In his advice to pregnant women, the Confucian doctor Inō Kōken (1610–80) wrote:

> When reading books, choose those of which neither the words nor pictures will cause agitation; books such as *Yamato shōgaku* or *Kagamigusa* are permissible but on no account should works such as *The Tale of Genji* be read.[47]

---

44. For a full account of the debate over the moral advisability of women reading *The Tale of Genji*, see P. F. Kornicki, "Unsuitable Books for Women: *Genji Monogatari* and *Ise Monogatari* in Late Seventeenth-Century Japan," *Monumenta Nipponica* 60.2 (2005): 147–93.

45. On Kumazawa Banzan, see James McMullen, *Idealism, Protest and The Tale of Genji* (Oxford: Oxford University Press, 1999). On Andō Tameakira, see Satoko Naito, "Seven Essays on Murasaki Shikibu," in Harper and Shirane, *Reading The Tale of Genji*, 392–411.

46. There is a photograph of one such item from the middle of the Edo period in Tsurumi Daigaku Toshokan, *Tsurumi Daigaku Toshokan zō kichō shoten mokuroku*, 10. From a slightly earlier period, see the trousseau copy traditionally attributed to Sanjōnishi Saneki (1511–79) in the collection of the Waseda University Library: https://www.wul.waseda. ac.jp/TENJI/virtual/genji/genji.html (Japanese) https://www.wul.waseda.ac.jp/collect/ wa/he2-4867-e.html (English).

47. "Taikyō," section one of Inō Kōken's *Inago gusa* (1690), in *Nihon kyōiku bunko*, ed. Kurokawa Mamichi and Otaki Jun (Dōbunkan, 1911), 12:50. *Yamato shōgaku* (1659) by Tsujihara Genpo (1622–?) and *Kagamigusa* (1647) by Nakae Tōju (1608–48) were moralizing tracts derived from Chinese Confucian texts and designed for a female readership.

The Confucian scholar Kaibara Ekiken (1630–1714) was of a similar opinion:

> One must be selective in what one allows young women to read. There is no harm in those books depicting the events of the past. Do not allow them to read *kouta* and *jōruri* books: they do not teach the true way of the sages and are tinged with frivolity. Moreover, one should not readily allow them to read such books as *Ise monogatari*, *Genji monogatari* and their ilk, which, although possessed of a literary elegance, depict licentious behavior.[48]

While Confucian scholars might debate the advisability of women of leisure reading *monogatari*, for the professional woman of higher rank, familiarity with *Genji* was an essential accomplishment. Though digests must often have sufficed for this purpose, there are also accounts of such women sending for impoverished court nobles to read *Genji* and other classical texts to them.[49] Perhaps some even managed to read *Genji* by themselves: a scene from "Mina no kawa" (Men and Women Getting Together), a series of woodblock prints by Numata Gabimaru (1787–1864), shows a prostitute at her work; on the other side of a pile of rumpled bedding can be seen a large box, labeled somewhat emphatically "Kogetsushō zen," that is, "The Kogetsushō Complete." A volume lies open on her desk, and beside it a writing brush and inkstone, as if to suggest that the arrival of a customer has momentarily called her away from her study of *Genji*.[50]

Kigin's *Kogetsushō* makes another appearance in *Seirō hiru no sekai: Nishiki no ura* (A Brothel in the Light of Day: The Other Side of the Brocade, 1791), *asharebon* by Santō Kyōden (1761–1816) which is set in a brothel:

---

48. Kaibara Ekiken, "Joshi o oshiyuru hō," in *Wazoku dōji kun,* ed. Ishikawa Ken (Iwanami Shoten, 1961), 268–69.

49. Noguchi, *Genji monogatari,* 5–6. See also the examples in Markus, "Representations of *Genji monogatari*," 16–17.

50. Fukuda Kazuhiko, ed., *Ehon ukiyoe sen* (Kawade Shobō Shinsha, 1990), 74. Numata was apparently in the service of the Nagoya domain, but in what capacity is not known.

Meanwhile, in Yūgiri's room the juniors have been getting out
the chopstick boxes and gold-lacquered trays, and setting out tea
bowls. Steam is whistling from a kettle hanging over a brazier.
They put some tea on top of a copy of *Kogetsushū* [an alternative
title for *Kogetsushō*] nearby, pull out the drawers of the smoking
set, and fill the tobacco pouches.[51]

No further mention of the commentary is made. Unopened and serving as a cupstand, the *Kogetsushō* appears along with poem-cards
and tortoise-shell hairpins, essential to the decor of a well-furnished
boudoir.

For the female reader of the Edo period, then, familiarity with
The Tale of Genji might improve her behavior as daughter, wife, and
mother; might "endanger" her physical and moral well-being; might
enhance her reputation as cultivated prostitute. Whatever the results,
however, *Genji* remained for them what it had been for all women
since the time of its creation. For Ōgimachi Machiko as much as for
Kanzawa Tami, it remained an avocation, an adjunct of their recrea-
tional reading. The great scholars of the work, their male contemporaries of the Edo period, came from the world of *Genji* as a classic. Any
woman who might presume to join their number—as did "Kamoko"
and "Keriko"—is a figure of fun.

Akiko's childhood reading too has much in common with what
we can glean of earlier female readers of *Genji*. Indeed Akiko herself
suggests a parallel with Takasue no Musume, the *Sarashina* diarist.
For both young women, *The Tale of Genji* was everything that *monogatari* had always been: absorbing, transporting, ultimately escapist.
And yet, for both of them, it was this childhood reading that nurtured
abilities that later led to greater accomplishments—as a "novelist" for
the Sarashina diarist; and as a scholar for Akiko:

> From the time that she was a young woman living in the coun-
> tryside in an eastern province, the author of *The Sarashina diary*
> read works of literature and, in as much as she had been born a

---

51. Translation by Peter F. Kornicki, *"Nishiki no Ura:* An Instance of Censorship and the
Structure of a *Sharebon," Monumenta Nipponica* 32.2 (Summer 1977): 176.

woman, she wanted somehow or other to grow up to be a beautiful woman, like Yūgao or Ukifune in *The Tale of Genji,* and be loved, even if only briefly, by a sensitive man like the Shining Genji, and with that in mind she cultivated herself accordingly. Ultimately she achieved her aim of going up to the capital, where she wrote *The Tale of Sagoromo* and other such novels. It is unfortunate that young women these days do not have such self-confidence. (14:111)

In a similar manner, Akiko's lifelong relationship with *Genji* might be characterized as a movement from the world of *Genji*-as romance to the world of *Genji*-as-classic. But for Akiko to do what only men had been able to do in the past—make a career of *Genji*—presupposed many external changes, changes in old categories. Chapter three will attempt to account for those changes. But it is to a description of Akiko's childhood reading that we must first turn.

Chapter Two:
Secret Joy: Akiko's Childhood Reading

わが十二ものゝ哀れを知りかほに読みたる源氏枕の草子
Waga jūni mono no aware o shirigao ni
yomitaru Genji Makura no sōshi. (2:393)[1]
At twelve, with "sensitivity" written all over my face,
I read *Genji* and *The Pillow Book.*

源氏をば十二三にて読みしのち思はれじとぞ見つれ男を
Genji oba jūnisan nite yomishi nochi
omowareji to zo mitsure otoko o. (3:194)
At twelve or thirteen I read *Genji;* and thereafter
hoped I should never be loved by any man I then knew!

And while Akiko was reading *Genji*—at about the same age and in the same frame of mind as the Sarashina diarist nearly a thousand years earlier—what were her contemporaries reading? At least a partial answer to this question can be found in a survey of sixty-nine notables of the literary world (only one of whom, alas, was female) compiled in 1889 by Tokutomi Sohō (1863–1957).[2] No more than twenty-four of the sixty-nine, or just over a third of those who submitted replies, included a work of classical Japanese literature—one written before 1600—in their lists. This compares with twenty-seven who mentioned a work of Edo period literature, twenty-eight a work of Western literature, and no fewer than thirty

---

1. This poem is possibly an allusion to the section of the 'Kochō' (Butterflies) chapter in which Genji lectures Ukon and Tamakazura on correct form in replying to letters from potential suitors. See 3:170; S 425.
2. Tokutomi Sohō, ed., "Shomoku jisshu," *Kokumin no tomo,* no. 48 (supplement: April 1889): 1–18; no. 49 (May 1889): 30–32; and no. 54 (July 1889): 28–29.

who listed a work of Chinese literature (not including philosophy) among their favorites.[3]

Akiko was only ten years old in 1889 when these surveys were published, but in 1922, when she was old enough to look back and remember what she had been reading at that time, she wrote the following account:

> At the age of eleven or twelve, I read the historical works of the Heian period—Eiga *monogatari, Ōkagami, Masukagami* and such, and at the same time I also read the more purely literary works such as *Genji, Utsuho, Sagoromo* and *Makura no sōshi.* I didn't understand them at first, but as I read on, I came in the natural course of things to understand them clearly, and this was my secret joy.
>
> After I had finished reading Heian history and literature, I moved on to the Nara period, and by the time I was seventeen or eighteen, I had more or less read the whole of Kamakura- and Edo-period literature and history. Meagerly informed though they were, the judgments that I arrived at were at least my own. There was much Edo-period writing that was trivial and did not attract me: I skimmed through it. After I had read Chikamatsu and Saikaku, I could not feel that Eakin and Tanehiko were good writers. And having read *Kokinshū, Man'yōshū,* Saigyō and Rihaku [Li Po], it goes without saying that I found it impossible to consider Mabuchi and Kageki, or even Basho outstanding poets. (18:432-33)

Akiko is quite specific about what she read, and what she liked and did not like. She also reveals that her reading was a private, even a hidden pleasure. How do her reading experience and her taste compare with other literary figures of the day? The results of the "Shomoku jisshu" surveys—even allowing for some inevitable emphasis on the highbrow in readers' responses—suggest that her extensive familiarity with Heian literature and her low opinion of Edo works put her in

---

3. Peter F. Kornicki, "The Survival of Tokugawa Fiction in the Meiji Period," *Harvard Journal of Asiatic Studies41.2* (December 1981): 461–82, esp. 478–80.

a minority. Akiko would probably concur in this assessment of the evidence.

In the two poems cited above, we see Akiko recalling with amusement the early reading of *The Tale of Genji* that, in her own mind at least, set her apart from the world into which she had been born. The frequency with which she harks back to her childhood reading in the essays and poetry of her adulthood attests the importance she attached to this solitary pleasure.

This chapter, therefore, will first examine Akiko's childhood reading in the context of her upbringing and education, making such comparisons with her Meiji contemporaries as the sources permit. Thereafter the focus shifts to the effects of that reading. The purpose of this juxtaposition is to suggest that Akiko's spectacular leap from provincial comfort, circumscribed by daughterly duty, to a literary career in the capital was not the result of a desire to overturn tradition, or to be true to some modern "sense of self." Rather, I shall argue, Akiko's was a flight inspired by fiction, a real-life romance she had already rehearsed in fantasies born of her childhood reading of *Genji*.

Akiko was born on 7 December 1878, the eleventh year of Meiji, to the Hō[4] family, who were second-generation proprietors of a sweetshop, the Surugaya of Sakai.[5] Akiko's name appears in the family register as Shō rendered in *kana;* she did not have a Chinese character with which to write her name until sometime around the turn of the century when she adopted the character Shō "translucent, bright" and reinvented herself as "Akiko."[6]

---

4. Although Akiko occasionally read her maiden name as Ōtori, the correct reading is Hō. See Shinma Shin'ichi, *Yosano Akiko* (Ōfūsha, 1981), 13, who speculates that "Hō" is a new name, invented in the early Meiji period.

5. See the reproductions of a Meiji period wood-block print of the Surugaya, its sweetwrappers and advertisements, and a later watercolor by Kishiya Seizō (1899–1980) in the exhibition catalogue *Yosano Akiko—sono shōgai to sakuhin—*, ed. Sakai Hakubutsukan (Sakai: Sakai Hakubutsukan, 1991), 10–12.

6. An early use of the resulting pen name "Akiko" is her signature to a letter addressed to poet Kawai Suimei (1874–1965) and dated 6 January 1900. See the photograph in ibid., 15. "Shō" remained Akiko's legal name: her Japanese Empire Passport (Nippon Teikoku Kaigai Ryoken), for example, issued on Meiji 45 (1912).3.26, gives her name as Yosano Shō.

It would appear that she was at least a third-generation book-worm. In Mori Fujiko's (1919–) account of her mother Akiko's early life, she notes that Akiko's uncle, her father's elder brother, had been permitted by his mother to spend his entire life doing as he pleased— which was to retreat to his room and read. Akiko's grandfather, too, was apparently a younger son whose elder brother had preferred a life of reading to the drudgery of doing business.[7] Akiko grew up in a house that had always supported at least one full-time reader.

The Surugaya was run in the main by Akiko's grandmother Shizu and mother Tsune, with the help of the female children.[8] There was nothing unusual about this arrangement: its antecedents are to be found at least as early as the Muromachi period and throughout the Edo period.[9] Unfortunately, the Surugaya was destroyed by fire during the Second World War and the post-war building was demolished when the Osaka-Sakai railway link was constructed; a memorial poem-plaque now marks the spot with one of Akiko's most famous poems:

海こひし潮の遠鳴りかぞへつゝ少女となりし父母の家
Umi koishi shio no tōnari kazoetsutsu
  otome to narishi chichi haha no ie. (1:127)
How I long for the sea! And for the house of my father and mother
  where I grew to girlhood, counting the distant roll of the waves.

Her father, too, loved books and spent his time dabbling in various pursuits: he submitted *haiku* to newspapers and magazines, tried his hand at painting and decided that the Surugaya should sell Western liquor as well as the traditional sweet *yōkan*.[10] Thus Akiko had access not only to the considerable library amassed by her peculiar bookish forebears, but also to current newspapers and literary magazines subscribed to by her father or sent down from Tokyo by her older brother who was studying at Tokyo University. She recalled that *Shigarami*

7. Mori Fujiko, *Midaregami* (Rukkusha, 1967), 9–10.
8. Akiko had two older half-sisters, children of Akiko's father by his first wife. Sōshichi (at the behest of his mother, according to some accounts) had divorced their mother but kept the daughters, who worked in the shop until they were old enough to be married.
9. Wakita Haruko, trans. G. G. Rowley, "The Japanese Woman in the Premodern Merchant Household," *Women's History Review* 19.2 (2010): 259–82.
10. Mori, *Midaregami*, 12.

zōshi (1889–94) and *Mesamashigusa* (1896–1902), both edited by
Mori Ōgai (1862–1922); and *Bungakkai* (1893–98), edited by Togawa
Shūkotsu (1870–1939) and others, were particular favorites.[11] There
was also a circulating library *(kashihon'ya)* not far from the shop
where the family lived. Akiko describes the family library as consisting of "a large amount of assorted literary material from the Eda period
that my grandmother had read" (18:433). It is hard to imagine Shizu
having had the time to read so much that a collection was formed, but
all commentators seem to agree that there was a considerable amount
of reading matter in the Hō house.[12]

Sakai, the city where Akiko was born, lies on the Inland Sea
about fifteen kilometers south of Osaka, of which it is now, adminis-
tratively at least, a part. During the period of civil war preceding the
closing of the country early in the seventeenth century, Sakai was a
prosperous trading port, but by the end of the Tokugawa period its
importance had been usurped by Osaka.[13] Sakai-born poet Kawai
Suimei, a close friend of Akiko all her life, described the city as it was
when the two were young:

> Sakai was at that time a city which appeared to be sound asleep. It
> was conservative and old ways were valued. Tea ceremony, flower
> arranging, the chanting of Noh and so on were practiced; and the

11. Yosano Akiko, "Yabukōji," (1906–7) cited in Fukuda Kiyoto and Hamana Hiroko, *Yosano Akiko,* Hito to sakuhin series (Shimizu Shain, 1968), 25.
12. Mori, *Midaregami,* 18; Shinma Shin'ichi, "Yosano Akiko to *Genji monogatari,*" in *Genji monogatari to sono eikyō: kenkyū to shiryō—kodai bungaku ronsō dairokushū,* ed. Murasaki Shikibu Gakkai (Musashino Shain, 1978), 250.
13. For an account of Sakai's development from two neighboring *shōen* (one in the province of Settsu, the other in Izumi, thus the name Sakai "border") to a port city that pros-
pered from both domestic and foreign trade, through 1569 when the city submitted to a war tax of 20,000 *kan* and became a direct holding of Oda Nobunaga, see two arti-
cles by V. Dixon Morris: "Sakai: From Shōen to Port City," in *Japan in the Muromachi Age,* ed. John W. Hall and Toyoda Takeshi (Berkeley: University of California Press, 1977), 145–58; and "The City of Sakai and Urban Autonomy," in *Warlords, Artists, and Commoners: Japan in the Sixteenth Century,* ed. George Elison and Bardwell L. Smith (Honolulu: The University Press of Hawaii, 1981), 23–54.

reciting of *gidayū*, as well as classical dance, koto, shamisen and the like were enjoyed by every family.[14]

Akiko herself took lessons in koto, shamisen, and classical dancing. Her father also sent her to an academy of Chinese studies for a few years, which would have acquainted her with the basics of the Chinese classics. It is doubtful that her education in this subject would have extended to the study of Po Chü-i's *Song of Everlasting Sorrow,* as Satō Haruo surmises.[15] But it certainly would have prepared her to read the poem later in life, as her poetic oeuvre shows she did:

> あなかしこ楊貴妃のごと斬られむと思ひたちしは十五の少女
> *Anakashiko Yōkihi no goto kiraremu to*
>   *omoitachishi wa jūgo no otome.* (2:30)
> Such distress! The fifteen-year-old virgin
>   convinced she will be cut up just like Yang Kuei-fei.

After completing primary school in 1888 she began to attend the newly established Sakai Women's School. In conservative Sakai at that time it was unusual for the children of a sweet-maker to go on to higher education, writes Mori, who sees Akiko's extended schooling as evidence of her father Sōshichi's regard for scholarship.[16] Sōshichi's enthusiasm for education was possibly also influenced by the efforts of the Japanese government, which in a series of Education Acts and ordinances issued from 1872 on, had aimed to centralize and standardize education throughout the

14. Kawai Suimei, "Akiko-san no Sakai jidai," *Shomotsu tenbō* 12.7 July 1942): 72–73. See also Mori, *Midaregami,* 32–33. In Akiko's own description of her hometown, "Sakai no shigai," written in 1915 for the young readers of *Shinshojo* and collected in *Watakushi no oidachi* (1985; reprint, Kankōsha, 1990), 95–101, she outlines the shape of the city—its bridges and streets, its shrines and temples, the mountains in the distance and the sea close by—without conveying much of a sense of what it was like to grow up there, and so I have preferred here Suimei's oft-cited description of the city.

15. Satō Haruo, *Akiko mandara* (Kōdansha, 1954), 11–13.

16. Mori, *Midaregami,* 16.

nation, exhorting every man to "subordinate all other matters to the education of his children."[17]

Akiko, however, remained dissatisfied with her education. Sewing and home economics formed the core of the curriculum at school; at home, her older sisters were married off and she, aged eleven, took their place behind the counter of the family shop:

> My older brother and younger sister and brother received their education at school, but my mother and I were tied down by the busy family business and I did not go to school.[18]

While this account is somewhat exaggerated—Akiko graduated from the Sakai Women's School in 1892 and continued on to the Supplementary Course *(hoshūka)* for a further two years—it is clear that her schooling "was not enough to satisfy her intellectual cravings," as one critic has put it:

> Moreover, there were the constraints of her work helping in the family business. For the spirited Akiko, single-handed study of the Japanese classics and immersion in newly published novels was the only road left to her.[19]

Inevitably, there was not enough time to enjoy this reading. "I was brought up in a sweetshop wrapping *yōkan* in bamboo leaves," she wrote:

> I waited for the end of the evening meal and then under the electric light that went off at twelve midnight, hidden from my parents, I made use of the short hour or half hour of light to read stealthily the works of Sei Shōnagon and Murasaki Shikibu. (14:60-61)

---

17. From the proclamation to the Education Act of 1872, cited in G. B. Sansom, *The Western World and Japan* (1930; reprint, Rutland, Vt. & Tokyo: Charles E. Tuttle, 1977), 456.

18. Yosano Akiko, "Yoriaibanashi," (1909) cited in Shinma, "Yosano Akiko to *Genji monogatari*," 249.

19. Shinma Shin'ichi, "Yosano Akiko shū kaisetsu," in *Nihon kindai bungaku taikei*, vol. 17, ed. Sakamoto Masachika, Moriwaki Kazuo, and Mukawa Chūichi (Kadokawa Shoten, 1971), 9. Akiko herself describes the schooling she received as boring and useless in her 1922 essay "Dokugaku to dokusho" *(TYAZ* 18:434).

Her parents' disapproval of her reading is mentioned several times in Akiko's accounts of her childhood.[20] Opposition seems to have come mainly from her mother, "infuriatingly over-anxious about her daughter who was now of marriageable age."[21] Although at least one of Akiko's accounts specifically mentions both parents' disapproval of her reading,[22] Mori is surely correct to see the principal opposition to days spent immersed in books as coming from Akiko's mother. Then, as now, it was the responsibility of the daughter-in-law (yome)—in this case Akiko's mother—to ensure the survival of the family. Useful though Akiko undoubtedly was around the shop, it was her younger brother who would inherit the business; if she should be deemed unmarriageably bookish, she was a liability. One cannot but be reminded of the very similar maternal antagonism encountered by Higuchi Ichiyō (1872–1896) as she was growing up.[23]

Despite her responsibilities in the shop and her mother's disapproval, Akiko managed to read vast amounts, as we have seen. In retrospect, even she was surprised by her youthful voracity. "Thinking about it now," she wrote in 1922, "I find it strange that in spite of my parents' objections I could have read that much when I was young" (18:43 3). Although she read from the entire corpus of Japanese literature, she was particularly attracted to Murasaki Shikibu's *Tale of Genji*:

> From the age of eleven or twelve, Murasaki Shikibu has been my teacher. I have no idea how many times I read through *The Tale of Genji* before I turned twenty. Her writing captivated me that much. I was entirely self taught; Murasaki Shikibu and I faced one another with no intermediary, just the two of us; and so I feel that I have had *The Tale of Genji* from the very mouth of this great woman of letters. (19:258)

20. See also Akiko's essays "Kyōshin tōgo," (1915, *TYAZ* 14:438); "Dokugaku to dokusho," (1922, *TYAZ* 18:433); and her defense of a woman's right to read in "Dokusho no shūkan," (1924, *TYAZ* 19:155–57).

21. Mori, *Midaregami*, 47.

22. Yosano Akiko, "Sei Shōnagon no kotodomo," (1911, *TYAZ* 14:61).

23. See the section from Ichiyō's diary "Chirino naka," ed. Wada Yoshie, *MBZ* 30:271. The passage is translated and discussed in Robert Lyons Danly, *In the Shade of Spring Leaves* (New Haven: Yale University Press, 1981), 14–15.

In Meiji Japan there were certainly others, even other young women, who loved to read as much as Akiko. But did they share this enthusiasm for *Genji?* Let us examine some accounts of the reading enjoyed by Akiko's female contemporaries.

Miyake Kaho [neé Tanabe Tatsuko] (1868–1943), Higuchi Ichiyō's fellow student at Nakajima Utako's (1841–1903) Haginoya poetry school,[24] and author of the successful *shōsetsu Yabu no uguisu* (Warbler in the Grove, 1888), recalls her childhood reading thus:

> I began reading *shōsetsu* when I was six or seven. Someone from one of those old circulating libraries would come with a mountainous load of books on his back for the household retainers, who crowded into the entrance hall. I became "addicted," as they say, to reading the books he would leave behind. From weighty tomes like *Kanso gundan, Sangokushi* and *Hakkenden;* to lighter works such as *Umegoyomi* or *Hizakurige,* I raced through them one after the other. I was happy with anything just so long as it had writing on it [25]

Kaho reveals that she for one grew up engrossed in the fiction of the recent past: the *Kanso magai mitate gundan* (The Genpei Wars a la War Tales of Han and Ch'u) is a *gōkanbon,* a series of complexly plotted stories in simple language by Kyokutei [Takizawa] Bakin (1767–1848), published 1829–31. *Sangokushi* most likely refers to the *Ehon tsūzoku Sangokushi,* published 1836–41, a popular illustrated edition of the seventeenth-century Japanese translation from Chinese of *San kuo chih yen-i* (The Romance of the Three Kingdoms). *Hakkenden* is of course the series of historical adventure stories *(yomihon)* by Bakin, *Nansō Satomi hakkenden* (The Eight Dog-Knights of the Kazusa Satomi), published 1814–42. *Shunshoku umegoyomi* (Spring Voluptuousness: A Plum Blossom Almanac) is a romantic fiction *(ninjōbon)* by Tamenaga Shunsui (1790–1843), published 1832–33. And *Tōkaidō dōchū hizakurige* (Hoofing it Down the Tōkaidō) is a

24. The Haginoya is discussed in Danly, *Spring Leaves,* esp. 15–16.
25. Miyake Kaho, "Ochanomizu jidai," ed. Shiota Ryōhei, *MBZ* 81:408.

series of comic adventure stories *(kokkeibon)* by Jippensha Ikku (1765–1831), published 1802–22.[26]

Ichiyō is less specific than Kaho, but her account of what she loved most is clearly a description of Edo fiction rather than earlier court literature:

> From the time that I was six, I used to love storybooks *(kusazōsht)*. Games of ball and shuttlecock didn't interest me. All I wanted was to read, and what I loved to read most were stories of the great and the valorous. Heroic exploits, full of honor and virtue, had quite an effect on me. I was spellbound by anything brave or spectacular.[27]

Ichiyō came to *Genji* when she began studying poetry at the Haginoya, and thereafter the work became one of the prime influences on her literary output.[28] In this sense she shares Akiko's fondness for *Genji.* The ways in which these two young women first read *Genji,* however, are markedly different. Left to her own devices, Ichiyō had preferred to read "stories of the great and the valorous," that is, edifying Edo fiction; she read *Genji* as part of her lessons in classical poetry at the Haginoya. For Akiko, on the other hand, *Genji* was her preferred reading, and she chose to read it long before she had any ideas of writing poetry.

A glimpse of the reading habits of other women writers, only slightly older than Akiko, is afforded by a survey entitled "Keishū shōsetsuka no kotae" (Responses From Lady Novelists), which appeared in five consecutive issues of *Jogaku zasshi* in March and April of 1890.[29]

26. I am indebted to Markus, *Willow in Autumn,* for his inspired English translations of the titles of *Hakkenden* and *Shunshoku umegoyomi.*

27. Higuchi Ichiyō, "Chirino naka," *MBZ* 30:270. Translation by Danly, *Spring Leaves,* 12.

28. See Shioda Ryōhei, "Katen to Meiji ikō no bungaku," in *Iwanami kōza Nihon bungakushi,* ed. Iwanami Yūjirō (Iwanami Shoten, 1959), vol. 14, part 6:13–14, 28; and Itō Hiroshi, "Genji monogatari to kindai bungaku," *Kokubungaku: kaishaku to kanshō* 48.10 (July 1983): 135–38.

29. *See Jogaku zasshi,* no. 204 (15 March 1890): 104, for the questions; the replies appear in no. 205 (22 March 1890): 127–28; no. 206 (29 March 1890): 158–59; no. 207 (5 April 1890): 187–90; no. 208 (12 April 1890): 216; and no. 209 (19 April 1890): 247. I am indebted to Ochi Haruo's *Kindai bungaku no tanjō* (Kōdansha:, 1975), 55–56, for directing me to this survey. In English, see Rebecca L. Copeland, "The Meiji Woman Writer 'Amidst a Forest of Beards'," *Harvard Journal of Asiatic Studies* 57.2 (1997): 383–418.

The magazine surveyed five "women writers prominent in the world of *shōsetsu*": Koganei Kimi (1871–1956), a regular contributor to her brother Mori Ōgai's *Shigarami zōshi*;[30] "Akebono Joshi" [neé Kimura Eiko] (1872–90), author of *Fujo no kagami* (A Mirror for Womanhood, 1889), the first *shōsetsu* by a woman to be serialized in the *Yomiuri* newspaper;[31] Wakamatsu Shizuko (1864–96), a writer and translator now best known for her Japanese version of Frances Hodgson Burnett's *Little Lord Fauntleroy*;[32] Sasaki Masako, also known as Chikuhakuen Joshi;[33] and Tanabe Tatsuko [Miyake Kaho]. These women were asked to tell of their experiences as writers; their ideals, hopes, and theories concerning the *shōsetsu* form; their opinions of recent *shōsetsu* literature. Their replies form a fascinating document, worthy of further study; but it is the answers to question three—"Over the years, which are the *shōsetsu* you have most enjoyed reading?"—that are of most direct relevance here.

30. Names are as they appear *in Jogaku zasshi*. Koganei's name appears elsewhere as "Kimiko."
31. I am grateful to Margaret Mitsutani for sharing her delightful adaptation of Akebono's story with me. Her version appeared in *The Magazine* 3.5 (1988): 50–55 and 3.6 (1988): 51–54.
32. Translated as *Shōkōshi* (1890–92). Wakamatsu Shizuko was the pen name of Shimada Kashiko. She married the editor of *Jogaku zasshi*, Iwamoto Yoshiharu (1863–1943), in 1889.
33. Pronounced "Nagizono," this was the poetic *nom de plume* used by *waka* poet and scholar of Japanese literature Sasaki Hirotsuna (1828–91), and succeeded to by his son Sasaki Nobutsuna (1872–1963). The *nagi* is a tall evergreen tree [Deceusocarpus nagi (Thunb.) de Laubenf.] found in the warmer regions of Japan. When Nobutsuna founded a poetry society in 1891 following his father's death, he simply took his father's *nom de plume* and used the Sino-Japanese reading of the two characters used to write *nagi* as its name, producing "Chikuhaku-kai." In later years he seems to have preferred to pronounce his own *nom de plume* "Chikuhakuen," retaining the *kanji* but departing from the customary pronunciation of his father. I therefore follow this practice in reading Masako's pen name. Sasaki Masako is described *in Jogaku zasshi* as the author of "Mune no omoi," published in the literary journal *Miyako no hana*. But according to Professor Sasaki Yukitsuna, present head of the Sasaki family, there was no one by the name of "Masako" in the family. OHirotsuna had no female offspring; Nobutsuna was only eighteen years old in 1890 and as yet unmarried. The name of the woman he eventually married was Yukiko. Professor Sasaki also detects a "strong scent of Nobutsuna" about the *Jogaku zasshi* piece and suggests that although "Chikuhakuen Joshi" is not one of Nobutsuna's known styles, there is a strong possibility that "Masako" is none other than the youthful Nobutsuna playing the "latter-day Tsurayuki." Conversation, 20 May 1992.

Of the five, Tanabe—that is, Miyake Kaho, whose favorite reading has been examined above—is the only one who has nothing at all to say on the subject of her reading.[34] Akebono writes that she still has little experience of Western books and finds them difficult; recently, however, she has read translations of Shakespeare and other greats and found their detailed depiction of human emotions (ninjō) most interesting. Kyōden and Bakin are the only two Japanese authors whose names appear in her reply and there is no mention of classical Japanese literature.[35] Wakamatsu's reply is by far the longest and her list of (Western) authors impresses. She has read Dickens's *The Old Curiosity Shop* and *David Copperfield*, and Lytton's *Zanoni* more than once, and Mrs. [Elizabeth Barrett] Browning's *Aurora Leigh* again and again. Of *shōsetsu* in the Japanese language, she has read just three or four by Eakin (no titles are mentioned); several *monogatari* (again, no titles are mentioned); and little of more recent works, although she mentions three publications from the previous year, 1889, as *shōsetsu* she had particularly enjoyed: *Hatsukoi* by Saganoya Omura (1863–1947), *Saikun* by Tsubouchi Shōyō (1859–1935), and *Fūryūbutsu* by Kōda Rohan (1867–1947).[36]

When we come to the replies of Koganei Kimi and "Sasaki Masako," however, the picture is a very different one. Both are lovers of *Genji*. Koganei writes, "It is none other than a *shōsetsu* of our own country, *The Tale of Genji*, which I customarily have by my side and have read about twenty times." She goes on to list the tales, diaries, essays and *kagamimono* of the Japanese classical canon, which, "it goes without saying" she has read. At one time she was fond of Eakin, though she does not look at his work now. Her list concludes with the two works of English literature she has read most carefully: Frances [Fanny] Burney's *Evelina* and Elizabeth Hamilton's *The Cottagers of Glenburnie*.[37] For "Masako," *Genji* is the *only* reading "she" enjoys

34. "Keishū shōsetsuka no kotae," *Jogaku zasshi*, no. 209 (19 April 1890): 247.

35. Ibid., no. 206 (29 March 1890): 158.

36. Ibid., no. 207 (5 April 1890): 189.

37. Ibid., no. 205 (22 March 1890): 128. In 1897, Koganei Kimi published an essay entitled "Yubi kuitaru onna" (The woman who bit a finger) in Mori Rintarō [Ōgai], ed., *Kagekusa* (Shun'yōdō, 1897), 614–17. Shimauchi Keiji, *Bungō no kotenryoku: Sōseki, Ōgai wa*

(konomite yomu wa Genji nomi nite), and in particular "she" rereads the "Rainy Night Ranking" of women from the 'Hahakigi' chapter, as well as the 'Wakamurasaki' (Lavender), 'Otome' (The Maiden), and 'Tenarai' (At Writing Practice) chapters.[38] Given Professor Sasaki's comments, and in the absence of further evidence, we must question the authenticity of this "woman writer's" professed fondness for *Genji.* Nobutsuna's little joke can nonetheless be read as his attempt to pronounce upon what a woman should be reading: *The Tale of Genji.* And the tally of Akiko's female literary contemporaries of whose reading we have an account thus yields one avid reader of *Genji,* three who preferred literature from the more recent past, and one, Wakamatsu Shizuko, who read principally Western novels.

Returning for a closer look at the preferences of the men of the "Shomoku jisshu" surveys, we find that the *Genji* readers among them are but a minority within a minority. Seventeen different works of classical Japanese literature are cited by the twenty-four readers who include such reading matter on their lists. The most frequently mentioned work is *Heike monogatari,* cited nine times, closely followed by *Tsurezuregusa* (eight) and then *Genji monogatari* (seven). Beyond this, all unanimity of taste disappears: *Kokinshū* receives four mentions, *Makura no sōshi* and *Taiheiki* three each, and there are single mentions of such works as *Taketori monogatari, Ōkagami, Shinkokinshū,* and *Genpei seisuiki.*

Neither is there anything that distinguishes the seven men who do cite *Genji* from their fellows. All include works of Chinese

---

Genji o yonda ka (Bungei Shunjū, 2002), 89, identifies the Austrian actor and playwright Ferdinand Raimund (1790–1836) she mentions; a careful reading reveals that the essay is not a discussion of one of Raimund's works, however, but of the "real story" (*jitsu no monogatari*) of his relationships with two women: his wife, the soubrette Luise Gleich (1798–1855), who bit his finger on what was to be their wedding day, necessitating a postponement; and his lover, Antonie (Toni) Wagner (1799–1879). The characters of the two women remind Koganei of those in the cautionary tales told by Uma no Kami in the "Rainy Night Ranking of Women" section of the 'Hahakigi' chapter of *Genji* (1:147–56; S 27–32), and she concludes, "in China, Japan, and in other countries, so one gathers, a woman may have this or that quality, but there are very few who have the full complement of virtues."

38. Ibid., no. 208 (12 April 1890): 216.

literature in their lists, yet only two, Yamada Bimyō (1868–1910) and the scholar of law Kōmyōji Saburō (1849–93), also list Western books. Yoda Gakkai (1833–1909), a government official, scholar of Chinese and writer of new *kabuki,* and the National Learning scholar Konakamura Kiyonori (1821–95), provide commentaries to their lists, which reveal something of their individual reading practices. Gakkai reports that he has always loved *Genji:*

> [I]n the course of reading this work from my youth, I generally consulted *Kogetsushō* for help in understanding difficult passages. If I was unable to understand even then, I simply left it at that: it is enough that one understands most of it.[39]

This approach to *Genji,* haphazard perhaps, but founded on a love for the work and a trust in an instinctive understanding of the text, closely resembles Akiko's experience of reading. Konakamura too had always been fond of *Genji,* but being a specialist in National Learning (*kokugaku*), he "read *[Kogetsushō]* with particular care, and added [his own] annotations throughout the fifty-four chapters."[40]

The response to this survey provided by the only woman to appear in the series is also illuminating for the breadth of interest it displays and her curiosity about a world that she could only hope to explore by reading. The lone female respondent was Shimada Utako (1854–193 7), a poet, as her name suggests, and founder of educational institutions for women. Shimada, preferring to reply discursively, does not provide a list of her favorite reading matter. The only works actually referred to in her response are the classics of Chinese history and philosophy that, deeming herself "shallow in learning and without talent," she has only skimmed.[41] She later began reading Japanese works, in the course of which she felt the need to acquire some understanding of Buddhism, which "naturally" led her to India and thence to the world of Occidental books. After becoming a student of Western

39. Tokutomi, "Shomoku jisshu," 6.
40. Ibid., 12.
41. Ibid., 15.

studies she found her preferences changing daily, and thus it was difficult for her to say with any confidence which books were her favorites.
   The reading of these six Meiji literary women and the sixty
eight men of the "Shomoku jisshu" survey provides at least a sketchy
background against which to view Akiko's accounts of her early reading. As we might expect, her preferences differ markedly from those
of most of her male contemporaries. And her single-minded devotion
to *Genji* and the Heian classics seems to be shared by only one of the
Jogaku zasshi five, Koganei Kimi. Clearly the evidence is too slight
to draw any firm conclusions about the popularity, or lack thereof,
of *Genji* among female readers of the Meiji period. It does suggest,
how ever, that in her choice of reading material, at least, Akiko had
good reason for believing, as she later said, that "the self-education
that I received through reading" was "atypical" (18:434).
   In other respects, however, Akiko's childhood reading seems
to mark her as entirely typical of the "modern" reader, as described
by Maeda Ai. She is not of that earlier generation whose "memories
of reading begin with memories of the voices of family members."[42]
Nowhere is there any mention of her father or mother reading to her,
or of other family members reading to each other.[43] She seems to
have learned to read at primary school. Her silent and solitary reading
reflects the gradual eclipse of "traditional" readers "for whom virtue
was living according to the norms passed down to them by their parents and teachers" and the rise of "modern" readers "who derived their
sense of values from the printed word, which opened up for them solitary adventures into unknown worlds."[44]

   What, then, were the effects of this childhood reading? Akiko's
"secret joy" in reading the Japanese classics seems certainly to have
fostered attitudes and values different from those of her merchant class

---

42. Maeda Ai, *Kindai dokusha no seiritsu* (Yūseidō, 1973), 127.
43. In her 1916 story "Watakushi no mita shōjo: Minami-san," in *Watakushi no oidachi*, 111,
   Akiko recalls that it was rare for her father to speak to her even three times in a month.
44. Maeda, *Kindai dokusha,* 126. Analogous developments in Western reading practices are
   discussed in Alberto Manguel, *A History of Reading* (London: HarperCollins, 1996),
   especially the chapter "Learning to Read," 67–83.

family and her provincial home town. "I abhorred the conservatism of my family and my home town," she says, "their hypocrisy, corruption, ignorance and vulgarity, as well as the melancholy atmosphere I was caught up in" (13:37–38). *The Tale of Genji* was an escape from all this; it also provided Akiko with heroines she could identify with, fantasies of beautiful lives, and roles of significance. "While my body was occupied with the busy life of work in the shop," she recalls, "in my mind I was transformed into a high-born lady from *The Tale of Genji*" (13:256):

> From the age of twelve I was fond of historical and literary works, and hidden away from people at home I immersed myself in them, envious of the pristine dignity of the lives of virgin empresses, like Amaterasu Ōmikami. I was drawn, too, to the vestals of the Ise and the Kamo shrines. Despite the grim reality that I faced, I regarded my future in vastly different terms, as something beautiful and ideal. I wanted to live my whole life as an unsullied virgin, like an angel. Such were my feelings then, I can see in retrospect.
>
> There was also something grown up about the way I felt. Partly that was because I managed the shop more or less by myself, helping my sickly mother in place of my irresponsible father; but it also seems to have been because I came to understand human nature early in life, through my intimacy with historical and literary works. In the midst of this busy life, I developed a degree of mental leeway that allowed me to look down on it all a bit.
>
> And so, grown up as I was, from about the age of twelve I was able to imagine what it was like to be in love, thanks to those works of literature. There were times when I would smile to myself, comparing myself with various of the women in *The Tale of Genji*. But whatever feelings of like or dislike for the opposite sex I might have had, in reality I had no opportunity to experience any that could be called love until I was twenty-three years old. I always felt that all of the men and women around me were impure; and so I felt close only to men and women in books. (14:374–75)

Akiko's letters from this period reveal even more vividly the strength of her identification with characters from *Genji*. In January 1900 she began corresponding with Kōno Tetsunan (1874–1940), son of a priest at a nearby temple in Sakai.[45] In a letter dated 5 April 1900 she writes indignantly:

> Even reading such things as *Genji*, well, people like Murasaki I can accept, but I simply can't work up much sympathy for those beautiful women of no great rank like Yūgao and Akashi. And even when reading about them in books, men who are cruel to women are hateful, hateful, I can't bear them. Isn't it just detestable how, when he leaves someone who means as much to him as Murasaki in the capital crying, and then is recalled to the capital from Akashi, he writes "I lament no less than when I left the capital in spring"![46]

In another letter Kōno apparently asked her which of the women in *Genji* she felt the greatest affinity for. Her reply:

> More even than the peerless Murasaki, I envy Ōigimi of Uji. To make one such as Kaoru cry that much, to be desired that much, and then to die so soon and be endlessly longed for, if only I could be loved like that—that is how I feel.[47]

Her fervor, her (at least imagined) desire to suffer for the sake of romance, is perhaps most reminiscent of the *Sarashina* diarist, who, in her early fifties, looked back at her youth and recalled that "[i]n those days most people began to read the sutras and to perform religious

45. Tetsunan is one of several men of Akiko's acquaintance who has been suggested as the subject of her early "michi o toku kimi" poem *(1YAZ* 1:6), cited in the introduction, p. 7. Kubo Kazuko lists the competing candidates in "Yosano Akiko: nazo," *Kokubungaku: kaishaku to kyōzai no kenkyū* 31.11 (September 1986): 133.
46. Quoted in Shinma, "Yosano Akiko to *Genji monogatari,*" 251. In her letter, Akiko quotes only the upper hemistich of Genji's poem to the Akashi Nyūdō in the 'Akashi' chapter:

    Toshi ideshi haru no nageki ni otorameya
        toshi furu ura o wakarenuru aki. (2:259; S 268)
    I lament no less than when I left the capital in spring,
        parting in autumn from these shores where years have passed.
47. Letter dated 15 March 1900. Quoted in Shinma, "Yosano Akiko to *Genji monogatari,*" 2 51; fuller text in Itsumi Kumi, "Yosano Akiko no *Genji monogatari* kōgoyaku ni tsuite," *Kokugakuin zasshi* 94.1 (January 1993): 15–16.

devotions at age sixteen or seventeen, but such things did not in the least interest me":

> All that I could manage to think of was how I might live hidden away in the mountains like Ukifune. And there would be some very noble and handsome gentleman, like Genji in the novel, who would call upon me perhaps once in a year. In my loneliness I would gaze out upon the cherry blossoms, the autumn leaves, the moon, or the snow, while I waited for one of his charming letters.[48]

In these early days Akiko seems to have been content to live out her fantasies in poetry-writing. As Kumasaka Atsuko has suggested, "[a]t the outset, Akiko's poems did not spring from the actual experience of life; she wrote of the world of the emotions by drawing upon desires and fantasies that had their origin in her reading."[49] Akiko herself admits as much. In a later account of her awakening to the possibilities of poetry, she states that although she was first moved to compose when she chanced upon some *tanka* by Tekkan in the *Yomiuri* newspaper one year, her initial subject matter was drawn from her fantasies and imaginings:

> Until I was twenty, I never thought about composing poetry. From the age of about ten, in my secret reading at home of various historical and literary works, I had read collections of *haiku* and *waka,* but I didn't like the finicky rules of decorum and the secret teachings that seemed to be involved. I thought that their content was inferior to that of Chinese poetry and they seemed to me to be of no particular significance; I regarded them with indifference. Then one year (about Meiji 30 [1897]), in spring, by chance I saw some poetry by my present husband in the *Yomiuri* newspaper.[50] There were a number of poems like the following one:

48. Translation by T. J. Harper, "Motoori Norinaga's Criticism of the *Genji monogatari:* A Study of the Background and Critical Content of his *Genji monogatari Tama no ogushi*" (Ph.D. diss., University of Michigan, 1971), 35. Japanese text in *NKBZ* 18:317.
49. Kumasaka Atsuko, "Yosano Akiko," *Kokubungaku: kaishaku to kanshō* 37.10 (August 1972): 117.
50. The poems to which Akiko refers were actually published in *Yomiuri shinbun,* 10 April 1898. Itsumi Kumi, *Hyōden Yosano Tekkan Akiko* (Yagi Shoten, 1975), *570.*

春浅き道灌山の一つ茶屋に餅食う書生袴着けたり
Haru asaki Dōkanyama no hitotsu chaya ni
   mochi kū shosei hakama tsuketari.
Early spring: at a tea-house in Dōkanyama, a student,
   wearing hakama, chews on sticky rice cakes.

... Looking at these poems, I thought that, if it would suffice to compose with such easy frankness, unconcerned with the ornaments of form, then I too could compose poetry. And so two or three years passed. In the autumn of Meiji 32 [1899] Yosano formed the Shinshisha (New Poetry Society);[51] at the opportunity provided by this new movement for *tanka* reform, I suddenly felt a desire to create and I sent some drafts of poems to the Society.

At that time, in order to escape the gloomy atmosphere of home, I drew hints from the various reading I have mentioned and from the beautiful scenery and ways of the Kinai area. I was immersed in ideals and fantasies of my own construction; having lived a life full of yearning, I dashed off poetry expressing the feelings that rose from my ideals and fantasies, exactly as suggested to me by Yosano's poetry. (13:31–32)

Akiko's account of her initial urge to write poetry is clearly romanticized, for we know that she had been publishing both newstyle poetry and *tanka* in various local literary magazines long before she sent her first batch of poems to *Myōjō*.[52] Nonetheless, the publication of her poems in *Myōjō* and subsequent meeting with Tekkan were turning points in her life. At last, longing could become reality:

As time wore on, I could no longer be satisfied by the fantasy world of books. I came to want to be a completely free individual. Then, by an uncanny coincidence of opportunity, at the same time as I screwed up my courage and won the freedom of love, I was able to escape from the cage of my old-fashioned family where my individuality had long been confined. Moreover, at the same time I was miraculously able to turn my thoughts into poems in my own

51. The Shinshisha was formed on 3 November 1899. Itsumi, *Hyōden*, 572.
52. Akiko's poems, collected under the title "Hanagatami," appear in *Myōjō*, no. 2 (May 1900): 11.

words. At a single stroke, I achieved three important freedoms,
those of love *(ren'ai),* morality *(rinri),* and art *(geijutsu).* (14:438)

Many have seen Akiko's flight from Sakai to Tokyo as an
archetypal gesture of modernity. Certainly running away from a com-
fortable if constricting merchant-class family to live in poverty with
her lover required courage. But mere "modernity"? Might not Akiko's
elopement also be seen as the enactment of fantasies that had their
origin in her reading of *Genji?*

In a letter to Tekkan written less than a month before her elopement, she explicitly identifies him as her "Genji," and herself as a
Genji heroine. As we shall see in chapter six, this fantasy, arising from
her childhood reading, survived years of privation, the birth of thirteen
children, her own fame and her husband's philandering—and for all
we know may never have been abandoned.

Chapter Three:
The Tale of Genji in the Meiji Period

文章経国之大業、不朽之盛事
Bunshō wa keikoku no taigyō, fukyū no seiji.
Literature: a vital force in the ordering of the state,
a glorious achievement that never grows old.[1]

Wei Wen-ti, "T'ien lun"

抑、源語は国家無上の至宝として万国に誇るに足るべきものなり。
*Somosomo, Gengo wa kokka mujō no shihō toshite bankoku ni hokoru
ni tarubeki mono nari.*
The Tale of Genji, then, is the unrivaled treasure of our nation and, as such,
something worth boasting about to all the nations of the world.

Sassa Seisetsu, *Shinshaku Genji monogatari* (1911)

By the end of the century, while Akiko was still spinning the fantasies of which she would later weave large portions of her life, both professional and domestic, *The Tale of Genji* was generating quite another sort of interest among the literati of mid-Meiji. These were the writers, scholars, and educators who looked to *Genji* as a new "cultural scripture" of the "new Japan" they were so earnestly attempting to build. They were also the pillars of the literary world in which Akiko was to make her debut as a translator of *Genji.* If we are to appreciate fully the nature and impact of her first major published work on *Genji,* we must first examine the attitudes and accomplishments of her senior colleagues in this endeavor.

The first modern Japanese translation of *The Tale of Genji,* Akiko's four-volume *Shin'yaku Genji monogatari,* was published by

1. *Wen hsüan* 52, translation by Burton Watson, *Early Chinese Literature* (New York: Columbia University Press, 1962), epigraph facing title page.

Kanao Bun'endō in 1912 and 1913.[2] It was an immediate commercial
success with the rapidly expanding reading public and the object of
extravagant praise from some of the most eminent members of the literary establishment, Mori Ōgai and Ueda Bin (1874–1916) among them.
Laudatory reviews, unfortunately anonymous, abounded in major
newspapers and literary journals.[3] To some extent this unprecedented
enthusiasm for a translation of *Genji* can be explained by the talent,
learning, and dedication that Akiko herself brought to the task. Yet in
the company of other literary landmarks of the same years—Nagai
Kafū's translations of French symbolist poetry, Arishima Takeo's
"Glimpse of a Certain Woman," the first Japanese performances of
Ibsen's "A Doll's House" and "The Wild Duck"—the translation of
an eleventh-century classic seems somehow out of place, out of date.[4]

For Ueda Bin, however, Akiko's *Shin'yaku* was no anomaly: it
was the work of "the right person at the right time."[5] Ōgai, too, opined
that no one was better suited to the task of translating *Genji* than
Akiko, and claimed that he had long felt a need for a modern translation of *Genji*.[6] That Akiko should be seen as the "right person" seems
explicable; and as we shall see in the next chapter, her knowledge of
Genji and her willingness to elucidate it for others were well known to
Bin and Ōgai. But what was it about the time—1912—that made the
publication of the *Shin'yaku* seem so "right," so "desirable," to these
two pillars of the Meiji literary establishment? I would suggest that the

2. Here I use the terms "modern Japanese" and "modern colloquial" interchangeably as translations of Japanese *gendaigo*, in contradistinction to "literary," "classical," or "ancient"
   (bungo, kotengo, or *kogo) Japanese.* According to the list of translations and versions *(yakubun hon'an)* in Fujita Tokutarō, *Genji monogatari kenkyū shomoku yōran*
   (Rokubunkan, 1932), 88–95, there were at least three attempts at complete translations
   of *The Tale of Genji* in the Edo period. Only one achieved partial publication in a woodblock edition, however, and most of the other manuscripts seem since to have been lost.
   Fujita himself hails Akiko's translation as "the first complete translation into the modern
   colloquial" (p. 93) and I follow him in this designation here.
3. The critical reception of the *Shin'yaku* will be discussed in chapter four.
4. Nagai Kafū, *Sangoshū* (Coral Collection, 1913). Arishima Takeo, "Aru onna no gurinpusu,"
   serialized in *Shirakaba* between January 1911 and March 1913. "A Doll's House" and
   "The Wild Duck" were first performed in September 1911 and May 1913, respectively.
5. Ueda Bin, untitled preface to Yosano Akiko, *Shin'yaku Genji monogatari* (Kanao Bun'endō,
   1912), 1:1.
6. Mori Rintarō [Ōgai], untitled preface in ibid., 1:2–4.

commercial and critical success of this translated classic in an age of "new-style poetry" *(shintaishi),* "new drama" *(shingeki)* and the novel *(shōsetsu)* alerts us to a little-noticed aspect of the national identity-building project then underway in Japan; and this in turn suggests that the success of Akiko's *Shin'yaku* is the result not only of the gifts of its author but also of the political uses to which *The Tale of Genji* was put in the latter half of the Meiji period.

The process is complex but the broad outlines are clearly discernible. We see the Meiji descendants of Eda period scholars of National Learning returning the text of *Genji* to circulation; establishing institutions to train a new generation of custodians of the canon; articulating the principles of their project; and attempting, through translation, to transform *Genji* into an instrument for the edification of the new mass readership of the new Japan.

In 1890, after a hiatus of almost two hundred years, there was a sudden rush of reprints of *The Tale of Genji:* three complete movable type editions appeared in 1890–91, with a further two following in 1903–6 and 1909–10.[7] Moreover, most of the ancillary aids to the reading of *Genji* that appeared in the Meiji period were published after this 1890 watershed. There were digests in the style of the popular Eda period genre.[8] There were translations of famous passages into simple literary Japanese,[9] into *kanbun,* and even into the twelve syllable lines of *shintaishi.*[10] For female students, there were readers *(tokuhon)*

7. Kokuritsu Kokkai Toshokan, ed., *Meiji-ki kankō tosho mokuroku: Kokuritsu Kokkai Toshokan shozō,* 6 vols. (Kokkai Toshokan, 1971–76) lists these editions as: Hagino Yoshiyuki, Ochiai Naobumi, and Konakamura Yoshikata, eds., *Nihon bungaku zensho,* vols. 8–12 (Hakubunkan, 1890–91); Oda Sugao and Shikada Genzō, eds., *Kōsei hochū kokubun zensho,* vols. 1–8 (Osaka: Kokubunkan, 1890–91); Inokuma Natsuki, ed., *Teisei zōchū Genji monogatari Kogetsushō,* 5 vols. (Osaka: Tosha Shuppan, 1890–91); Maruoka Katsura and Matsushita Daizaburō, eds., *Kokubun taikan,* vols. 1–2 (Itakuraya, 1903–6); and Motoori Toyokai and Furuya Chishin, eds., *Kokumin bunko,* 1st ser., vols. 7–8 (Kokumin Bunko Kankōkai, 1909–11).
8. Chō Tsuratsune, *Genji monogatari kōgai* (Shinchōsha, 1906); Onoe Torako, *Genji monogatari tai'i* (Daidōkan, 1911).
9. Masuda Yukinobu, *Shinpen shishi,* 10 vols. (various publishers, 1888–1904); Shimano Enkō, *Ese Genji* (Keigyōsha, 1892).
10. Into *kanbun:* Kawai Jirō, *Shishi* Oinrian, 1893); into *shintaishi:* Mizoguchi Hakuyō, *Katei shinshi Genji monogatari* (Okamura Shoten, Fukuoka Shoten, 1906).

containing selections from the early chapters of *Genji* with commentary and notes in an easy classical style.[11] Articles about *Genji* and Murasaki Shikibu began to appear frequently in women's magazines.[12] And transcripts of lectures on *Genji* seem to have been enthusiastically received by young provincials with aspirations to culture.[13]

Since Akiko was only eleven or twelve years old when she began reading *The Tale of Genji*—in 1888–89, just prior to the watershed—the text she first encountered must have been a woodblock printed edition from the Edo period, most likely a copy of the *Kogetsushō*.[14] Soon thereafter she was also reading it in modern movable type. As she writes in 1922:

> I borrowed old woodblock printed editions *(kohanpon)* of works from the Heian and other periods from friends, and I also bought Hakubunkan editions *(Hakubunkanbon)* as well as other Meiji movable type editions *(shinpan)* and read those too. (18:433)

How, then, are we to account for this spate of new editions of *Genji* that suddenly made the text so much more accessible, not only to Akiko but to the entire reading public? Why did so many scholars suddenly decide to expend so much energy editing, explicating, and otherwise attempting to rescue *Genji* from obscurity? It is to the authors and editors of these works that we must turn for answers.

11. Suzuki Hiroyasu, *Jogakkō yō tokuhon: Genji monogatari bassui,* 5 vols. (Chūgaidō, 1888); Ōwada Tateki, *Genji tokuhon,* 2 vols. (Uehara Shobō, 1901).
12. The most complete list of Meiji period journal articles about Murasaki Shikibu and *The Tale of Genji* is, so far as I know, Sakurai Yūizō, "Genji monogatari kenkyū bunken mokuroku—zasshi kankei—," *Kokugo to kokubungaku,* no. 390 (October 1956): 164–66. Pages 166–87 continue the listing through 1955.
13. Mitani Kuniaki, "Meiji-ki no *Genji monogatari* kenkyū," *Kokubungaku: kaishaku to kanshō* 48.10 (July 1983): 53. Published lecture notes include Suzuki Hiroyasu, *Genji monogatari kōgi,* 9 vols. (Chūgaidō, 1884–88); and Iida Takesato, "Genji monogatari," *Kokugo kōgiroku,* vol. *ha* (no publisher indicated, 1890).
14. Kannotō Akio, "Yosano Akiko no yonda *Genji monogatari*," in *Genji monogatari e Genji monogatari kara,* ed. Nagai Kazuko (Kasama Shoin, 2007), 284–90, convincingly argues that the text of *Genji* Akiko first encountered was most likely the illustrated small-format woodblock-printed edition from the early Kanbun period (ca. 1661) that she used throughout her life.

It is a commonplace of Japanese literary history that the third decade of the Meiji period (that is, from 1887–96) is one of conservative reaction to Westernization.[15] To some scholars this tendency alone has seemed a sufficient explanation of the concurrent renewal of interest in classical Japanese literature. But a "public reaction to the excesses of Japan's Westernizing policies"[16] hardly suffices to explain the successive publication of five complete new editions of *Genji* after a hiatus of two centuries. The motivation for this sudden surge of reprints lies, I think, in a less conspicuous but more complex aspect of the modernization process. Carol Gluck aptly describes this as an "ideological momentum" which gathered force in the 1880s:

> [An] outburst of nation-mindedness [which] included explorations of national character, reassertions of indigenous ways, and projections of Japan into the world order as the nineteenth-century West defined it. Invocations of nation included, more and more pressingly, the effort to draw all the people into the state, to have them thinking national thoughts, to make *kokumin* of them, new Japanese for what was called "the new Japan."[17]

To scholars of Japanese literature, heirs to a seemingly moribund tradition of Edo-period National Learning, this atmosphere of "nation-mindedness" offered a chance to make *their* literature—and in particular *The Tale of Genji*—a "vital force in the ordering of the state." In the classical canon they would find the source of the national (and self) identity they needed to ensure for themselves and their scholarship a place of prominence, perhaps even influence, in

---

15. See Donald H. Shively, "The Japanization of the Middle Meiji," in *Tradition and Modernization in Japanese Culture*, ed. Donald H. Shively (Princeton: Princeton University Press, 1971), 77–119, for an overview of the "nativistic reaction to Japanese 'Westernization'" (117). Much earlier, Ikari Akira, *Ken'yūsha no bungaku* (Hanawa Shobō, 1961), 13–17, showed how various was the response to the first twenty years of "Westernization."

16. Michael C. Brownstein, "From *Kokugaku* to *Kokubungaku*: Canon–Formation in the Meiji Period," *Harvard Journal of Asiatic Studies* 47.2 (December 1987): 436.

17. Carol Gluck, *Japan's Modern Myths: Ideology in the Late Meiji Period* (Princeton: Princeton University Press, 1985), 23.

"the new Japan." In *The Tale of Genji* they would find both the guidance needed to make a *kokumin* of their people, and the "projection of Japan" they would present to the world. Their *Genji* would become a "treasure" not only of the nation Japan, but of the whole world. Before *Genji* could be put to these new tasks, however, not only the text but also the now depleted supply of scholars would have to be saved from oblivion.

Concern on the part of several scholars about the possible extinction of the National Learning tradition led to the establishment, in 1882, of a *Koten kōshū–ka* (Classics Training Course) in the Faculty of Letters at Tokyo University.[18] From the vantage point of the present, when the discipline of "National Literature" *(kokubungaku)* is such a well-established part not only of Japanese academic life but also the cultural life of the nation, it might seem that it should have been a simple matter for National Learning scholars of the Edo period to find and train their Meiji disciples. This evidently was not the case. Wada Hidematsu (1865–1937) recalls that in his year, 1884, the number of dropouts from the Classics Training Course was so high that a second intake of students was necessary:

> [I]t seemed to be because the nature of a Department of National Books was not generally well understood. I have heard that my relatives often asked, "What on earth can Hidematsu be intending

18. In March 1886 "Tōkyō Daigaku" was renamed "Teikoku Daigaku." A further adjustment of nomenclature in June 1897 resulted in "Tōkyō Teikoku Daigaku." For the sake of clarity I refer to the institution as Tokyo University throughout.
    The basic source of information on the *Koten kōshū-ka* is *Tōkyō Teikoku Daigaku gojūnenshi* (Tōkyō Teikoku Daigaku, 1932), 1:721–47. My discussion is also based on the following sources: Sasaki Nobutsuna, "Kotenka jidai no omoide," and Wada Hidematsu, "Koten kōshūka jidai," both in *Kokugo to kokubungaku* 11.8 (August 1934): 23–31 and 32–39, respectively; the 'Koten fukkō' section of Shioda Ryōhei, "Koten to Meiji ikō no bungaku," in *Iwanami kōza Nihon bungakushi*, ed. Iwanami Yūjirō (Iwanami Shoten, 1959), 14:3–5; the 'Meiji shinkokugaku undō e no tenbō' section of Haga Noboru, "Bakumatsu henkakki ni okeru kokugakusha no undō to ronri," *Nihon shisō taikei*, vol. 51, ed. Haga Noboru and Matsumoto Sannosuke (Iwanami Shoten, 1971), 707–14; *Tōkyō Daigaku hyakunenshi* Henshū Iinkai, ed., *Tōkyō Daigaku hyakunenshi: bukyokushi* (Tōkyō Daigaku Shuppankai, 1986), 1: 712–16; and Brownstein, "From *Kokugaku* to *Kokubungaku*," 436–38. "Classics Training Course" is Brownstein's translation of *Koten kōshū-ka*.

to do, studying such a thing as *kokugaku?* Surely he doesn't intend to become a Shinto priest?" It was a period when *kokugaku* was in decline, and so such doubts were inevitable.[19]

Although for budgetary and other reasons the Classics Training Course was abolished after only six years, its name is in structive. *Koten* in Chinese usage meant ancient precedent, ceremony, or text. Motoori Norinaga had used this combination of characters, glossed *inishiebumi* (old texts), in his *Tamakatsuma.* In *Kojikiden,* he glossed the same characters *furukifumi* (ancient texts).[20] Then in the Meiji period the word was exhumed and its meaning extended to translate the word "classics," on the model of the Greek and Roman classics.[21] Thus the compound at least, if not the reading, had blue-blooded National Learning lineage that underlined the ideological respectability of the Classics Training Course and at the same time implied an equivalence between Japanese literature and the classics of the West. And the very name of the course indicates that this new use of *koten* had achieved currency at least by the second decade of the Meiji period.

What then were the classics at this time? Shiota Ryōhei offers the following list:

> At that time *koten* meant the *Kojiki,* the *Nihongi,* the *Man'yōshū,* the first eight Imperial anthologies of poetry, *Taketori, Ise, Utsuho,*

19. Wada, "Koten kōshūka jidai," 35. In 1884, the *Koten kōshū–ka* was divided into a Department of National Books *(Kokushoka)* and a Department of Chinese Books *(Kanshoka).* See *Tōkyō Teikoku Daigaku gojūnenshi,* 1: 733–3 6, on the establishment of the Chinese section.
20. For *inishiebumi,* see *Motoori Norinaga zenshū,* vol. 1, ed. Ōkubo Tadashi (Chikuma Shobō, 1968), 87. *Tamakatsuma* consists of a series of essays composed between 1793 and Norinaga's death in 1801, and published serially between 1794 and 1812. For *furuki-fumi,* see *Motoori Norinaga zenshū,* vol. 9, ed. Ōno Susumu, 62.
21. See Morohashi Tetsuji, *Daikanwa jiten* (Taishūkan Shoten, 1955), 2:735 and Shinmura Izuru, ed., *Kōjien,* 3rd ed. (Iwanami Shoten, 1983), 881. The earliest example of the use of *koten* to mean "classics," cited in *Nihon kokugo daijiten* (Shōgakukan, 1974), 8:260, is from Shimazaki Tōson's *Rakubaishū* (Fallen Plum Blossom Collection, 1901). In the section "Suiyōbi no sōbetsu" (Wednesday Parting, 1898) he writes *"kimi wa haya koten no arakata o mo osameowaritsu"* (you had already mastered most of the classics). It is clear, however, that *koten* had meant "classics" for some time prior to Tōson's use of the word.

Kagerō, and the Heian period tales, diaries, and essays which followed [these], down to *Tsurezuregusa.* Anything after that did not count as a classic, but was [simply] literature of the previous age. With their strongly medieval cast, Bashō's *haikai* and *haibun* were treated as pure *koten;* but Saikaku, Akinari, and the like were regarded merely as distant antecedents of contemporary literature.[22]

The curriculum of the Classics Training Course seems to have corresponded closely to the canon described above. In addition to literary classics, however, works studied in the course spanned the whole range of the National Learning project to include texts on Japanese language, ancient court and military practices *(yūsokukojitsu),* and history. Wada remembers lectures on the *Kojiki* and the *Nihongi* as well as other early histories; the *Man'yōshū; Genji, Eiga,* and *Utsuho monogatari;* the *Ōkagami, Imakagami, Masukagami* and *Azumakagami;* and works on the Japanese language such as Norinaga's *Kotoba no tama no o* (1779).[23]

In 1882, the year that the Classics Training Course began accepting students, another similarly named institution, the *Kōten kōkyūsho* (Institute for the Study of Imperial Classics), opened its doors.[24] The Institute was part and parcel of the government's attempts to propagate a version of Shinto that would aid the achievement of national unity. Accordingly, a course for the training of Shinto priests was established and a system of examinations for Shinto functionaries inaugurated. Whereas the Classics Training Course had been founded to arrest a perceived decline in National Learning scholarship, the need for an

22. Shiota, "Koten to Meiji ikō no bungaku," 5.
23. Wada, "Koten kōshūka jidai," 36–37.
24. The Institute for the Study of Imperial Classics gave rise to, but was not replaced by, Kokugakuin (Academy of National Learning), established in 1890. In 1906 the Academy became a university with the name Kokugakuin Daigaku. The Institute continued its activities until 25 January 1946 when it was dissolved by the Allied Occupation authorities. See Fujii Sadafumi, "Kōten Kōkyūsho," in *Kokushi Daijiten* Henshū Iinkai, ed., *Kokushi daijiten* (Yoshikawa Kōbunkan, 1985), 5:459, upon which my discussion is based. In *Daikanwa jiten,* 8:79, *kōten* is defined as *"Kōkoku no tenseki. Waga kuni no koten"* (The imperial canon. The classical literary canon of our nation). No Chinese source for the compound is given; it is clearly a Japanese construction.

Institute for the Study of Imperial Classics was felt by politicians who were alarmed at the fervor of the People's Rights movement and by the agitation for a constitution. The decree establishing the Institute promulgated by its first president, Prince Arisugawa (1812–1886), defined the purpose of study at the Institute as the "clarification of the national polity *(kokutai)* in order to strengthen the foundations of the state."[25] Despite differing emphases, there were some connections between the two institutions. In 1888, for example, a former student of the Classics Training Course, Ochiai Naobumi (1861–1903), began teaching at the Institute for the Study of Imperial Classics. He later joined the staff of Kokugakuin, where he edited the renowned *Kotoba no izumi* dictionary, published in 1901. The simultaneous establishment in 1882 of the Classics Training Course and the Institute for the Study of Imperial Classics, the similarity of their missions, and the congruence of scholarly interest and political purpose suggest that this was one of those moments in history when conservative scholars and politicians alike were in agreement as to what the goals of the nation should be and how they might be attained.

Short-lived though the Classics Training Course was, its students were to produce the first series of "complete works" of Japanese literature, thus ratifying for the Meiji period the classical canon of their Edo-period forebears. This was the influential *Nihon bungaku zensho,* published by Hakubunkan in twenty-four volumes from 1890 to 1892 and edited by Hagino Yoshiyuki (1860–1924), Ochiai Naobumi, and Konakamura Yoshikata (1864–1923), the adopted son of one of the mainstays of the Classics Training Course, Konakamura Kiyonori.[26] With a degree of hindsight, all commentators agree that these former students of the Course (Ochiai for one left before he could graduate), with their colleagues from the Department of Japanese Literature,[27]

25. Cited in *Kokushi daijiten,* 5:459.
26. In 1897, Konakamura Yoshikata decided to revert to using the name of the family he was born to, Ikebe. Thus his family name appears as Konakamura in work published before that date, and as Ikebe in subsequent publications. Konakamura Kiyonori was a disciple of Motoori Uchitō (1792–1855), who was himself the adopted son, of Motoori Norinaga's adopted son, Motoori Ōhira (1756–1833).
27. A department of Japanese and Chinese literature *(Wakan bungaku-ka)* was part of the Faculty of Letters when Tokyo University was founded in 1877; the dearth of students in

were Japan's first scholars of National Literature *(kokubungakusha)*. Thirty years into the Meiji period, a new generation of scholars of the classical canon had been recruited, trained, and employed; and a new discipline had been created. National Learning scholar Konakamura Kiyonori, adoptive father of one and teacher of all three of the editors, officially bestowed his approval on one of the first products of the new discipline by contributing the opening preface to the *Nihon bungaku zensho*.

The *Nihon bungaku zensho* provided the Meiji reading public with some of the first complete texts of the classics to be printed in movable type. Shiota ascribes the success of the series to its affordability (initially twenty–five *sen* per volume at a time when a month's subscription to the *Asahi shinbun* cost twenty-eight *sen* and ten kilograms of rice was selling for approximately fifty *sen),*[28] convenient size, and the ease of reading movable type as compared with manuscripts or woodblock printed texts. Many Meiji period writers first encountered the Japanese classics in the form of the Hakubunkan series: Ozaki Kōyō (1867–1903), Kunikida Doppo (1871–1908), and Higuchi Ichiyō were among them. It was apparently this series, too, that revealed to ordinary Tokyoites the existence of a *Genji* other than Tanehiko's parodic *Nise murasaki inaka Genji.*[29]

The twenty-four volumes of the *Nihon bungaku zensho* consisted largely of Heian period literature, five volumes of which were devoted to *The Tale of Genji.* In their preface to the first volume, the editors explain the purpose of their publishing venture as follows:

> Books of old literature are scarce, difficult to obtain, and even the
> rare volume that comes to light is full of errors and not easy to

---

the department was one factor in the establishment of the *Koten kōshū-ka* in 1882. When the two components of the *Wakan bungaku-ka* were separated in 1885, with students being required to choose a major in either Japanese or Chinese after a combined course in their first year, the *Koten kōshū-ka* perhaps came to seem superfluous, and this may have been another reason for the termination of the course in 1888.

28. These figures are taken from *Nedan-shi nenpyō: Meiji, Taishō, Shōwa,* ed. *Shūkan Asahi* (Asahi Shinbunsha, 1988).

29. Both of these points are made by Shiota, "Koren to Meiji ikō no bungaku," 4, and Hisamatsu Sen'ichi, *Nihon bungaku kenkyūshi* (Yamada Shoin, 1957), 75.

understand. The reason we publish this series now is to make these books more easily obtainable, more easily readable, and to demonstrate the excellence of the national literature, which stands head and shoulders above Chinese and Western literature in a class by itself.[30]

They will rescue the canon from neglect, and the canon will show the nation what makes Japan great and what makes it unique.

Scholars of National Literature were not the only participants in this project. Another group, termed by Gluck *"minkan* nationalists" and including men such as Kuga Katsunan (1857–1907), Shiga Shigetaka (1863–1927), and Yamaji Aizan (1864–1917), also felt that a recognition of past achievements could serve as a bulwark against the dilution of Japan's distinctive national character *(kokuminsei).*[31] In his influential essay of 1891 entitled *Shin–zen-bi Nihonjin* (The Japanese and Truth, Goodness, and Beauty), one such *minkan* nationalist, Miyake Setsurei (1860–1945), offered a justification for the preservation and development of Japanese culture. The essay has been much discussed by scholars of the period;[32] it is of interest here as an example of the way in which *The Tale of Genji* was beginning to be called upon to serve national ends. Having praised Bakin for his prodigious output, Miyake continues:

> Moreover, when we turn our gaze to female writers, the fifty [sic] chapters of *Genji* produced by Murasaki Shikibu [depicting] a superior and extraordinary elegance which briefly flowered at a time when only a fraction of the country—the Kinki region and areas to the west—was within the reach of civilization: the existence of a work such as this must be attributed to her truly astonishing intellectual power. Although I am not suggesting that in other countries there is a dearth of great works by talented women writers, just how many could be ranked with Shikibu?[33]

30. "Hanrei," (Introductory Notes) in Hagino et al., *Nihon bungaku zensho,* 1:1.
31. *Gluck, Japan's Modern Myths,* 112–14.
32. See Kenneth B. Pyle, *The New Generation in Meiji Japan: Problems of Cultural Identity, 1885–1895* (Stanford: Stanford University Press, 1969), 150–56; and Shively, "The Japanization of the Middle Meiji," 103–4.
33. *Gendai Nihon bungaku zenshū* (Kaizōsha, 1931), 5:221.

Nationalists like Miyake saw a direct link between pride in native genius of the past and a national strength that would allow "independence in the commerce among nations,"[34] namely the revision of the Ansei unequal treaties of 1858. Repealed article by article over a period of more than thirty years of intense diplomatic effort, complete rescission of the treaties was not finally accomplished until 1911.

In this context it is significant that the first English version of *The Tale of Genji*—a partial translation published in London by Trübner & Co. in 1882—was by none other than Suematsu Kenchō (1855–1920), attaché to the Japanese legation in England and student at the University of Cambridge.[35] As author of a series of "informal reports on British and European politics"[36] for Itō Hirobumi (1841–1909), Suematsu was keenly aware of Western attitudes toward Japan and the importance of a coordinated approach to the task of treaty revision. In his introduction to the translation, Suematsu accordingly maintained that his purpose was:

> not so much to amuse my readers as to present them with a study of human nature, and to give them information on the history of the social and political condition of my native country nearly a thousand years ago. They will be able to compare it with the condition of mediaeval and modern Europe.[37]

By subtly reminding his Victorian readers that Murasaki Shikibu had produced *The Tale of Genji* at a time when Anglo-Saxons were still, as Virginia Woolf was later to remark, "squatting in their huts,"[38] Suematsu provided further evidence in support of Japan's claim for equal treatment.

34. Gluck, *Japan's Modern Myths*, 114.
35. Margaret Mehl, "Suematsu Kenchō in Britain, 1878–1886," *Japan Forum* 5.2 (October 1993): 173–93.
36. Ibid., 177.
37. Suematsu Kenchō, *Genji Monogatari* (1882; reprint, Rutland, Vt. and Tokyo: Charles E. Tuttle, 1974), 17. On Suematsu's translation of *Genji*, see Rebekah Clements, "Suematsu Kenchō and the First English Translation of *Genji monogatari*: Translation, Tactics, and the 'Women's Question'," *Japan Forum* 23.1 (2011): 25–47.
38. Virginia Woolf, "The Tale of Genji: The First Volume of Mr Arthur Waley's Translation of a Great Japanese Novel by the Lady Murasaki," *Vogue* 66.2 (1925): 53.

Suematsu's translation also suggests the direction that Meiji scholars of Japanese literature were to take. As we have seen, the new scholars of National Literature conceived of themselves as "custodians of a tradition of scholarship, a body of texts, and 'Japaneseness.'"[39] This conception of their mission also implied a new mission for a prime object of their energies, *The Tale of Genji*.

This new generation of scholars was quick to see that if *Genji* was to function as the cultural scripture they meant it to be, it had to be made accessible to a much larger reading public than it had ever reached before. The digests, readers, and lectures noted above might contribute to the cause, but the best way to take the text itself to the people was through translation. Curiously, however, the only attempt to produce a modern colloquial version of *The Tale of Genji* that predates Akiko's *Shin'yaku* was the first volume of the *Shinshaku Genji monogatari* (A New Exegesis of The Tale of Genji), published in 1911. This edition printed the text of *Genji* together with commentary and a modern Japanese translation. Volume one contained the eight chapters from 'Kiritsubo' (The Paulownia Court) to 'Hana no En' (The Festival of the Cherry Blossoms); a second volume published in 1914 contained a further six chapters, bringing the work up to the end of 'Miotsukushi' (Channel Buoys). Here, for reasons unknown, the project was terminated.

The four editors of *Shinshaku Genji monogatari* were all students at Tokyo University between 1890 and 1900: Fujii Shiei (1868–1945), Sassa Seisetsu (1872–1917), and Nunami Keion (1877–1927) graduated from the Department of National Literature, Sasakawa Rinpū (1870–1949) from the Department of National History.[40] All also went on to earn their living teaching Japanese literature at high

---

39. Brownstein, "From *Kokugaku* to *Kokubungaku*," 438.
40. Shigematsu Nobuhiro notes that although Shiei is listed as an editor, he did not actually have a hand in the translation. The contributions of the other three editors are compared in Shigematsu Nobuhiro, *Shinkō Genji monogatari kenkyūshi* (Kazama Shobō, 1961), 433–35.

schools and universities. Recent accounts of their lives emphasize their activities as *haikai* poets (all were members of the Tsukubakai poetry society founded by Tokyo University students in 1894), but fail to mention their edition and translation of *Genji*.[41] The omission is unfortunate, for it obscures the mission these young scholars envisaged for themselves and their version of *Genji*. In a grandiloquent preface to the initial volume of the *Shinshaku*, Sassa Seisetsu sets forth the principles and ideals that underlay the translation project, and in doing so articulates the agenda of virtually his entire generation of National Literature scholars.[42] This document thus deserves close attention:

> Whether or not they possess any acquaintance with the text, there can be none who are unaware of the name of *The Tale of Genji*. For the great majority, however, this amounts to no more than a vague consciousness that it is the greatest treasure of our national literature. Of its style, of its structure, of the thought that informs it, they know not the first thing.... Nay, we would not hesitate to claim that even amongst specialists in the language and literature of our land, most have read no further than (the twelfth chapter] 'Suma.' (1)[43]

41. Compare, for example, the article on Sassa in *Daijinmeijiten* (Heibonsha, 1957), 3:129, with accounts given in Itō Sei et al., eds., *Shinchō Nihon bungaku shōjiten* (Shinchōsha, 1968), 519–20, or Odagiri Susumu, ed., *Nihon kindai bungaku daijiten* (Kōdansha, 1977), 2:116. An understanding of *Genji* had always been a prerequisite of *haikai* composition; Kitamura Kigin's *Kogetsushō* is but the most famous product of this concern.

42. Sassa Seisetsu, "Jo," in *Shinshaku Genji monogatari,* ed. Sassa Seisetsu et al. (Shinchōsha, 1911), 1:1–11. For a complete translation of Sassa's preface, see G. G. Rowley, trans., "Preface to *A New Exegesis of The Tale of Genji,*" in Harper and Shirane, *Reading the Tale of Genji,* 550–56.

43. Confirmation of Sassa's sense that *Genji* remained largely unread is provided by W. G. Aston, who remarks in his *A History of Japanese Literature* (New York: D. Appleton and Company, 1899), 117, that "[b]oth the *Genji monogatari* and the *Makura Zōshi* [sic] are only imperfectly intelligible even to educated Japanese, and they are little read at the present day." Masamune Hakuchō (1879–1962), too, recalls the late Meiji "reign of the Naturalists" *(shizenshugi jidat)* in his 1951 essay "Dokusho zakki (8)" and asserts confidently that among members of the literary world at the time, virtually no one had read *Genji* right through. *"The Tale of Genji* was something that scholars of National Learning were supposed to read," he writes. "It was not regarded as something that writers of modern literature should read." *Masamune Hakuchō zenshū* (Shinchōsha, 1965), 9:306.

What might be the cause of this lamentable state of affairs?

> For one thing, it is because ordinary people are plagued by dif-
> ficulties in understanding the language of the work. For another, it
> is because they dismiss it as a curiosity, they fail to realize that in
> fact it is a book every citizen *(kokumin)* ought to read. (2)

These, then, are the principal problems classical scholars must address.
The first, Sassa and his colleagues feel, can be solved with relative
ease—through translation:

> [I]n this *Shinshaku* we make *The Tale of Genji* comprehensible
> and accessible; we translate it employing ordinary everyday lan-
> guage. The purpose of this book is simply to make *Genji* com-
> prehensible. Accordingly, for those planning to study the tale as a
> classic, this book will by no means be adequate. If, however, as a
> citizen, you are satisfied to understand what sort of work *Genji* is,
> to become conversant with its style, its structure, and the thought
> that informs it, then this simple *Shinshaku* is probably the most
> suitable work. (2)

Their audience is distinctly defined: they address not scholars but "ordinary people," "citizens." Their method is clear-cut: they will translate
Genji into "ordinary everyday language." And their hopes are high:

> Our project, if it is not too much to hope for, is once and for all
> to make the incomprehensible *Genji* a thing of the past. At that
> point, if readers still do not flock to *Genji*, it can only be because
> they do not fully appreciate the worth of *Genji*, that they do not
> comprehend fully why it is a book that every citizen ought to read.
> We who propose to make *Genji* comprehensible thus have a duty
> to explain its true worth. (2–3)

Sassa's insistence on the necessity of every "citizen" actually becoming acquainted with *Genji* implies a belief that the text is now part of
the "all–national heritage" of Japan.[44] The task of wresting control of

44. E. J. Hobsbawm, *Nations and Nationalism Since 1870: Programme, Myth, Reality,* 2d ed.
   (Cambridge: Cambridge University Press/Canto, 1992), 90.

Genji from its aristocratic custodians had been begun by Edo period scholars of National Learning;[45] Sassa and his colleagues are determined to discharge their inherited obligation. But their confidence in the citizenry's willingness to partake of the newly comprehensible *Genji* was perhaps not so strong as their belief in the efficacy of the text. For the remaining three-quarters of Sassa's preface is devoted to an impassioned explanation of the reasons every citizen was duty-bound to read *Genji*.

In the phrase cited as the second epigraph to this chapter, Sassa harks back to Ichijō Kaneyoshi's (1402–81) encomium of 1472 (Bunmei 4), but with a significant difference. Whereas Kaneyoshi praises *Genji* as "the unrivaled treasure of our land," Sassa, in keeping with his nationbuilding agenda, praises it as "the unrivaled treasure of our nation and as such, something worth boasting about to all the nations of the world" (3).[46] Indeed, even Japan's spirit of *bushidō*, so much admired both at home and abroad, he claims has its roots in the culture that produced *Genji*. For "if military men had not cultivated *mono no aware*, they would have been but heartless warriors, war-loving barbarians" (3). Neither is the preeminence of the culture of the Heian court to be judged by purely national standards:

> According to what we hear, Rome should be regarded as the epitome of a culture based upon reason, whereas the culture of Greece is a culture of beauty and feeling. This, however, is but a relative evaluation. When in the world, where in the world, has there been a culture like that of our Heian court, so utterly ruled by sensibility? Where in the world have the moon and the flowers been so admired? In what age has there been such fondness for *mono no aware*? (5)

The political implications of the comparison with ancient Greece and Rome are obvious. If Japan is to hold its head high among

45. See T. J. Harper, *"The Tale of Genji* in the Eighteenth Century!"
46. Kaneyoshi's encomium reads *"Wagakuni no shihō wa Genji no monogatari ni sugitaru wa nakarubeshi,"* (As the unrivaled treasure of our land nothing surpasses *The Tale of Genji)* in *Kachō yosei,* ed. Ii Haruki, *Genji monogatari kochū shūsei,* 1st ser., 1 (Ōfūsha, 1978), 9.

the nations of the world it has so recently rejoined, then it is important that its culture be rooted in soil at least as rich as that of the nations of Europe. For Sassa and his colleagues, the nourishing soil of all Japanese culture is the Heian court—which so far as they are concerned not only equals but excels the world of the Greek and Roman classics. But again there is the problem of *bushidō*:

> The world misunderstands our *bushidō;* they say that we are a war-loving people. And yet the unique culture of our nation is this emotionalism, this love of beauty; in our opinion, the most refined culture in the world is the culture of our own Heian court. And our *Tale of Genji* is truly the epitome of this culture.... . [T]hose who would investigate our true national character must first of all look back to the Heian court and to *The Tale of Genji.* (5–6)

Clearly he is keen to counter the image—perhaps the result of victory in the Russo-Japanese War of 1904–5—of the Japanese as a race of battle-hungry samurai. The *true* Japanese is a lover of beauty, a person of gentility and feeling, in other words, a latter-day Heian courtier. *The Tale of Genji,* as the "epitome of this culture," thus has important tasks to perform. It is to make "every citizen" aware of his or her "true national character" and provide proof of a certain cultural superiority. *The Tale of Genji,* in short, ought to be one of the prime movers in the Meiji project of forging a national identity:

> As for the period in which the work was composed, around the Kankō era [1004–12] during the reign of the Ichijō emperor, is it not more than three hundred years prior to the age in which the poet Chaucer, whom Tsubouchi Shōyō has called the English Murasaki Shikibu, first laid the foundations of English literature? Excepting the ancient literature of Greece and Rome in the West, and of India and China in the East, is this an age in which it is possible to find literature worthy of attention anywhere else in the world? It is not. The Kankō era, which corresponds to the beginning of the eleventh century A.D., is an era when, both in the East and in the West, it is impossible to find a single realistic tale (*shajitsu monogatari*) or novel depicting human emotions (*ninjō shōsetsu*). In this sense, *The Tale of Genji* is not only the unrivaled treasure of Japanese literature; more than that, it should truly be called an unrivaled treasure of world literature. (6–7)

Sassa's argument here takes an interesting twist. He is not content merely to establish *Genji* as a classic on a par with those of Greece and Rome, the quintessence of a culture unique in the world; he is determined to prove its superiority in terms of the literary vocabulary of the West: *Genji* must also be "modern," the world's first exemplar of true "realism."

The venerable term *ninjō*, "human emotions," the depiction of which Sassa equates with *shajitsu*, is, of course, a key term in Tsubouchi Shōyō's *Shōsetsu shinzui* (The Essence of the Novel, 1885–86), and moreover had long been used in discussions of *Genji*. In combination with *shōsetsu*, however, Sassa's reference to the critical discourse established by Shōyō is unmistakable. On the other hand, *shajitsu*, "realism," is not a word used in *Shōsetsu shinzui*, where the preferred term is *mosha* "imitation." But by 1890—the watershed date again—just five years after *Shōsetsu shinzui* began to appear, *Genji* had become a *shajitsu shōsetsu*: in the first major Meiji period account of Japanese literary history, Mikami Sanji (1865–1939) and Takatsu Kuwasaburō (1864–1921), both graduates of the Department of Japanese Literature at Tokyo University, describe *Genji* as "our consummate realistic novel *(kanzen naru waga shajitsu-ryū shōsetsu).*"[47] In discerning both *ninjō* and *shajitsu* in *The Tale of Genji*, therefore, Sassa extracts *Genji* from the past and relocates it in the "modern" world.

Sassa's preface is thus much more than a justification of the *Shinshaku* project. It is a vigorous polemic: in arguing for the preeminence of the culture delineated in and exemplified by *The Tale of Genji*, Sassa and his colleagues attempt to resituate Japan in the world. At the same time, Sassa's description of the culture of the Heian period—"in the full maturity of peace, the sole, unrivaled pursuits of ladies and gentlemen were poetry and music" (4)—is his wishful solution to the problem of national identity. Drawing upon an idealized antiquity, he propounds a definition of "national character" that stands in opposition both to the warrior rule of the Tokugawa past, and the martial values of the Meiji present. The wellspring of "national character" posited by the scholars of National Literature is, of course, a fantasy. But by advancing the *mono no aware* view of Heian court culture and *The Tale*

47. Mikami Sanji and Takatsu Kuwasaburō, *Nihon bungakushi* (Kinkōdō, 1890), 1:265.

of Genji in this way, Sassa seeks to redefine the "national character" in the minds of his readers: "With our work on the *Shinshaku* … it is our earnest hope that we have succeeded in providing our fellow citizens with the opportunity to reflect anew upon the national character" (11). A knowledge of *Genji,* he suggests, will assist readers to know better who they are. And he is realistic enough to recognize that his readers will require a translation in order to fulfill their patriotic duty.

Sassa describes the language into which he and his colleagues translate *Genji* as a "modern colloquial style which closely follows the original."[48] They recognize that the didactic purposes of their translation will best be served by the new language of fiction and education that had been developed during the decades preceding the publication of the *Shinshaku—the* so-called *genbun'itchi* style. This style of written language conformed more closely to the spoken word, and gained ground as literacy increased and the Sino-Japanese and Russo-Japanese Wars generated new readerships and conspicuous expansion in the publishing industry.[49]

The volume of *shōsetsu* employing the *genbun'itchi* style grew exponentially. A study based on a count of *shōsetsu* published in the literary journals *Bungei kurabu* (launched 1895) and *Shinshōsetsu* (relaunched 1896) estimates that in 1896 twenty-four percent were written in modern colloquial, increasing to thirty-six percent in 1897, forty-five percent in 1898, fifty-seven percent in 1899, and reaching sixty-one percent by the turn of the century. Less than a decade later, in 1908, *all* of the *shōsetsu* carried in these two magazines were written in the *genbun'itchi* style.[50]

---

48. Sassa Seisetsu, "Hanrei," in *Shinshaku,* 1:1.

49. Nakamura Yukihiko, "Kinsei no dokusha," *Nakamura Yukihiko chojutsushū* (Chūō Kōronsha, 1983), 14:40–41, estimates that literacy doubled between the beginning of the Meiji period and the end of the Meiji thirties (1906). On the new readership created by the Sino-Japanese War, see Jay Rubin, *Injurious to Public Morals: Writers and the Meiji State* (Seattle and London: University of Washington Press, 1984), 41–42. The expansion of both readership and publishing in the late Meiji period is noted by Gluck, *Japans Modern Myths,* 171–73.

50. Yamamoto Masahide, "Kindai kōgobuntai no seiritsu to tenkai," *Kōza Nihon bungaku* (Sanseidō, 1969), 9:153, 158.

Pedagogical changes lagged only slightly behind. In 1901, a recommendation by the *genbun'itchi* sub-committee of the Imperial Committee on Education that a study be made concerning the implementation of the modern colloquial was accepted by both houses of the Diet.[51] By 1903–4, much of the material in elementary school readers approved by the Ministry of Education was written in the *genbun'itchi* style.[52] A new generation was emerging, educated in a modern colloquial that gave them access to growing amounts of reading matter—and increased the distance between them and the language of the Heian court. If, therefore, *The Tale of Genji,* the "unrivaled treasure" of the Japanese literary canon and the world's first "realistic novel," was to make its fullest possible contribution to the forging of a nation, if its beneficial influence was to reach the widest possible audience in readily comprehensible form, this newly fashioned literary language was the language into which it must be translated.

The period of two decades or so when the events just described were in train coincides almost precisely with the years between Akiko's initial encounter with *Genji* and the publication of her first modern translation of it. Given the loftiness of the ideals of the scholars involved, the national urgency of the need they perceived, and the magnitude of their efforts to bring their project to fruition, one might expect that by the time Akiko's translation was complete, it would have been but one of several modern versions of *Genji* available for the edification of the citizenry. In fact it was the only one. As already mentioned, the *Shinshaku* project was never completed; nor would it have been a readable modern-language *Genji* if it had been. The same may be said of a number of less ambitious projects. Chapter five will examine in more detail some of these attempts to make *Genji* accessible. Here it remains only to note the irony that, in the end, it was

51. Kugimoto Hisaharu, "Kōgotai undō: Meiji no kokugo kaikaku undō," *Kindai bungaku kōza*, ed. Nakano Shigeharu (Kawade Shobō, 1952), 1:145–46.
52. Yamamoto Masahide, "Genbun'itchi," *Nihon kindai bungaku daijiten,* 4:140–42. The standard English account of the adoption of the colloquial style in school textbooks is Nanette Twine, *Language and the Modern State: The Reform of Written Japanese* (London: Routledge, 1991), 81–88, 104–7, and 170–71.

Yosano Akiko—self–taught, a disciple of no one, and with no ideological axe to grind—who actually achieved what scholars of National
Literature had been aiming to do since they published the first movable type editions of *Genji* in 1890. To their credit, the Meiji literati
seem to have seen that Akiko's work was the perfect instrument of
their purposes—the instrument they themselves had failed to produce.
It does not detract from her accomplishment, I think, to suggest that
the receptiveness to such a project that scholars of National Learning
and National Literature had nurtured may have contributed to the commercial and critical success of Akiko's translation. It is in this sense
that, in Ueda Bin's phrase, Akiko was not only the "right person" to
produce a new *Genji* for the "new Japan," but that her talents were
brought to bear upon the work at precisely "the right time."

Chapter Four:
A Murasaki Shikibu for the Meiji Period

わがよはひ盛りになれどいまだかの源氏の君のとひまさぬかな
Waga yowai sakari ni naredo imada kano
   Genji no kimi no toimasanu kana, (2:96)[1]
Though at my age I have reached my prime
   Prince Genji has yet to honor me with a visit.

寛弘の女房たちに値すとしばしば聞けばそれもうとまし
Kankō no nyōbotachi ni atai su to
   shibashiba kikeba sore mo utomashi. (2:201)[2]
"As worthy as the ladies of the era of the *Genji*"
   yet heard too often even that grows wearisome.

Touring France in the summer of 1912, Akiko made a special point of
visiting the studio of the sculptor Auguste Rodin (1840–1917) in order
to present him with copies of the first two volumes of her *Shin'yaku
Genji monogatari*. She describes their encounter in her afterword to
the final volume of the translation:

1. As Ichikawa notes in "Yosano Akiko no koten *sesshu—Sarashina nikki, Tsurezuregusa—*,"
   Namiki no sato, no. 38 June 1993): 5, Akiko's poem recalls the Sarashina diarist's
   "*Sakari ni naraba, katachi mo kagirinaku yoku, kami mo imijiku nagaku narinamu.
   Hikaru no Genji no Yūgao, Uji no Taishō no Ukifune no onnagimi no yō ni koso arame to
   omoikeru kokoro, mazu ito hakanaku asamashi.*" *NKBZ* 18:302–3. T. J. Harper, "Motoori
   Norinaga's Criticism of the *Genji monogatari*: A Study of the Background and Critical
   Content of his *Genji monogatari Tama no ogushi*" (Ph.D. diss., University of Michigan,
   1971), 34, translates: "… when I grew up I would be beautiful with very long hair. Surely
   I would grow up to be like Genji's Yūgao or Kaoru's Ukifune, I thought, silly fool that
   I was."
2. The title of the collection in which this poem appears, *Seigaiha* (Waves of the Blue Ocean,
   1912) is the same as the name of the dance performed by Genji in the 'Momiji no Ga' (An
   Autumn Excursion) chapter, and a further example of the way Akiko's work is permeated
   with references to *Genji*.

Rodin Sensei looked through the illustrations and, exclaiming all the while over the beauty of the Japanese woodblock prints, he said, "The number of people in France and in Japan studying the language and thought of our two countries will gradually increase. I bitterly regret being unable to read Japanese, but I trust that one day in the future I shall be able to appreciate the thought of this book through the medium of a friend's translation." The memory of his words is still fresh in my mind.[3]

It was the sort of meeting that perhaps surpassed even Sassa's fondest hopes: Akiko abroad as unofficial cultural ambassador, successfully expediting the transformation of *The Tale of Genji* into a symbol of Japan.

How had Akiko, seemingly so untouched by the politicization of *Genji*, come to be so prominent a participant in the project of bringing *Genji* first to the "citizenry" and then the world? This chapter will sketch the process by which, as "Meiji period Murasaki Shikibu,"[4] she was able to produce her landmark first translation and turn her love of *Genji* into a paying profession. It concludes with a brief discussion of the reception of the *Shin'yaku.*

Akiko's professional involvement with *Genji* began early in her working life. It soon developed into a significant source of income and occupied a steadily increasing amount of her energy. At the same time it generated commissions for work on other classics, and in her latter years became the principal object of her attention. The fruits of this work include two translations of *Genji;* a commentary on *Genji* that does not survive; numerous articles on the life of Murasaki Shikibu, both journalistic and academic; series of lectures on *Genji;* a scholarly edition of the text; and several other related activities.[5]

---

3. Yosano Akiko, "Shin'yaku Genji monogatari no nochi ni," in *Shin'yaku Genji monogatari* (Kanao Bun'endō, 1912–13), 4:7. On Akiko's meeting with Rodin, see her account "Rodan-ō ni atta hi," first published in the June 1916 issue of *Shinchō* and later collected in *Warera nani o motomuru ka* (1917); TYAZ 15:336–42.

4. The phrase is Sasaki Nobutsuna's. For the full quotation, see below, p. 81.

5. A list of Akiko's publications on *Genji* and other works from the classical canon may be found in Appendix A.

Before describing these projects, however, it may be well to say something of the need for the income it produced. This is not to suggest that she undertook this work merely for the sake of money. Nevertheless, the payment she received appears to have been vital to the survival of her family. Akiko's husband Hiroshi was rarely in conventional employment and hence her writing was the financial mainstay of their large household.[6] In eleven pregnancies between 1902 and 1919, she bore thirteen children: one was stillborn and another died soon after birth, leaving eleven, all of whom survived childhood. The Taishō years were particularly lean for the Yosanos; they chose to bring up their five boys themselves but sent away three of their six girls, Sahoko (born 1910), Uchiko (born 1911) and Hélène (born 1915), to be brought up by other, unrelated families as foster children (*satogo*).[7] As Akiko herself explains, the very idea that her writing might provide the means of alleviating their financial distress was suggested to her by her reading of the classics:

> I took hints from the way talented women lived in the Heian period, learning that the independence of women's lives depends upon an economic independence of their own making, and because of this, I support the working women of society, I delight in the increase in work available to women, and I rejoice at the new social climate in which educated young women go out to take their places in various jobs. I myself have my own work, and I work hard to meet the expenses of my household. (14:440)

She further points out that it was her childhood reading that developed some of the abilities that made possible her later work on the classics: her philological confidence and a strong memory:

> That I was early able to understand what Japanese literature is about is because Murasaki Shikibu was my teacher. Moreover,

6. In April 1919, after the birth of the Yosanos' last child Fujiko in March 1919, Hiroshi finally obtained a teaching post at Keio University, a position he held until his retirement in March 1932.
7. Yosano Uchiko's tart memoir *Murasakigusa—haha Akiko to satogo no watakushi* (Shintōsha, 1967) explains how the system worked, and something of its effects.

because of this, as a young girl the strength of my memory and my powers of comprehension were developed, and as a result, after I had read *Genji* I didn't find reading other classical works in the least bit difficult. To this day I know much of *Genji* by heart; I remember the representative literary and historical works from each period in great detail; and I am able to lecture to students—all because at the beginning I had the good fortune to read Murasaki Shikibu carefully. (19:258)

The "comprehension" of which she speaks is not merely that of a highly competent reader, but that of a textual critic. Akiko's first known publication on a work of classical literature is her contribution to a discussion of *Ise monogatari* published in *Myōjō* in August and September 1901, immediately after her arrival in Tokyo from Sakai.[8]

In 1906, concluding a review of stories by Iwaya Sazanami (1870–1933) and Kosugi Tengai (1865–1952), Akiko could not help but compare their work unfavorably to *Genji*:

Contemporary writers, as if compelled to make their readers feel sympathy whether they like it or not, are very careful to set forth the reasons why readers should sympathize, but for us nothing could be more excruciating. The love affair between Genji and the Akashi lady, as it develops, arouses no sympathy whatsoever, because the reader's heart is still full of Murasaki, who in tears said, "I would exchange my life for yours without regret if it might postpone/just a little while longer this parting we face." And having left someone like this back in the capital, when it comes time to return, how dare he say, "Sorry I was that spring

8. With Ochiai Naobumi, Yosano Tekkan, and other members of the Shinshisha, Hō Akiko is listed as one of the authors of "Ise monogatari hyōwa," *Myōjō*, no. 14 (August 1901): 21–26, and *Myōjō*, no. 15 (September 1901): 60–63. A stimulating account of Tekkan's admiration for the "male romance" of the Narihira legend is provided by Katagiri Yōichi, "Yosano Akiko no koten kenkyū," *Joshidai bungaku: kokubun hen*, no. 43 (March 1992): 19–29. Katagiri (p. 24) speculates that the reason Akiko did no further work on *Ise monogatari* was because she was put off by the narcissism and shallowness of the *Myōjō* men's enthusiasm for the tale; and because Tekkan had earlier laid claim to the work in his "Nihon o saru uta" (Song of farewell to Japan), published in *Myōjō*, no. 10 January 1901): 104–8, cited in Katagiri, "Yosano Akiko no koten kenkyū," 24. The second stanza of his poem reads in part: "Ah my country Japan/ Ah my forefathers' country Japan/ The country which bore Nichiren/ The country which bore Hideyoshi/ The country which bore my revered old friend Narihira …"

I left the capital; sorrier I am / this autumn to farewell these shores where I have made my home"]! Genji is hateful. By rights we should hate the Akashi lady too, but in the section describing their first night together it says, "she reminded him strongly of the Ise Miyasudokoro" [i.e. the Rokujō lady], and with just these few words one is completely taken with her.[9]

The following year, in the May 1907 issue of *Myōjō*, she published a detailed review of the seventeen-volume *Eiga monogatari shōkai* by Wada Hidematsu and Satō Kyū.[10] Although lavish in her praise of their thoroughgoing commentary, the bulk of the review consists of suggested corrections to the work of these eminent scholars. She concludes briskly: "Apart from the above points there are no glaring errors. By making these corrections when the work is reprinted, the authors will have produced a commentary without peer."[11]

Akiko's work with *The Tale of Genji* began with lectures to students. Her first public appearance as a *Genji* specialist was in June 1907, just three months after the birth of her twin daughters Yatsuo and Nanase, when she was asked to teach Japanese classics and poetic composition to the short-lived Keishū Bungakkai (Ladies' Literary Association), an organization established with the dual aims of deepening women's understanding of Japanese and foreign literatures and the fostering of female writers.[12] Advertisements for the lecture

9. Yosano Akiko, "Shōsetsu ni san," *Myōjō* 7.1 (January 1906): 172. Akiko quotes most of Murasaki's last poem to Genji before he goes into exile in the 'Suma' chapter, 2:178; S 229; the upper hemistich of Genji's poem to the Akashi Nyūdō in the 'Akashi' chapter, 2:259; S 268; and Genji's reaction to the Akashi lady's barely visible form in the darkness of their first night together in the 'Akashi' chapter, 2:247; S 263.

10. Wada Hidematsu and Satō Kyū, *Eiga monogatari shōkai*, 17 vols. (Meiji Shoin, 1899–1907).

11. Yosano Akiko, "Eiga monogatari shōkai," *Myōjō* (May 1907): 106. Matsumura Hiroji provides a point-by-point assessment of Akiko's comments in "Yosano Akiko no *Eiga monogatari* hihyō," *Heian bungaku kenkyū*, no. 20 (September 1957): 39–46, and no. 21 (June 1958): 16–25.

12. The following discussion is based on the accounts in Itsumi Kumi, *Hyōden Yosano Tekkan Akiko* (Yagi Shoten, 1975), 427–29, 483; and Itsumi Kumi, "Hiroshi, Akiko no tegami kara mita Akiko Genji," *Komabano*, no. 33 (Tōkyō-to Kindai Bungaku Hakubutsukan, March 1982): 4.

series in *Myōjō* indicate that Akiko was responsible for classes on *Genji, Ōkagami,* and *Shinkokinshū.* People connected with Hiroshi's Shinshisha poetry society formed the core of the teaching staff at the Keishū Bungakkai. Akiko's early repute as an expert on *Genji* most likely dates from 1904–5. Over a period of fourteen months, she participated in a *Genji* reading circle organized by Shinshisha members and advertised in the pages of *Myōjō;* together they read from 'Kiritsubo' to 'Aoi' (Heartvine). Through this, Akiko's profound understanding of *Genji* had become common knowledge, which surely influenced the decision of those organizing the Keishū Bungakkai to appoint her to lecture on the classics.

Itsumi Kumi suggests that Akiko was also chosen as an exemplar of a successful female writer. The state of high anticipation with which Hiratsuka Raichō (1886–1971) looked forward to Akiko's lectures amply corroborates this suggestion. But Raichō was disappointed with Akiko's performance, and recalls in her autobiography:

> The impression I had the first time I saw Yosano Sensei was so different from the person I had imagined that I was shocked. I had imagined that since she was the author of the liberated, extravagant poems of *Midaregami*, she would be a flamboyant person just to look at, but the Yosano Sensei who appeared before us gave the impression of having been dragged there against her will.
> ... Her figure as she stood there with her knees bent, looking ill at ease, was so pitiful I could hardly bear to look at her.
> ... At last Yosano Sensei's lecture on *The Tale of Genji* began, but it was as if she were talking to herself, and furthermore she delivered it in the Kansai dialect and so nobody could understand more than a few words of what she said.[13]

According to Raichō, the lecturers were unsalaried. And, for reasons which remain unclear, the entire series was abandoned after only four months. It had not been a promising start to a teaching career.

Less than two years later, however, Akiko was again lecturing on *Genji,* this time to students in her own home. The final issue of

---

13. Hiratsuka Raichō, *Genshi, josei wa taiyō de atta* (Ōtsuki Shoten, 1971), 1:203–4.

Myōjō had appeared in November 1908; in April 1909, just a month after the birth of their fifth child, a son they named Rin, the Yosanos began a year-long lecture series in their house at Surugadai.[14] The cost was advertised as two yen per month and initially the series seems to have attracted some twenty students. Classes were held twice a week until November, when a notice in the literary magazine *Subaru* announced that henceforward lectures would be held only once a week, and the cost reduced accordingly. Perhaps support for the lectures was waning. In any case Akiko was pregnant again; their sixth child, Sahoko, was born on the first day of March in 1910 and immediately fostered out.

In one way or another Akiko was lecturing on *Genji* for the rest of her life. Her first published writing on *Genji* consisted of excerpts from a lecture she had given about the 'Kagerō' (The Drake Fly) chapter.[15] And she taught *Genji* at the Bunka Gakuin from the time of the school's inception in 1921 until her final illness.[16]

The work for which she is best known, of course, is her translations of *Genji*. The idea for her first translation came from the critic and translator Uchida Roan (1868–1929). Akiko's publisher, Kanao Tanejirō (1879–1947), recalls the meeting at which Uchida made his suggestion:

> The first volume of *Shin'yaku Genji* appeared in February 1912, so I think it must have been two or three years before that. I had called upon Uchida Roan Sensei, and during a conversation on various matters having to do with the publishing world he said, "Why don't you get Yosano Akiko to translate *Genji* and you publish it? I'm sure it would be splendid. She's just the right person!" His being so good as to suggest this was the impetus behind the *Genji* venture. Truly it was all Roan Sensei's doing. Straightaway

---

14. Itsumi, *Hyōden*, 483–87.
15. Yosano Akiko, "Te no ue no kōri," *Joshi bundan* 4.5 (April 1908): 5–8.
16. The Bunka Gakuin was a school founded on liberal principles by Nishimura Isaku (1884–1963). A useful account of Akiko's involvement with the school is provided by Laurel Rasplica Rodd, "Yosano Akiko and the Bunkagakuin: 'Educating Free Individuals'," *Journal of the Association of Teachers of Japanese* 25.1 (April 1991): 75–89.

I went to get Akiko's agreement... . [She said that] as long as
Uchida Sensei had said so, she would give it a try.[17]

In her afterword to the final volume of the *Shin'yaku*, Akiko
writes that she began work on the project in January of 1911.[18] The first
volume, containing the twenty-one chapters 'Kiritsubo' to 'Otome,'
appeared in February 1912, although, in a desperate attempt to keep
up with requests for her work, she had already published drafts of two
chapters, 'Sekiya' (The Gatehouse) and 'Tamakazura' (The Jeweled
Chaplet), as short stories.[19]

Her account of six days in March 1912 allows us a glimpse of
the frenetic pace of her life at that time:

7th March
... My head felt heavy today. Just as I had written seven or
so pages of 'Fuji no uraba' (Wisteria Leaves) from *Genji*, someone from [the magazine publisher] Gahōsha came to take photographs. Nanase and [Yatsuo][20] protested and so I had them take
me with Rin only. Since I had just changed my kimono, and since
I couldn't think anyway, I decided that I might as well go out and
do some shopping. I had simmered *kōyadōfu* and flavored *nori* for
lunch and left the house... .

8th
... Taking out the children's bedding my head began to ache
so badly I thought I would collapse. Still in my daytime kimono
I got into bed at the same time as the children. I felt as if I might
sleep, so when Momo [the maid?] said that she was going out to
shop for tomorrow there seemed no reason to stop her and with an
"all right" I let her go. Momo slid the door to the entryway shut

---

17. Kanao Tanejirō, "Akiko fujin to *Genji monogatari*," *Dokusho to bunken* 2.8 (August
    1942): 8.
18. Yosano, "Shin'yaku Genji monogatari no nochi ni," 1.
19. Yosano Akiko, "Genji Tamakazura," *Mitsukoshi* 1.9 (October 1911); "Genji Sekiya,"
    Subaru 4.1 January 1912). Cited in Shinma Shin'ichi, "Yosano Akiko to *Genji mono-
    gatari*," in *Genji monogatari to sono eikyō: kenkyū to shiryō—kodai bungaku ronsō
    dairokushū*, ed. Murasaki Shikibu Gakkai (Musashino Shoin, 1978), 260.
20. The *furigana* in the *Bunshō sekai* text incorrectly give the name of Akiko's eldest daughter
    as "Yatsumine" instead of "Yatsuo."

and left. It was nine o'clock when I woke from a terrifying dream. I called Momo but she did not seem to have returned yet. The wind blowing against the door was making an awful sound. Wondering how to combat the terror, I lay there full of the feelings aroused by the dream I had just had. I was glad when Momo came back about fifteen minutes later. My headache was gone. I let Momo go to bed and set to work again. At about eleven o'clock I finished 'Fuji no uraba' and then I wrote a letter to Paris.[21]

9th

I slept fitfully until about six o'clock and today too I felt exhausted. Thinking that I would make the selection of poems that I was supposed to send off to a certain magazine yesterday, I began, but my heart was not in it, and as I sat there next to the brazier Kanao-san dropped in. Saying that it was to celebrate the reprinting of [the first volume of my] *Genji,* he was kind enough to bring me a box of cigarettes wrapped in twelve different colors... [22] Since it was Saturday, in the afternoon Hikaru and [Shigeru][23] went out to play, the one to the Kinoshitas and the other to the Hondas. It was after three o'clock before I eventually finished the manuscript of the selection of poems. When I remembered that there was another piece of work waiting for me I felt even more exhausted; leaning against my desk I watched the garden being blown about by the wind....

11th

Putting away the bedding and cleaning the sitting room I suddenly felt that today I wanted to have a breakfast just like everyone else. So I stopped [the maid] from putting oatmeal on the

21. Hiroshi had left for Europe in November 1911 and Akiko was making plans to join him there. The entry for the eighth reveals Akiko's disappointment that ambassador Katō, who was returning to England and whom she had hoped to accompany on the transSiberian railway, had decided to travel by ship instead. On Akiko's trip to Paris in 1912, see Janine Beichman, "Akiko Goes to Paris: The European Poems," *Journal of the Association of Teachers of Japanese* 25.1 (1991): 123–45; and "Portrait of a Marriage: The How and Why of Yosano Akiko's Paris Foray," *Transactions of the Asiatic Society of Japan*, 5th series, vol. 8 (2016): 135–55; as well as Kannotō Akiko, "Akiko, *Genji*, Pari," *Kokubungaku kenkyū* no. 182 (2017): 1–17.
22. Twelve-colored cigarettes like the twelve–layered kimono *(jūnihitoe)* of the Heian period, perhaps?
23. Another mistake in the *furigana:* the name should be read "Shigeru" not "Hiizu." Hikaru is Akiko's eldest son, born 1902; Shigeru is her second son, born 1904.

fire and, with the children, ate warm rice... I wrote poems for
the *Nichinichi [Tōkyō nichinichi shinbun]* and selected poems for
the *Manchōhō [Yorozu chōhō]*. The fish soup we had for lunch did
not taste good. Perhaps it was because we had had rice for breakfast. Just as I was preparing a fair copy of the *Genji* manuscript,
Hirokawa-san came by [24]

Akiko was hurrying to complete the manuscript of the second
volume of her *Shin'yaku* before she set off in May 1912 to join her
husband in Paris. The second volume was published in June, a month
after her departure, and contained the eighteen chapters 'Tamakazura'
to 'Yūgiri' (Evening Mist).

No sooner did she arrive in Europe than she became pregnant
again and had to return to Japan after only four months, traveling home
alone in October 1912. The rest of the manuscript was completed following her return and published in two further volumes in August and
November of 1913. After it was finished she wrote:

> During these few short years, I was unable to spend all of my time
> preparing the translation. I was perpetually pushed to the limit
> by the pressure of work, both with my family and in my study.
> During this time I traveled to Europe and I was twice confined;
> one of these confinements was a difficult birth in which my life
> was at risk.[25] Nonetheless, sustained by the interest I have had in
> the original work since I was twelve or so, the translation has been
> the core of my work for the past three years, and by dint of these
> meager efforts, I have been able to complete it earlier than we had
> initially planned. In retrospect, I am not without a feeling of relief
> that I have managed to accomplish this overly ambitious feat.[26]

Akiko was keen that the *Shin'yaku* be a success. Her publisher Kanao recalled that as a surprise for her he had ordered from
the Mitsukoshi department store a twelve-layer set of formal kimono

24. Yosano Akiko, "Muikakan (nikki)," *Bunshō sekai* 7.5 (April 1912): 74–79.
25. This refers to the birth, in February 1911, of a second set of twins, one of whom was still-
    born. The surviving child was the Yosanos' seventh, their fourth daughter Uchiko. Then
    in April 1913 Akiko gave birth to a son they named Augyusuto after Auguste Rodin. In
    1933 he changed his name to Iku.
26. Yosano, "Shin'yaku Genji monogatari no nochi ni," 1–2.

(*jūnihitoe no haregi*) such as Murasaki Shikibu herself might have worn. But somehow she got wind of the plan and told him he might better put the money towards advertising her *Genji*.[27] She was not ready yet to take on Murasaki's mantle, but Kanao for one already saw her in that role.

Sasaki Nobutsuna was another who was moved to recall Murasaki in connection with Akiko. Publication of volume two of the *Shin'yaku* coincided with an issue of *Chūō kōron* which featured a special section devoted to discussion of Akiko's work. The articles are brief and in the main, laudatory, though Kōda Rohan for one is said to have responded to the request for a comment with the remark that he could not remain indifferent to her poetry: he either loved it or hated it.[28] Perhaps because they had been commissioned before the *Shin'yaku* began to appear, none of the essays makes any mention of Akiko's translation of *Genji*. Sasaki Nobutsuna's article is, however, tantalizingly titled "Akiko to Ichiyō to wa Meiji no Sei-Shi," (Akiko and Ichiyō: the Sei Shōnagon and Murasaki Shikibu of the Meiji period).[29] But he does not elaborate the comparison. How interesting it would be if, he writes, like Murasaki commenting on Sei Shōnagon, Ichiyō should have something to say about Akiko in her forthcoming diaries—ignoring (perhaps mischievously) the fact that when Ichiyō died in 1896 she could not possibly have been aware even of Akiko's existence. The title of his article is instead perhaps intended to evoke that period when women dominated the literary scene, and thus to suggest that because of the work of such writers as Ichiyō and Akiko, the present age was similarly glorious.

Nobutsuna graduated from the Classics Training Course at Tokyo University in 1888 when he was only seventeen years old. He went on to found the poetry magazine *Kokoro no hana* in 1898, and at the time of his remarks on Akiko he was also a lecturer at Tokyo University[30] as well as author/compiler of several massive scholarly works on Japanese poetry, including the twenty-four-volume *Nihon*

27. Kanao, "Akiko fujin to *Genji monogatari*," 9.
28. *Chūō kōron* 27.6 June 1912): 144.
29. Ibid., 141–42.
30. When the Meiji emperor made his last imperial progress to Tokyo University in July 1912, Nobutsuna was selected to explicate manuscripts of the *Man'yōshū* for him.

kagaku zensho (1890–92; 1898–1900) begun by his father Hirotsuna. That *Chūō kōron* was able to prevail upon Nobutsuna for his opinion of Akiko is revealing not only of the esteem with which such an establishment figure now viewed her work; for, it will be recalled, the outraged review of *Midaregami* cited in the introduction appeared (anonymously) in Nobutsuna's *Kokoro no hana*. It also suggests, I think, that in the late Meiji period, *tanka* and *tanka* poets still mattered, and that scholars of poetry, even the most eminent, still wrote poetry themselves and kept up with developments in that world.

A further example of the way in which Akiko was nudged into the role of Meiji period Murasaki Shikibu is to be found in Mori Ōgai's preface to her *Shin'yaku Genji monogatari*. He writes:

> [I]f one were to search the contemporary world for a person suitable to translate *The Tale of Genji*, it would be impossible to find anyone better than Yosano Akiko. For it seems to me that this translation of *The Tale of Genji* comes from the hand of a "congenial" person.[31]

Ōgai writes the word "congenial" in English here, *addingfurigana* in *katakana,* and Shinma Shin'ichi suggests that the expression is to be understood quite literally: by his use of "congenial," Ōgai implies that Akiko's talent is such that she "shares the genius" of Murasaki Shikibu and ought to be ranked alongside her.[32]

Ōgai's friendship with Akiko and her husband was of long standing.[33] He was an early admirer of her poetry and apparently took copies of her collections *Koōgi* (Little Fan, 1904) and *Koigoromo* (Love's Raiment, 1905)—as well as editions of the *Man'yōshū* and the *Kokinshū*—*with* him when he was sent to the front during the

---

31. Mori Rintarō, untitled preface to Yosano, *Shin'yaku Genji monogatari,* 1:4. In common with Edo period custom, page numbering is restarted for both prefaces, for the table of contents, and again for the text itself.

32. Shinma, "Yosano Akiko to *Genji monogatari*," 258.

33. See Shinma Shin'ichi, "Akiko to Ōgai, Takuboku," *Kindai tankashi ran* (Yūseidō, 1969), 177–82; and Kaneko Sachiyo, "Yosano Akiko to Mori Ōgai," *Ōgai to josei—Mori Ōgai ronkyū*—(Daitō Shuppansha, 1992), 282–301, for detailed accounts of the relationship.

Russo-Japanese War.[34] He was also *nazukeoya* (godfather) to the Yosanos' twin girls, born March 1907. Hearing of their safe delivery, he had sent the following congratulatory poem:

むこ来ませ一人は山のやつをこえひとりは川の七瀬わたりて
Muko kimase hitori wa yama no yatsuo koe
hitori wa kawa no nanase watarite.[35]
Husbands, approach!
One surmounting the eight peaks, one crossing the seven river fords.

Akiko was so delighted that she named the girls Yatsuo "eight peaks" and Nanase "seven fords" accordingly.

Not only did Ōgai provide one of the prefaces that accompanied the first volume of the *Shin'yaku;* he also took the trouble to check the proofs of volume two for her. On 2 May 1912 he noted in his diary, "Began proofreading the translated *Tale of Genji* for Yosano Akiko," but this is the only mention of the chore.[36] Akiko's publisher Kanao recalls what actually happened:

> Bit by bit I sent more than four hundred pages to the Professor for checking, but as nothing was returned to me I went often to the Ministry of War to urge him on. For a long time he was unable to do it because he was busy. As it was impossible to wait any longer, one evening I called upon him at his house in Sendagi to entreat with him about the matter. I don't know whether he sat up several nights without sleep, but all at once the four hundred pages of corrected proofs were returned to me.[37]

Ōgai's willingness to go out of his way to assist Akiko in the preparation of the *Shin'yaku* for publication is a measure of his respect for both the translator and the translation project itself.

34. Shinma, "Akiko to Ōgai," 178; Kaneko, "Yosano Akiko to Mori Ōgai," 288.
35. Cited in Shinma, "Akiko to Ōgai," 180. Ōgai alludes to two poems from the *Man'yōshū:* for *yatsuo* see no. 1262 *(NKBZ* 2:247, but note that as far as Ōgai was concerned a more likely interpretation of this poem is offered in the *Nihon kokugo daijiten,* 2:423d entry for *iwaizuma);* and for *nanase* no. 3303 *(NKBZ* 3:414–15).
36. Cited in Shinma, "Akiko to Ōgai," 180.
37. Kanao, "Akiko fujin to *Genji monogatari,*" 9.

Ueda Bin begins his preface with a sentiment similar to that which Ōgai had expressed in his introduction:

> When I heard that a modern language translation of *The Tale of Genji* from the pen of Yosano Akiko would be published, I rejoiced that this endeavor had found the person perfectly befitting it. That at the right time, the right person has accomplished this interesting yet by no means simple task is cause for celebration by the literary establishment.[38]

Bin had followed Akiko's career with interest.[39] In October 1901 he published a favorable assessment of some of the *Midaregami* poems in *Myōjō*.[40] He did not sign the article, but his friendship with the Yosanos was such that the following year he acted as *nazukeoya* to their first-born son Hikaru. In 1904 he put his name to a preface for *Dokusō* (Poison Grass), a collection of new-style verse and *tanka* by both Akiko and Hiroshi.[41] Bin also wrote the preface to her 1911 collection of poetry, *Shundeishū* (Spring Thaw).[42] Thus it was his abundant knowledge of her poetic abilities that underwrote his endorsement of her translation of *Genji*.

If I have seemed to dwell overlong upon Akiko's relationship with the two men who wrote the prefaces to her first venture into the world of *Genji*, it is because I think it important that not only the translation but also the translator be seen in context. Accounts of post-Restoration literary history have tended to concentrate on the development of the modern Japanese novel, and since Akiko wrote not

---

38. Ueda Bin, untitled preface to Yosano, *Shin'yaku Genji monogatari*, 1:1.
39. See Shinma Shin'ichi, "Bin to Hiroshi, Akiko," *Teihon Ueda Bin zenshū geppō*, no. 8 (1980): 9–12, for details.
40. Nanigashi, "Midaregami o yomu," *Myōjō*, no. 16 (1901). Reprinted in *Teihon Ueda Bin zenshū*, ed. Yano Hōjin (Kyōiku Shuppan Sentaa, 1980), 7:2 75–81.
41. Ueda Bin, "Dokusō jo" (1904), *Teihon Ueda Bin zenshū*, 9:315–16.
42. Ueda Bin, "Shundeishū no hajime ni" (1911), *Teihon Ueda Bin zenshū*, 9:335–39. I am indebted to Jay Rubin, *Injurious to Public Morals: Writers and the Meiji State* (Seattle and London: University of Washington Press, 1984), 213, for the translation of *Shundeishū* as "Spring Thaw."

shōsetsu but *tanka,* she has in recent decades been seen as, at best, a figure peripheral to mainstream literary culture.[43] The *Chūō kōron* special issue devoted to commentary on her work; the close relationships she enjoyed with Mori Ōgai and Ueda Bin, exemplified by the prefaces they wrote for her—all these suggest that throughout her lifetime, she and the literary form for which she is best known were anything but peripheral.

In the context of her time, the prefaces to the *Shin'yaku* by Ōgai and Bin are much more than mere introductions to her work. From Ōgai, the modern incarnation of the scholar-official of ancient tradition, and from Bin, Kyoto University professor and acclaimed translator of Western verse, Akiko and her *Genji* received a highly significant seal of approval from two of the most widely respected arbiters of Japanese culture.[44] Bin and Ōgai's prefaces are therefore crucially different from, say, Tsubouchi Shōyō's accreditation of Tanabe Kaho. When in 1888 Shōyō wrote a preface for Kaho's first published story, *Yabu no uguisu* (Warbler in the Grove), he was endorsing a much younger beginner in an art in which he was already accomplished.[45] Ōgai and Bin, on the other hand, write not as masters enthusiastic about the talent of a younger follower, but as elder statesmen of the Meiji literary world bestowing their approval upon an esteemed colleague's venture into a new literary form.

43. Consider, for example, the space allotted to Akiko in the three major postwar versions of the modern Japanese literary canon: she receives one quarter of one volume in *Gendai Nihon bungaku zenshū,* 99 vols. (Chikuma Shobo, 1953–58); a bare quarter of one volume in *Meiji bungaku zenshū;* and about a third of one volume in *Nihon kindai bungaku taikei,* 60 vols. (Kadokawa Shoten, 1970–75).

44. Trusted not only by the Meiji government, which appointed the two to the Committee on Literature (Bungei Iinkai) announced by the Ministry of Education on 17 May 1911 (and abolished two years later in June 1913); but also by their colleagues in the literary world: in separate complaints concerning the makeup of the committee, Tayama Katai (1871–1930), Baba Kochō (1869–1940), and Satō Kōroku (1874–1949) all remarked that Ōgai and Bin, with Shimamura Hōgetsu (1871–1918), a critic associated with the Naturalist movement, were the only worthy members of the sixteen–man body. On this point, see Rubin, *Injurious to Public Morals,* 199–219, esp. 207.

45. Tsubouchi Shōyō, "Harunoya shujin etsu," preface to *Yabu no uguisu,* by Tanabe Kaho (Kinkōdō, 1888), unnumbered pages before p. 1.

As it happens, these prefaces by Bin and Ōgai are also the first critical assessments of Akiko's translation, and thus must be the starting point of our examination of the contemporary reception of the *Shin'yaku.*

The conception of literature as a national asset and the locus of "true national character," made explicit in Sassa Seisetsu's preface to *Shinshaku Genji monogatari,* is implicit in Mori Ōgai's insistence that it is *The Tale of Genji* which, of all *monogatari,* most warrants translation. Ōgai begins his preface with the question: "Is there a need to translate *The Tale of Genji* into the modern colloquial language?" The rest of his introduction is his answer:

> Were I asked whether it would be desirable that *The Tale of Genji* be translated into the modern colloquial language, I would without hesitation answer yes. I am very keen to have a translation of this tale.... For translations of simple *kanbun* written by people of the Edo period, I see no need whatever. What I desire are translations of the truly ancient texts of this nation, such as the *Kojiki.* From a slightly later period, of the several fictions, a translation of *The Tale of Genji* is what is most needful.... Whenever I read *The Tale of Genji,* I always sense a certain resistance; and if that cannot be overcome, I cannot grasp the meaning of the words. *The Tale of Genji,* it seems to me, is written in a style that in itself, quite apart from the antiquity of the words, is by no means easy to understand.[46]

It would be wrong, I think, to take Ōgai's words entirely at face value. There is surely a fair bit of preface etiquette in his protestations of the difficulty he experiences in reading *Genji;* yet insofar as they serve to elevate Akiko's achievement, they may at least be taken as a measure of his enthusiasm for the project.

Bin, on the other hand, is not entirely happy with the notion of a *Genji* accessible to all. He makes light of the linguistic difficulties presented by the classical language and prefers to see Akiko's work as "a new stimulus even for those who are able to understand the beauty of the original," rather than as a version for those who, as Ōgai had

46. Mori Rintarō, untitled preface in Yosano, *Shin'yaku Genji monogatari,* 1:1–6.

put it, "sense a certain resistance." Bin is more interested in the transformation of *Genji,* in what happens when the classical language is
transmuted into modern Japanese.

What "strange perfume will be produced when ... that grace-
ful wonder of the classical language is transformed into the sprightly
modern way of saying things?" Bin, "overcome with curiosity" as to
how Akiko translates his favorite passages from *Genji,* proceeds to
quote them. There is the description of a chill autumnal dusk falling
on the grief-stricken Kiritsubo emperor from the chapter of that name;
excerpts from 'Hahakigi,' 'Yūgao' (Evening Faces), 'Momiji no Ga,'
'Suma,' and 'Akashi'; and two lines from the 'Hashihime' (The Lady
at the Bridge) chapter that describe Kaoru's first glimpse of the daughters of the Eighth Prince at Uji. Unfortunately, he does not compare
any of these passages with Akiko's modern language versions. Instead,
he moves on to a discussion of the style of *Genji,* defending it against
charges that it is ostentatious, overwrought, or frivolous. It is almost
an early form of *genbun'itchi,* he writes, so much so that some of its
phrases could as well come from the mouth of a present day lady of
quality; and, except for the honorifics, it is rather closer to the modern
spoken language than the stiff, formulaic styles of later ages:

> When one is compiling an anthology of exquisite examples of the
> ancient language, whether for study or for delectation, the origi-
> nal language is best. Nonetheless, in order that the lush beauty of
> the whole may be enjoyed ... a modern transformation is inevi-
> tably necessary. Here lies the *raison d'etre* of Mrs. Yosano's new
> translation.
>
> This new translation, then, is no reckless modernization of
> the ancient language, bringing it down to the level of the com-
> mon reader. It is no popularization; rather, it is a new song sung
> by a contemporary poet who has transformed ancient tempos into
> the rhythms of today. Though it may well be useful as a sort of
> "Child's Guide," it will also be a new stimulus even for those who
> are able to understand the beauty of the original; [it is] of immense
> interest, and moreover, a work that is extremely useful... . It is
> inevitable that something will be lost in the modernization of the
> ancient language. But if we were to accept the opinions of those
> who hold that only old things are precious, [if we were to] strive
> solely for elegance, and in so doing, abandon the passion that flows

through this tale, we would instead end up losing the distinction of the original.... It delights me that, far from rendering the gentle flow of the original flaccid and lukewarm, it has been transformed into a brisk, strong, modern, colloquial style. This new translation is a success.[47]

We shall return to the subject of the language of Akiko's *Genji* in the next chapter. For the moment we may note that Bin's assessment was upheld by his contemporaries: the *Shin'yaku* was indeed a success. It was enthusiastically reviewed by most of the major newspapers and literary journals of the period.[48] And it was reprinted many times in various forms and by different publishers during the decades that followed, remaining in print for twenty-five years, until the *Shin-shin'yaku Genji monogatari* began to appear in October 1938.[49]

In reviews of the *Shin'yaku*, the sentiments most often expressed are those of delight and gratitude. At long last there is a *Genji* that is easy to read; thanks are due to Akiko for providing it. There is universal praise for Nakazawa Hiromitsu's illustrations—each chapter of the *Shin'yaku* was preceded by a vividly colored woodblock printed illustration—although the lavish endpapers *(mikaeshi)* are too gaudy for the *Shinchō* reviewer.[50] Citing Ōgai and/or Bin, most of the reviews agree that the translator could not have been better chosen. There is also praise for the language of the translation. The *Yomiuri* describes it as a *genbun'itchi* style which, without losing any of the ancient feel of the original, conveys many of the overtones of the Heian court era. The *Shinchō* reviewer is delighted to report that, though he or she had

---

47. Ueda Bin, untitled preface in Yosano, *Shin'yaku Genji monogatari,* 1: 1–10.
48. Reviews of the *Shin'yaku* appeared in the following newspapers: *Ōsaka jiji shinpō* 26 February 1912, 3; *Tōkyō yomiuri shinbun* 11 March 1912, 1; and *Tōkyō nichinichi shinbun* 21 March 1912, 4. Reviews were also carried by the journals *Shinchō* 16.3 (March 1912): 126; *Bunshō sekai* 7.3 (March 1912): 126; *Hototogisu* 15.7 (April 1912): 22; *Joshi bundan* 8.4 (April 1912): 294; and *Shinshōsetsu* 18.9 (September 1913): 78.
49. On the printing history of the *Shin'yaku* and the *Shin-shin'yaku*, see Tamura Sachi, "Yosano Akiko yaku *Genji monogatari* shoshi," *Tsurumi Daigaku kiyō* no. 32 (1995): 157–98.
50. Nakazawa Hiromitsu (1874–1964) was trained in Western art and designed the bindings for several of Akiko's poetry collections. He also provided cover illustrations for the works of other contemporary literary figures.

been apprehensive whether the language of *Genji* could be made to harmonize with the modern, colloquial language, such fears proved groundless: the translation reads fluently and difficult passages are smoothed out in a pleasing manner. The *Nichinichi* review is by far the longest of the newspaper notices. In it, the famous opening section, "which everyone knows by heart," is cited alongside Akiko's version as an example of her style, but without any further comment. Then a longer quotation, from the beginning of the 'Suetsumuhana' (The Safflower) chapter, is followed by Akiko's translation of the same passage, together with remarks by the reviewer:

> [In Akiko's version] two or three lines containing words or phrases of interest have been omitted, but this is surely unavoidable when one translates into the modern language. In so far as the feeling (*kibun*) one receives from the abbreviated passage is the same as that of the original, [the missing lines] are completely unnecessary. Those who delight in the subtle beauty of the words used in the ancient language must of course read it in the ancient language. There may well be criticism from those who feel that translating the ancient language into the modern, colloquial style deprives it of its historical flavor, and thus abominate translations as offensive. Yet in terms of feeling and in terms of plot, it seems to me that in the *Shin'yaku Genji monogatari* everything that could be done has been done with aplomb.[51]

As far as I have been able to ascertain, the *Shin'yaku* attracted only one unfavorable notice, "Evaluating Akiko's Shin'yaku Genji monogatari" by Hinata Kimu (1884–1967).[52] The review is a detailed

---

51. *Tōkyō nichinichi shinbun* 21 March 1912, 4.
52. Hinata Kimu, "Akiko-shi no Shin'yaku Genji monogatari o hyō su," *Joshi bundan* 9.13 (November 1913): 81–84; 9.14 (December 1913): 42–43; 10.1 January 1914): 60–63; and 10.2 (February 1914): 34–37. The existence of a first installment in the October 1913 issue of *Joshi bundan* is likely, but unfortunately no public library in Japan seems to hold this particular issue. References are to *Joshi bundan* published by Fujin Bungeisha, not the identically named journal published by Joshi Bundansha. My thanks to Koyama Noboru of the Cambridge University Library for tracking down these references. For a biography of Hinata, later Hayashi Kimu(ko), see Mori Mayumi, *Taishō bijinden: Hayashi Kimuko no shōgai* (Bungei Shunjū, 2000).

but cranky comparison of Akiko's rendering of the 'Wakamurasaki' (Lavender) chapter with the original, in which Hinata not only takes Akiko to task for her many omissions, but offers her own translation of these passages, rendering them in a semi-classical style that stands in sharp contrast to the *genbun'itchi* of the *Shin'yaku*. If Akiko saw this review, she took no notice of it.

The enthusiastic reception accorded Akiko's first *gendaigo-yaku* led to the appearance, in swift succession, of her translations of *Eiga monogatari* (1914–15), *Murasaki Shikibu nikki* and *Izumi Shikibu nikki* (1916), all published by Kanao Bun'endō. For a different publisher, she also produced a translation of *Tsurezuregusa* (1916).[53] Moreover, reviews of *Shin'yaku Eiga monogatari,* as her rendition of *Eiga* was called, began by referring to the great service she had done the reading public by translating *Genji* so that the entire work could be enjoyed without difficulty.[54]

How is one to account for the overwhelmingly positive response to the *Shin'yaku?* Why were reviewers and scholars alike moved to describe her translation as such an epoch-making accomplishment? The *Shin'yaku* was not merely the "first complete translation in the colloquial language," but "one of the greatest products of the Meiji literary world." An examination of the nature of Akiko's transformation of the classical *Genji* into a *Genji* for her own time, and particularly the language that was the vehicle of this transformation, must therefore be the subject of the next chapter.

53. For publication details of this and the foregoing works, see Appendix A. For an assessment of *Shin'yaku Eiga monogatari* by the eminent postwar scholar of the Heian period work, see Matsumura Hiroji, "Kaisetsu," in *Eiga monogatari,* trans. Yosano Akiko, vol. 9 of *Katen Nihon bungaku zenshū* (Chikuma Shobō, 1962), 418–22.
54. See "Shinkan hihyō to shōkai," *Chūō kōron* 29.10 (September 1914): 95; and "Shinkan hihyō," *Mita bungaku* 5.9 (September 1914): 160.

Chapter Five:
The *Shin'yaku Genji monogatari*

*Masafumi o tadafumi ni shite Kokorouru koto wa, tada bunshō kaku tame
nomi ni mo arazu, furufumi o yoku kokoroen tame ni mo yokaramashi to
kataraishikaba, aru hito, Genji Hahakigi shinasadame no uchi, sukoshi
utsushite mote kitarite, ika ni, to iu. Makoto ni zoku ni kikoyu tote, waraite
kakitodomenu.* [1]

I once mentioned that translating classical texts into the colloquial
language helps one not only to write well, but also to understand the
ancient language better; whereupon someone brought me a short passage
from the ranking of women in the 'Broom Tree' chapter of *Genji*, and
asked what I thought of it. "Sounds dreadfully colloquial," I said; and
laughing, I copied it down.

Ban Kōkei (1733–1806)

*Shin'yaku Genji monogatari … Yosano Akiko … kōgo no zen'yaku no
saisho.* [2]

"A New Translation of The Tale of Genji" … [by] Yosano Akiko … the
first complete translation in the spoken language.

Fujita Tokutarō (1901–45)

The two quotations above mark a major shift in attitude to the
literary use of the colloquial language. For the Edo-period literatus
Ban Kōkei, the colloquial is *zokugo,* the "vulgar vernacular." By the
time of Akiko's contemporary Fujita Tokutarō, however, the colloquial has become simply *kōgo,* the "spoken language," a language not
merely acceptable in a work of literature, but positively commend-
able. It is precisely this new use of the spoken language, and this new

1. Ban Kōkei, "Utsushibumi warawa no satoshi" (1794), in *Ban Kōkei shū,* ed. Kazama Seishi,
   vol. 7 of *Sōsho Edo bunko,* ed. Takada Mamoru and Hara Michio (Kokusho Kankōkai,
   1993), 66. The translation Kōkei refers to is quoted on pp. 66–67.
2. Fujita Tokutarō, *Genji monogatari kenkyū shomoku yōran* (Rokubunkan, 1932), 93.

attitude, that lie at the heart of Akiko's work on *Genji* and the acclaim with which it was received.

As noted in chapter one, a good many "translations" of classical Japanese into the contemporary vernacular had appeared before Akiko turned her attention to the task.[3] In some of these, translation was the instrument of comedy or parody; in others, a mode of explication or instruction. But as many of the titles of Edo period vernacular versions of *Genji* suggest—"Murasaki's Writings in the Gibberish.of Fisherfolk" (*Shibun ama no saezuri*), "The Tale of Genji for Humble Folk" (*Genji monogatari shizu no odamaki*), "A Rustic Genji" (*Genji hinakotoba*), and so on—the colloquial quality of a translation had always to be explained away and apologized for. The *Shin'yaku* is the first unashamed colloquial translation. Deliberately colloquial, it is written for an audience that aspires to go no further than a modern language translation, and holds no other form of language to be superior. The present chapter will attempt to show how this shift in attitude in favor of the literary use of the vernacular is manifested in Akiko's first translation of *Genji*.

Even from a cursory glance, it is clear that the whole bent of Akiko's *Shin'yaku* differs markedly from that of the *Genji* projects of her contemporaries. Scholars of National Literature may well have wanted everyone to read *Genji*, but strictly on their own terms. This meant pages crowded with text, often topped by notes, and overlaid with circles and lines for emphasis. In Sassa's *Shinshaku*, the only gesture to visual modernity is a black and white illustration in the Japanese style at the head of each chapter; the volumes themselves come equipped with scholarly apparatus familiar from Edo period works: a critical essay at the beginning of each chapter and extensive headnotes in small print. The translation itself is only squeezed in after all this, as

---

3. See the list in ibid., 88–95. Rebekah Clements and Niimi Akihiko, ed., *Genji monogatari no kinsei: zokugoyaku, hon'an, e-iribon de yomu koten* (Bensei Shuppan, 2019), provide modern editions of some of the major texts. In English, see Rebekah Clements, "Rewriting Murasaki: Vernacular Translation and the Reception of *Genji Monogatari* during the Tokugawa Period," *Monumenta Nipponica* 68.1 (2013): 1–36; and "Cross-Dressing as Lady Murasaki: Concepts of Vernacular Translation in Early Modern Japan," *Testo a Fronte*, no. 51 (2014): 29–51.

though it were no more than another ancillary aid to the student. Only Mizoguchi Hakuyō's new-style verse version, a slim and colorful *Genji* digest, small enough to fit in the reader's pocket, departs from this venerable format.[4] Every other Meiji-period attempt to bring *Genji* to the citizenry is decked out in some array of academic apparatus.

Akiko dispensed with all of this. At her insistence, the *Shin'yaku* was illustrated in the Western style by Nakazawa Hiromitsu, the artist who had illustrated and/or designed the bindings for all but one of the six volumes of poetry she published between 1905 and 1911.[5] At three yen per volume, more than it cost to buy a copy of Sanseidō's *Kōjirin* dictionary,[6] the four-volume *Shin'yaku* was certainly not within the reach of every reader. But the clean layout of the text, with dialogue clearly distinguished from narrative by line-breaks and brackets, gave it the look and accessibility of a novel. The *Shin'yaku* was designed to be read straight through, from cover to cover, not pored over piecemeal like a commentary.

And then there is the language of the translation. Comparison of various Meiji versions of the opening passage of *Genji* demonstrates how different Akiko's rendition is. The *NKBZ* edition of the original renders the text as follows:

Izure no ohon-toki ni ka, nyōgo kōi amata saburaitamaikeru naka ni, ito yamugotonaki kiwa ni wa aranu ga, sugurete tokimekitamau arikeri.

(1:93; S 3)

4. Hakuyō's aim, he states in his preface, is the same as that of *Shinobugusa* and other digests of the Edo period: to condense *Genji* to its essentials *(tai'i)*. *Genji monogatari shinobugusa* is a digest of *Genji* compiled c. 1688 by Kitamura Koshun (1648–97), son of Kitamura Kigin. See Mizoguchi Hakuyō, "Jijutsu," in *Katei shinshi Genji monogatari* (Okamura Shoten, Fukuoka Shoten, 1906), unnumbered pages before p. l.
5. Akiko expressed her gratitude to Nakazawa in "Shin'yaku Genji monogatari no nochi ni," in *Shin'yaku Genji monogatari* (Kanao Bun'endō, 1912–13), 4:6; translation in Appendix B. Kanao Tanejirō, "Akiko fujin to *Genji monogatari*," *Dokusho to bunken* 2.8 (August 1942): 8, and Shinma Shin'ichi, "Yosano Akiko to *Genji monogatari*," in *Genji monogatari to sono eikyō: kenkyū to shiryō—kodai bungaku ronsō dairokushū*, ed. Murasaki Shikibu Gakkai (Musashino Shoin, 1978), 264, provide more detailed descriptions of the presentation of the *Shin'yaku*.
6. At the time a month's subscription to the *Asahi* was forry-five *sen*, a copy of *Chūō kōron* twenty *sen* and ten kilograms of rice one yen seventy-eight *sen*. Figures from *Nedan-shi nenpyō: Meiji, Taishō, Shōwa*, ed. *Shūkan Asahi* (Asahi Shinbunsha, 1988).

In which reign was it? Among the many women of several ranks
who served [the emperor] there was one, not of the highest rank,
who enjoyed the particular affections of the emperor.

Shinpen shishi (A New Edition of Murasaki's History, 1888), composed in the hope that *"The Tale of Genji* would be widely read and
understood by the general public,"[7] attempts to achieve this level of
comprehensibility by specifying grammatical subjects and plurals,
updating the occasional adjective *(tōtoki)* or verbal inflection *(tokime-
kishi)* and breaking the text into small segments. Romanized transcrip-
tions for this and the following examples replicate the *furigana* glosses
that are provided by most of the texts cited:

> *Izure no mikado no on-toki ni ka ariken. nyōgo kōi-domo amata
> saburaikeru naka ni. ito tōtoki kiwa ni wa aranedo. hito yori sug-
> urete. tokimekishi hitori no kōi ari.*[8]

Genji monogatari kōgai (A Digest of The Tale of Genji, 1906) is only
slightly more expository:

> *Izure no mikado no on-toki ni ka, nyōgo kōi nado amata saburai-
> keru naka ni, shikaku tōtoki mibun naranedo, sugurete tokimekishi
> Kiritsubo to yoberu kōi owashikeri.*[9]

Onoe Torako, whose *Genji monogatari tai'i* (The Essentials of The
Tale of Genji) appeared in 1911, writes in a prefatory note that she
had considered using the *genbun'itchi* style "because it is easy to
understand":

> But it is too modern *(imayō ni sugite),* and thinking that the ele-
> gance of the original would be lost, I decided that I would do it
> in the classical style *(gabuntai),* sticking close to the original and

7. Masuda Yukinobu, *Shinpen shishi* (Ōyashima Gakkai, 1888), 1:3.
8. Ibid., 1:29. The periods in this transcription represent the Japanese punctuation mark *maru.*
   Nowadays it is used only to represent a full stop; but in earlier times it was often used, as
   here, as an all-purpose punctuation mark.
9. Chō Tsuratsune, *Genji monogatari kōgai* (Shinchōsha, 1906), 1.

adding brief notes so that there should be no passages that are difficult to understand.[10]

Her rendition is as follows:

> *Izure no mikado no on-toki narikemu. Nyōgo kōi, amata saburaita-*
> *maikeru ga naka ni, ito yangotonaki kiwa ni wa aranedo, mikado*
> *no on-oboe, koto ni medetaki kōi arikeri.*[11]

In common with the two examples cited previously, Onoe's method is to translate by assigning Chinese characters to the Japanese vocabulary of the text: the character customarily read *tōtoki* is to be read *yangoto-naki,* that for *mibun* is to be read *kiwa.* In this way her version maintains much of the classical diction of the original, yet spares the reader (whose knowledge of *kanji* is sufficient) the trouble of looking up unfamiliar words in a dictionary. None of the three alter the word order of the original. Their translation strategies remain commentarial strategies, as if the interlinear glosses of a commentary had been moved into the text.

It is not until Sassa's *Shinshaku Genji monogatari* of 1911 that we encounter an attempt to transform classical grammar into the new written language of the Meiji period:

> *Aru miyo ni takusan no nyokan no naka de hitori toki no mikado*
> *no chō o moppara ni shite orareru kōi ga atta. Kore wa amari*
> *iegara no takai kata de wa nai.*[12]

Determined to produce a *Genji* for the edification of the masses, Sassa and his fellow translators use what they describe as a "modern colloquial style which closely follows the original."[13] Classical

---

10. Onoe Torako, "Reigen," (prefatory notes) *Genji monogatari tai'i* (Daidōkan, 1911), 1. The prefatory notes are numbered separately from the text.

11. Onoe, *Genji monogatari tai'i,* text, p. 1.

12. Sassa Seisetsu et al., *Shinshaku Genji monogatari* (Shinchōsha, 1911), 1:1.

13. Sassa et al., "Hanrei," in ibid., 1:1. The prefatory notes are numbered separately from the text.

verb endings give way to the clipped plain perfective or imperfective. Elsewhere other adjustments are made: the substitution of the general term *nyokan* (female officials) for *nyōgo kōi* (Junior Consort and Mistress of the Wardrobe) prepares the way for the specificity of *kōi* which appears later in the same sentence; *iegara* for *kiwa* brings the latter word up to date. Sassa's use of *-rare keigo* (in *moppara ni shite orareru kōi*) is interesting: much less deferential than the *-tamau* of Murasaki's narrator, it is as if Sassa wishes to convey the less-than-exalted status of the Kiritsubo consort by using honorifics that will make that distinction clear to the ear of a Meiji reader. Despite these attempts at modernization, however, it should be remembered that the *Shinshaku* translation only accompanies and does not replace the text of *Genji*. Each section of translation is preceded by the original text (the latter in larger print) and followed by a section of commentary; the translated passages are not meant to be read independently. For Sassa and his colleagues, translation performs essentially the same function as commentary: it is to be read as an adjunct to and not a substitute for the original text.

Akiko propounds none of the popularizing ideals of the *Shinshaku* translators; but she practices them, nevertheless, in a far more thoroughgoing manner. In her afterword to the final volume of the *Shin'yaku*, Akiko claims only that she hoped "to delineate the spirit of the original using the instrument of the modern language":

> I endeavored to be both scrupulous and bold *(saishin ni, mata daitan ni tsutometa)*. I did not always adhere to the expressions of the original author; I did not always translate literally. Having made the spirit of the original my own, I then ventured a free translation.[14]

Her *Shin'yaku* version of the opening lines of *Genji:*

> *Itsu no jidai de atta ka, mikado no kōkyū ni ōku no hihintachi ga atta. Kono naka ni hitori heika no sugureta chō o ukete iru hito ga aru. Kono hito wa kiwamete kenmon no shusshin to iu no demo*

14. Yosano, "Shin'yaku Genji monogatari no nochi ni," 2–3.

*naku, mata ima no chi'i ga kōkyū ni oite samade takai mono demo
nakatta.*[15]

What is most immediately striking about this passage is the sheer
distance between the language of the original and that of Akiko's
translation. It is not simply that classical verb forms have been recast
in the *genbun'itchi* style and grammatical subjects made explicit; the
text has been entirely rewritten. Honorifics have for the most part been
dispensed with, and extensive omissions and additions radically alter
the narrative. Let us examine these changes more closely.

Akiko's is the only version among those cited above in which
ohon-toki is translated without a deferential prefix. Instead of *saburaitamaikeru* she interpolates *mikado no kōkyū ni*. Where Murasaki made
her narrator both a participant in and an observer of the world of the
text through the use of deferential and humilific language, Akiko's
paring away of *keigo* marks her narrator as someone "outside" the
world of the text, distant from both the characters and the events. In
the *Shin'yaku* deferential forms are reserved for verbs indicating imperial action, and humilific forms are used only in dialogue. Later in the
'Kiritsubo' chapter, for example, Akiko's narrator uses a deferential
form to describe the emperor's feelings for Genji:

> *Heika wa sono haha o omou gotoku, daini ōji o aishitamau koto
> wa hijō na mono de atta.* (2–3)
> The love that His Majesty bestowed upon the Second Prince was
> of the same extreme sort that he felt for [the boy's] mother.

In contrast, the Kokiden consort's apprehension concerning Genji is
described in strictly "neutral" terms:

> *Sore o shitta Udaijin no musume no Kokiden no nyōgo wa, waga
> ko no ue ni fuan o kanzezu ni wa irarenai. Daini no ōji ga kōtaishi
> to naru no de wa arumai ka to omowazu ni wa irarenai.* (3)

15. Yosano Akiko, *Shin'yaku Genji monogatari* (1912–13; reprint Shinkōsha, 1935),
1. Hereafter, page numbers cited in the text are to this one-volume reprint of the *Shin'yaku*.

Once the Kokiden consort, daughter of the Minister of the Right, knew that [i.e. the Emperor's affection for Genji], she could not but feel uneasy about her own child. She could not but fear that the Second Prince [i.e. Genji] might become the Crown Prince.

An example of Akiko's use of honorific distinctions in dialogue occurs in the following passage, in which the emperor and the Kiritsubo consort exchange final words:

"Watashi no kokoromochi o sasshite kureru nara, watashi o nokoshite wa dairi o derarenai hazu da."
Konna dada mo o-ii ni naru yō ni naru.
"Shigo no sematta watashi da to omou to, tadaima no o-wakare no kurushii koto wa iiyō mo gozaimasen. Watashi wa ikitai, ikite itai."
... Kōi wa jikka e sagatta. (5-6. Cf. 1:98-99; S 6)
"If you understood how I feel, you would surely not be able to depart the palace leaving me behind."
It came to the point where he was uttering even nonsense of this sort.
"When I realize that I am close to death, the pain of this parting is beyond words. I want to live, to go on living."
... The lady left for her family home.

The emperor speaks in plain forms to the Kiritsubo consort; the narrator uses deferential language towards the emperor but plain forms for the consort; the consort speaks respectfully to the emperor.

These sorts of distinctions are maintained throughout the *Shin'yaku* text: the narrator is deferential only to members of the imperial family, and characters observe the humilific niceties that they would if they were speaking to each other in Meiji Japan. It is only after Genji is made Jun-Daijō Tennō in the 'Fuji no Uraba' chapter that his actions are unfailingly described with deferential forms.[16] This stripping away

---

16. We are informed of Genji's "promotion" in the following sentence: *"Aki ni Genji no Kimi wa Jun-Daijō Tennō no senji o o-uke ni natta"* (671). Akiko takes her cue from Murasaki Shikibu, who also "promotes" Genji to the deepest of deferential forms at this point in the narrative: when Suzaku-in and the Reizei emperor visit Genji at the Rokujō-in, Genji is described as *"migokoro o tsukushi, me mo ayanaru migokoromōke o sesasetamau"* (Genji deigned to do his utmost to ensure that it would be dazzling). See 3:450; S 534.

of honorific language *(keigo)* is, like the visual distinctiveness of her volumes, a characteristic of Akiko's translation that clearly sets it apart from those of her Meiji predecessors. It would be wrong, however, to regard Akiko's departures simply as marks of her willingness to race headlong down a path along which others had ventured only timidly. Hers is a different path, with a different starting point. Masuda, Chō, Onoe, even Sassa and his collaborators, still under the spell of a centuries-old awe for Japan's "unrivaled literary treasure," could not conceive of tampering with anything but the peripherals of the text of *The Tale of Genji*. Akiko, on the other hand, creates a new *Genji* in what by contrast seems a different language. The depth and nature of the difference is well described by Richard Bowring in a percipient formulation of the *genbun'itchi* process: *genbun'itchi*, he writes, was not simply a matter of "taking *bungo*, chipping away all the more obvious old bits, and replacing them with spoken equivalents." It "involved something far more difficult: the forging of a new literary language *out of* the vernacular."[17] This describes precisely the fundamental difference between Akiko's language and that of her predecessors. Others had found the *genbun'itchi* style "too modern," had feared that "the elegance of the original would be lost;" to do more than "chip away at the old bits and replace them with spoken equivalents" would have constituted an affront to a classic. Akiko "ventured a free translation" *(jiyū yaku o aete shita)*—free not only in the sense that her rewriting was radical, but also in the sense that she worked *"out of* the vernacular" and not out of *bungo*.

The passages compared thus far only begin to suggest the extent of the "freedom" Akiko allows herself. Examination of a somewhat larger segment of the *Shin'yaku* reveals several more of her translation strategies—and among them a liberty so far beyond what might be expected that it demands special treatment in a subsequent chapter. Let us look, therefore, at the well-known passage from 'Hahakigi'

---

17. Richard Bowring, review of *Paragons of the Ordinary: The Biographical Literature of Mori Ōgai*, by Marvin Marcus, *Journal of Japanese Studies* 20.1 (Winter 1994): 233. Emphasis in original.

describing Genji's attempted conquest of the wife of the Governor of Iyo.

At last there comes a break in the long rains—the occasion of the famous "Rainy Night Ranking" of women—and Genji leaves the palace to pay a visit to the home of his father-in-law the Minister of the Left. Like the mood of the mansion, the mien of his wife, Aoi no Ue, is "strikingly elegant and utterly unflawed" *(kezayaka ni kedakaku, midaretaru tokoro majirazu)*. She is just the sort of woman his companion Sama no Kami had spoken of, a woman of real substance in whom a man might confidently place his trust. Yet for all her perfection, Genji finds her off-putting. She makes him feel inferior, he cannot relax in her presence; and so he spends his time bantering with two of the younger ladies of the house, Chūnagon and Nakatsukasa, who are charmed by the sight of him in dishabille. Then along comes the minister himself to greet his wayward son-in-law, at which Genji complains, "Oh, not in this heat." The ladies giggle, but Genji shushes them, pulls up an armrest and welcomes the minister with his usual easy charm (1:167–68; S 38).

Here we find an example of perhaps the most noticeable of Akiko's freedoms: she reduces this passage, so revealing of both Genji's attractions and his failings, to a single sentence, "Genji left the palace and went to the mansion of the Minister of Left" (38).

To some extent omissions of this sort can be explained in terms of the history of the *Shin'yaku* project. With her publisher Kanao, Akiko had agreed on a limit of a thousand pages for the translation, to be divided between three volumes. At first she cut boldly: the twenty-one chapters from 'Kiritsubo' to 'Otome' are drastically rewritten, with many "unnecessary" passages of this sort replaced by a simple bridging sentence. But apparently readers wrote to say that they wanted a more complete translation.[18] She complied, and, as we shall see, the later chapters were translated more thoroughly—though by no means in their entirety—necessitating a fourth volume. In her afterword to the *Shin'yaku* Akiko explained:

18. Kanao Tanejirō, "Akiko fujin to *Genji monogatari*," *Dokusho to bunken* 2.8 (August 1942): 8.

For the reason that I did not feel that any more was necessary, I have attempted a somewhat abbreviated translation of the chapters following the first chapter 'Kiritsubo,' as these are chapters that have long been widely read and offer few difficulties. From the second volume of the present work, however, for the benefit of those who might find it difficult to read the original, I have paid careful attention to the meaning and adopted the method of virtually complete translation. [19]

Somewhat belatedly she realized that many of her readers required more than a reminder of the main events of the original. In this particular passage they are deprived of a telling glimpse of the complexity of Genji's character.

At this point, Genji's visit is abruptly interrupted. One of his men, "a deeply superstitious retainer" *(meishin no fukai kerai no hitori),* Akiko adds, informs him that their route from the palace runs counter to that of the God of the Center for that day; they must not spend the night where they are. Genji protests, but ultimately is persuaded to leave when someone suggests that the newly refurbished garden of Ki no Kami, one of his entourage, might offer a pleasant place to escape the heat. Akiko's handling of the conversation between Genji and his subaltern is worth a closer look. The original reads:

> *Shinobi-shinobi no on-katatagae tokoro wa amata arinubekeredo, hisashiku hodo hete wataritamaeru ni, kata futagete hikitagae hokazama e to obosan wa itōshiki naru beshi. Ki no Kami ni ōsegoto tamaeba, uketamawarinagara, shirizokite "Iyo no Kami no Ason no ie ni tsutsushimu koto haberite, nyōbō nan makariutsureru koro nite, sebaki tokoro ni habereba, namege naru koto ya haberan" to shita ni nageku o kikitamaite, "Sono hito chikakaramu nan ureshikarubeki. Onna tōki tabine wa mono-osoroshiki*

---

19. Yosano, "Shin'yaku Genji monogatari no nochi ni," 3–4. The extent of Akiko's cuts is tabulated in Seki Reiko, *Ichiyō igo no josei hyōgen: sutairu, media, jendaa* (Kanrin Shobō, 2003), 306–7. See also Seki, "Uta, monogatari, hon'yaku: Yosano Akiko *Shin'yaku Genji monogatari* ga chokumen shita mono," in *Genji monogatari no gendaigoyaku to hon'yaku,* ed. Kawazoe Fusae, *Kōza Genji monogatari kenkyū* vol. 12 (Ōfū, 2008), 135–64.

kokochi subeki o. Tada sono kichō no ushiro ni" to, notamaeba,
"Ge ni, yoroshiki omashidokoro ni mo" tote, hito hashiraseyaru.
Ito shinobite, kotosara ni kotogotoshikaranu tokoro o to, isogiide-
tamaeba, otodo ni mo kikoetamawazu, on-tomo ni mo mutsuma-
shiki kagiri shite owashimashinu. (1:168–69; S 38–39)

There must surely have been many places he could visit secretly
to avoid this directional taboo; but having come here after such a
long absence, it would be a pity if she/they were to think that, his
way being blocked, he had betrayed her/them and gone elsewhere.
When Ki no Kami was informed of the command, although he
acquiesced, when he had withdrawn he lamented in a low voice,
"There has been a proscription at the home of Iyo no Kami and
the ladies have now moved [to my home]. As crowded as it is,
I wonder if he mightn't feel ill treated." Hearing this, Genji said,
"I should be delighted to have them nearby. I'd feel terribly frightened to sleep in a strange place, far from any women. But behind
their screens …"Whereupon everyone said, "Truly an excellent
place," and they sent a messenger ahead. Very stealthily, thinking
this was no occasion for any fanfare, he hurried away, saying nothing to the minister. With only his closest retainers in attendance
upon him, he arrived there.

Akiko translates:

Jitsu wa sonna ni kangaenaide mo Genji no Kimi no itte tomaru
ie wa nai de mo nai no de aru ga, tama ni kita no ni hoka no onna
.no ie e yuku no wa Aoi no Kimi ni taishite shinobinai tokoro mo
atta no de arō, Genji no Kimi wa sassoku Kii no Kami o yonde,
"Omae no ie e hōyoke ni itte tomete moraō to omou. "
to itta. Kii no Kami wa makoto ni menboku aru koto da to itte
shukun no mae wa sagarinagara,
"Sukoshi komaru no wa watashi no oya no Iyo no Kami no uchi
no onnatachi ga, uranaisha ni nanika iwarete, sono uchi ni izu ni
mina watashi no uchi ni kite iru no de, semai tokoro de wa aru shi
futsugō ga nai ka to shinpai suru. "
to kage de itte iru no o kiita Genji no Kimi wa,
"Sore ga ii no da onna ga takusan kite iru no wa nigiyaka de
watashi wa suki da. Sono onnatachi no iru kichō no ushiro e de mo
hitoban tomete moraeba ii."
nado to jōdan o itte ita. Kii no Kami wa sassoku tsukai o ie no hō
yatte, bantan no setsubi o saseta. Genji no Kimi wa sotto Sadaijin-
ke o dete, shi-gonin no tomo de Nakagawa no uchi e kita. (39–40)

Actually, it was hardly as if there were nowhere Genji could go and spend the night without giving great thought to the matter; yet if, despite coming so rarely, he were to go to the home of another woman, for Aoi this would be intolerable. Genji immediately called Kii no Kami and said, "I'd like to put up at your home to avoid this directional taboo." Kii no Kami said he should be truly honored, but as he withdrew from his lord's presence, he said aside, "What's a bit of a problem is that the women of the household of my father Iyo no Kami have been advised of something by a diviner, and have left his house and come to mine; it's crowded and I worry that it might be inconvenient." Hearing this, Genji said in jest, "That's fine! With a lot of women there, it will be lively; I like that. I'm happy to spend the night behind the screens where the women are." Kii no Kami forthwith sent a messenger to his house and had them make all the arrangements. Genji quietly left the mansion of the Minister of the Left and, with four or five retainers, arrived at the Nakagawa house.

We note first of all Akiko's continued modernization of honorifics. The narrator's deference to Genji is eliminated. *Wataritamaeru,* combining a verb used only of the movements of the highest ranking personages and a deferential auxiliary, is replaced by the modern neutral *kita;* the humilific *uketamawa*[*ru*] (to assent) is completely rephrased as *makoto ni menboku aru koto da to itte* (saying he should be truly honored). On the other hand, the difference in rank between Genji and Ki no Kami is by no means leveled: Genji addresses his retainer as *omae* and concludes his command with *-te moraō to omou* (lit. "I shall accept"). And having lost the directional indicators that inhere in the old honorifics, the grammatical subjects of these actions have had to be identified. In the case of Genji and Ki no Kami, this is a straightforward matter; but when it comes to the question of who might "think" *(obo*[*su*]*)* badly of Genji if he were to go and visit another woman, a choice has to be made. Akiko opts for Aoi rather than the Minister of Left, or, equally possible, both.

Even more noticeable, however, is the length of Akiko's translation. In contrast to the near total excision of the previous passage, this one actually expands upon the original. The increment is accounted for almost entirely by Akiko's attempts to clarify for the modern reader what would be obvious to a reader of the Heian court. As already noted, subjects are identified, and the psychological connotations of *uketamawa[ru]* are specified. In addition, she makes it clear that the places Genji might have gone to spend the night "in secret" are the homes of "other women;" that Iyo no Kami is Ki no Kami's father (and note too her use of the learned pronunciation of the province, "Kii," where the *NKBZ* text gives the popular pronunciation "Ki"); that the issuer of the "proscription" is a "diviner;" that Genji speaks "in jest;" that the messenger's mission is to have "arrangements" made; and that whereas the original says only that Genji takes his closest retainers, Akiko specifies "four or five."

Perhaps the most interesting alteration, however, involves hardly any increase in the word count. Whereas Murasaki Shikibu has Genji tell Ki no Kami that he would "feel terribly frightened to sleep in a strange place, far from any women," Akiko only allows him to say that he is happy to have the women around because they make it "lively," and he "likes that." The suggestion, only half in jest, that he could hardly be expected to sleep without female company is considerably tamed. In the only cuts in this passage, Akiko omits to mention that Aoi could feel "betrayed" if Genji were to go to the house of another woman, and that Genji neglects to inform his father-in-law of his departure.

The next passage Akiko condenses, once again, drastically. A description of the many charms of Ki no Kami's garden is entirely omitted, and the reader is hurried ahead to the point where Genji's men are shown to a gallery beneath which a stream flows, where they are served sake. Also omitted is Genji's thought, as he silently surveys the scene, that the women of the middle rank, of whom his companions of the previous night had spoken, must have come from just such homes as this. Which in turn leads on to less abstract thoughts—and deeds—which Akiko translates more fully:

> *Omoiagareru keshiki ni, kikiokitamaeru musume nareba, yukashi-*
> *kute, mimi todometamaeru ni, kono nishi-omote ni zo, hito no kehai*
> *suru. Kinu no otonai harahara to shite, wakaki koedomo niku-*
> *karazu. Sasuga ni shinobite warai nado suru kehai, kotosarabi-*
> *tari. Kōshi o agetarikeredo, Kami, "kokoro nashi" to mutsukarite,*
> *oroshitsureba, hi tomoshitaru sukikage, sōji no kami yori mori-*
> *taru ni, yaora yoritamaite, miyu ya to oboscdo, hima mo nakereba,*

shibashi kikitamau ni, kono chikaki moya ni tsudoiitarunarubeshi,
uchi sasameki iu kotodomo o kikitamaeba, waga on-ue narubeshi.
"Ito itō mamedachite, madaki ni yamugotonaki yosuga sadamari-
tamaeru koso, sōzōshikamumere" "Saredo, sarubeki kuma ni wa
yoku koso kakurearikitamau nare" nado iu ni mo, obosu koto nomi
kokoro ni kakaritamaeba, mazu mune tsuburete, kayō no tsuide ni
mo, hito no iimorasamu o kikitsuketaramu toki nado, oboetamau.

Kotonaru koto nakereba, kikisashitamaitsu. Shikibu Kyō no
Miya no himegimi ni, asagao tatematsuritamaishi uta nado o,
sukoshi hohoyugamete kataru mo kikoyu. Kutsurogigamashiku uta
zunjigachi ni mo aru kana, nao miotori wa shinan kashi to, obosu.

Kami idekite, tōro kakesoe, hi akaku kakage nado shite, on-
kudamono bakari maireri. "Tobarichō mo ikani zo wa. Saru
kata no kokoro mo nakute wa, mezamashiki aruji naramu" to,
notamaeba, ' "Nani yokemu' to mo e uketamawarazu" to, kashi-
komarite saburau. Hashitsukata no omashi ni, kari naru yō nite
ōtonogomoreba, hitobito mo shizumarinu. (1:170–71; S 40)

As the daughter, so he heard, had apparently been a woman of
high aspirations, he is curious, and as he listens carefully there
are sounds of people on the western side. The rustling of silks
and the young voices are not displeasing. Their suppressed laughing, as one would expect, seemed self-conscious. The shutter was
raised, but the Governor grumbled that "this would not do," and
they lower it. Thinking he might be able to see them, he moves
softly toward where a sliver of light shines out from above the sliding door, but there is no gap. He listens for a time and it sounds as
if they must have gathered in the nearby main hall. As he listens to
their whispered speech, it seems they are talking about him. "He
would appear to be very, very earnest. It seems a pity that they
have already found a high-ranking wife for him, even though he's
hardly grown up." "But I hear that he often contrives to go in secret
to certain out-of-the-way haunts," they are saying. Thereupon,
with that single longing ever on his mind, he immediately cringes,
wondering: if the time should come when even in such places as
this they should hear someone reveal his secret... .

As it was rather uninteresting, he stopped listening. He can hear
them discussing, and misquoting, the poem he sent with a morning
glory to the daughter of Prince Shikibu. Too quick to poetry and a
bit lax at it besides, are they? he thought; yes, to see them would
only prove disappointing.

The Governor came; he hung more lanterns, turned up the
lamps, and offered them sweets of some sort. "And what about the

curtains?" [Genji] said, "It would be poor hospitality not to attend
to that." "I cannot imagine what you might find to please you
here," he replied with due ceremony as he took his place. [Genji]
chose a place near the verandah to rest for the moment, and he lay
down. His men too grew quiet.

Akiko translates:

*Genji no Kimi wa Kii no Kami no imōto wa kiryō jiman no onna de
aru koto o mae ni kiita koto ga aru no de, mitai mono da to omotte
iru to, kono shinden no nishi no hō ni onnatachi no iru kehai ga
kikoeru. Fusuma no soba e yotte mita ga, hi no tomotte iru akari
dake ga sashite ite nani mo mienai. Shikashi onna no suru hiso-
hisobanashi wa kikoeru.*
*"Anmari hayaku go-bonsai ga o-kimari ni natta no de akkenai
koto ne. Keredo kakushigoto datte o-kirai no hō de wa nai sō yo."*
*nado to itte iru mono mo aru. Genji no Kimi wa Fujitsubo no
Miya ni arumajiki koi o shite fumi nado o okuru koto ga konna
hitotachi ni uwasa sarete iru no o kiitara to omowazu mi ga chi-
jinda. Heika no otōto no Shikibu Kyō no Miya no himegimi ni
okutta Genji no Kimi no uta nado mo hanashi no tane ni natte
iru.* (40–41)

Just as Genji was thinking that he would like to see the younger
sister of Kii no Kami, since he had heard that she is a woman who
takes pride in her good looks, he hears the sounds of women on the
west side of the main hall. He went up to the sliding door but only
a crack of light from the lamp is shining through and he can see
nothing. But he hears the whispered conversation of women. "It's
a shame that they found a wife for him so soon, isn't it? But I do
hear that he's not averse to a bit of secret dalliance,"
some of them are saying. If he were to hear women of this sort
gossiping about his carrying on an illicit love affair with the
Fujitsubo empress and sending letters to her ... Genji thought, and
involuntarily cringed. The letters Genji sent to the daughter of the
emperor's younger brother Prince Shikibu were also a subject of
their conversation.

It will be immediately obvious that Akiko reduces the length
of this passage by half. Her "freedoms" here, however, are far more
nuanced than any we have seen so far, and cannot be ascribed to the
exigencies of publishing. Rather, they are informed by a consistent

narrative logic, aimed at transforming a "story" *(monogatari)* that is told into a "novel" *(shōsetsu)* that is narrated. Just as Genji is thinking that he would like to get a glimpse of the visiting lady, he hears voices on the far side of the building. In the original, we are also told that he makes a point of listening, that the sounds he hears are those of rustling silks and young voices, and that he finds them not unpleasant. The teller of a tale, who can call upon the resources of facial and vocal expression to hold her audience's attention, can afford this sort of embroidery. Akiko the writer deletes it, and advances the action immediately to the point of Genji's next move, which is toward the light shining out from the room where the ladies sit. Neither does the modern novelist need to add that the ladies "seem to have gathered in the nearby main hall." Nor is it necessary to point out that Genji catches them "talking about him," for that will be perfectly obvious from the conversation that follows. *What* the ladies say of him, however, she reports in full, for that is of crucial interest to the reader. In short, Akiko here exemplifies precisely what she means when she calls *Genji* a *"shōsetsu"* and describes the act of translation as "writing *Genji*."

The only indiscriminate "cut" in this passage, then, is Genji's final bit of badinage directed at Ki no Kami. When the Governor returns with more refreshments for his guests, Genji chides him: "And what about the curtains?" His allusion is to a Saibara that goes:

Tobarichō o mo taretaru o,	The curtains are hung,
Ōkimi kimase, muko ni semu	Come my lord, be my son-in-law
Mi-sakana ni, nani yokemu	And to eat what would please you
Awabi, sadaoka, kase yokemu.	Abalone? Turbo? Sea Urchin?

Shellfish have a long history of service in Japanese literature as metaphors for the female genitalia. Here they provide Genji with the means to suggest to Ki no Kami that a good host would offer his guests not only drink and food but sexual companionship as well. It is a shame that Akiko deprives her readers of this further glimpse of the darker side of Genji's character.

The longish section that intervenes between Genji's first intimations of interest in Utsusemi and his actual invasion of her quarters is translated with surprisingly few "freedoms." Hardly a word is omitted from the conversation in which Ki no Kami relates the past history of Utsusemi and her younger brother Kogimi, and Genji remarks on the cruel fate of a woman who might once have aspired to the favor of the emperor ending up as the second wife of an old provincial governor. And apart from the excision of some disapproving remarks about the old governor's baser interests in his young wife, the same is true of the conversation leading up to Genji's inquiry as to the whereabouts of the lady.

Thereafter the scene shifts to the room where the boy and his sister are discussing Genji, unaware that he is eavesdropping upon them. This passage, though tightened by Akiko in the same dexterous manner as the previous narration of Genji's nocturnal prowlings, is rendered with its essence intact. The boy tells his sister that Genji is every bit as handsome as he had heard; the sister muses that she might have had a look for herself were it still light enough. But instead they find themselves a place to sleep, the boy in the corner of the room, and the sister just beyond the door. As she lies down, she asks after her maid Chūjō, for she "feels deserted and frightened." But Chūjō has gone to the bath. This Genji takes as his cue to make a move. He tries the door, finds it unlatched, and enters. Making his way through a jumble of wardrobe chests, he comes upon a lone, tiny figure, lying on the floor with a robe pulled over her. He pulls it back, uncovering her, and says:

"Chūjō meshitsureba nan. Hito shirenu omoi no shirushi aru kokochi shite" to notamau o, to mo kaku mo omoiwakarezu, mono ni osowaruru kokochi shite, ya to obiyuredo, kao ni kinu no sawarite, oto ni mo tatezu. "Uchitsuke ni, fukakaranu kokoro no hodo to mitamauran, kotowari naredo, toshigoro omoiwataru kokoro no uchi mo kikoeshirasemu tote nan. Kakaru ori o machiidetaru mo, sara ni asaku wa araji to omoinashitamae" to, ito yawaraka ni notamaite, onigami mo aradatsumajiki kehai nareba, hashitanaku, "Koko ni hito" to mo, e nonoshirazu. Kokochi hata wabishiku, arumajiki koto to amoeba, asamashiku, "Hitotagae ni koso haberumere" to iu mo, iki no shita nari. Kiemadoeru keshiki ito kokorogurushiku rōtage nareba, okashi to mitamaite, "Tagaubeku mo aranu kokoro no shirube o, omowazu ni mo obomeitamau kana. Sukigamashiki sama ni wa, yo ni mietatematsuraji. Omou koto sukoshi kikoyubeki zo" tote, ito chiisayaka nareba, kakiidakite sōji no moto ni idetamau ni *zo, motometsuru Chūjō-datsu hito kiaitaru. "Ya ya" to notamau ni ayashikute, saguriyoritaru ni zo, imijiku nioi michite, kao ni mo kuyurikakaru kokochi suru ni, omoiyorinu. Asamashū, ko wa ika naru koto zo to, omoimadowaruredo, kikoen kata nashi. Naminami no hito naraba koso, araraka ni mo hikikanagurame, sore dani hito no amata shiramu wa ikaga aran, kokoro mo sawagite shitaikitaredo, dō mo nakute, oku naru omashi ni iritamainu. Sōji o hikitatete, "Akatsuki ni on-mukae ni mono seyo" to, notamaeba.* (1:175–76; S 42)

"Since you called for a Captain ... I feel this must be the reward of my secret longings," he says. She felt utterly petrified, as if possessed by a demon, and gasped in fright, but her face was covered by her robes and no sound emerged. "Well may you take my feelings to be impulsive and of no great depth; but I have been waiting for just such an opportunity to let you know how I have longed for you for years. Pray understand how far from shallow this must be." And since he spoke so very gently that even a demon could not have been upset with him, her will weakens and she is unable even to call, "someone, come here." Her words, "you would seem to have mistaken me for someone else," are likewise uttered under her breath. The sight of her distressed to the point of perishing is so pitiably sweet that he finds it charming. "I'm hurt that you fail to realize that I am led here by my heart, which could never be mistaken. I have absolutely no intention of doing anything indecent. I just want to tell you something of how I feel." She was so very small that he picked her up and was about to head for the door, when a person, apparently the Chūjō who had been summoned, happened to come along. Thinking it strange when he said, "Hey there," she groped her way [toward him], whereupon his scent, so filling the air that it seemed a cloud of smoke about her face, told her who it was. She is so shocked, and perplexed as to what might be happening, that she cannot speak. Were this some ordinary person, she would be rid of him by force; but what if everyone were to learn of this? Her mind in turmoil, she followed after him, but he was unperturbed and went right on back to his place within. As he slides the door shut, he says, "Come get her in the morning."

Akiko translates:

"Chūjō o yonde oide ni natta kara, watashi ga hito shirezu omotte iru kokoro ga tsūjita to omotte kimashita. "
to Genji no Chūjō wa onna ni itta. Onna wa osowareru yō ni,

"Aa!"

to koe o tateta ga, kuchi no tokoro e kaketa yogi ga sawatte soto e
koe ga kikoenai.

"Fui ni konna busahō na koi o shikakeru to o-omoi ni naru deshō
ga, watashi wa hisashii mae kara anata o omotte ite, sono hanashi
o shitai tame ni kō iu kikai o tsukutta no desu. Keshite asai koi ja
arimasen. "

to yawaraka na chōshi de otoko wa iu.

"Sore wa hitochigai deshō."

to yatto onna wa itta. Mamamusume to machigaerareta to omotta
rashii.

Genji no Kimi wa onna no komatte iru yōsu ni omoshiromi o kan-
jiru no de atta.

"Hitochigai nado o suru koto mo nai no desu. Anata wa iikagen
na koto o o-ii ni naru. Sukoshi o-hanashi ga shitai no da kara."

Kō itte Genji no Kimi wa kogara na kono onna o daite jibun no
shinjo no hō e tsurete ikō to shita. Chōdo soko e Chūjō to iu onna
ga kita.

"Oi!"

to Genji no Kimi wa sono onna ni koe o kakete oite fusuma o shimete, "Akegata ni o-mukai ni oide."

to itta. Chūjō wa otoko ga otoko de aru kara, sawagu koto mo
dō suru koto mo dekinakatta no de aru. Onna wa shūya naite ita.
(45–46)

"Since you called for a Captain, I've come assuming that my secret
longings have made themselves known to you," Captain Genji said
to the woman. The woman, as if possessed, exclaimed,

"Aa!"

but muffled by the bedclothes that covered her mouth, her voice
was inaudible.

"I expect you think me impulsive, that I make love to you in so
rude a manner; but I have yearned for you since long past, and
I have taken this opportunity because I want to talk with you of
this. Mine is by no means a shallow love,"
the man said in gentle tones.

"There must be some mistake," she said at length. She seemed
to think she had been mistaken for her stepdaughter. The sight
of the woman in such distress aroused feelings of fascination
in Genji. "There is no chance whatever that I am mistaken. You
speak too hastily. [I am here] because I wish to talk with you about
something."

So saying, Genji picked up this tiny woman and was about to take
her away to the place where he was to sleep. Just then, the woman
called Chūjō came.
"Hey there,"
Genji called out to the woman, and as he was sliding the door shut,
"Come get her in the morning,"
he said. Men will be men, and so Chūjō was unable to raise a fuss
or do anything else. The woman cried the whole night through.

Genji's first speech is translated in its entirety, offering a further
example of Akiko's sensitive transformation of Heian dialogue into the
vernacular speech of her own day. She follows the wording of the original very closely; but when Genji justifies his intrusion on the basis of
an idea no longer current—that emotions can have consequences in the
"real world"—she has him say not that this opportunity must be the
result of his own yearning but that his yearning must somehow have
communicated itself to her. And since the modern reader could not be
expected to know that Genji at that time held the rank of Chūjō, she
explains that he is playing upon (and taking advantage of) the name
of the maid, Chūjō, by calling him "Genji no Chūjō." Throughout the
passage, despite her leveling tendencies in the honorific language of
the narrator, she scrupulously renders Genji's almost comical use of
honorifics in his attempt to seduce Utsusemi.

In the narrative that follows, Akiko again edits out the orna-
mentation of the storyteller. For example, when Genji "speaks gently" to Utsusemi, and Utsusemi counters his advances with the weak
suggestion that he must have mistaken her for someone else, Akiko
dispenses with the narrator's conceit that "even a demon could not
have been upset with him." In doing so, she both increases narrative
pace and tension while simultaneously removing the narrator from
the immediate company of her audience to the distance of the printed
page. Likewise with the description of the scent of Genji's robes as
"like a cloud of smoke," and Chūjō's musings as to how she would
dispose of any lesser personage than Genji "by force." Toward the end
of the passage, however, far from modernizing, Akiko seems herself to
step briefly into the role of the Heian narrator. In an authorial intrusion

of the sort that would be termed *sōshiji* in a Heian text, she comments, without basis in the original, that "men will be men," so there was nothing Chūjō could do to prevent him. Here again, then, we see the twentieth-century writer tightening up the text of a tenth-century teller of tales—reducing expansive narrative to its essences, turning up the tension, quickening the pace.

At the very end of the passage, however, the mode of analysis employed thus far totally breaks down. The reader may already have noticed that Akiko's final sentence, "The woman cried the whole night through," has no equivalent in the original text. The reason is simply that these seven words stand in the stead of a massive cut. Here, at the very climax of this long episode, Akiko suppresses the entire description of Genji's conquest of Utsusemi. Genji's unrelenting protestations of sincerity; Utsusemi's anguish and Genji's delight in it; her pathetic recognition of the hopelessness of her situation, and the hopelessness of trying to make Genji understand it; their final exchange of poems—a passage of about fifty lines in most modern texts—disappears without a trace. A cut of this magnitude and of such central importance to the narrative is utterly inexplicable in terms of the constraints of space or the narrative strategies of a modern novelist. Reasons of a radically different sort must be sought. One cannot but wonder, for example, whether Akiko, unconsciously at least, might for some reason be bent upon making Genji appear in a better light in her translation than he does in Murasaki Shikibu's original. But that is a question too large to be dealt with here. For the moment I shall address briefly the far more manageable question: how is it that Akiko had become so adept a practitioner of the skills that we have observed in her transformation of Murasaki Shikibu's *monogatari* into a modern *shōsetsu*?

Her long experience with the language of *Genji* and her extensive knowledge of the world of *Genji* have been discussed in previous chapters. But these were not the only skills she brought to the task of translating. As Shinma reminds us, Akiko, in addition to her other accomplishments, was also a successful writer of fiction:

> Between 1906 and the end of 1910, Akiko wrote approximately thirty short stories and plays in the modern colloquial. Even after

she began work on the translation of *Genji* in January of 1911,
she continued writing works of this sort ... . The introduction of
dialogue rooted in a liberated modern language, a concise, quick-
tempoed style and such were amply fostered by the practice of
writing these short stories, plays, and children's tales.[20]

By the time she turned her hand to the translation of *Genji,* therefore, Akiko was not only a proficient reader of the classical language,
but also a published writer of *genbun'itchi* prose. The language of her
translation rises from the same source as the language of her fiction: the
"modern colloquial." As we have seen in the case of Sassa's translation, a *"genbun'itchi* style" might as readily be forged from the literary
as from the spoken language. In beginning from the latter, Akiko created a language of translation dramatically different from any that had
yet been applied to the text of *The Tale of Genji.*

The combined effect of the characteristics of her *Shin'yaku* that
we have observed—the visual, the summarization and explication, the
repositioning of the narrator—is to extricate Murasaki's fiction from
the world of scholars and scholarship where it had long been enshrined
as a classic, and to transport it into the world of modern literature.
Akiko rewrote, and at times even reinvented *Genji* in the language of
the Meiji novelist—and more importantly, the Meiji reader.[21]

From the vantage of the present, with its plethora of *gendaigoyaku,* it is bound to seem banal to cite this as Akiko's accomplishment.
But, as Fujita Tokutarō reminds us, hers was the "very first colloquial
language *Genji.*" Against the background of the work of her Meiji predecessors, all of whom shared an earnest desire to bring *Genji* to the
masses yet could not bear to reduce it to a *shōsetsu,* virtually every
aspect of Akiko's language noted in this brief analysis comes to seem
an act of daring. What was perhaps her ultimate act of daring is the
subject of the next chapter.

20. Shinma, "Yosano Akiko to *Genji monogatari,*" 259–60.
21. Kawazoe Fusae, *Genji monogatari jikūron* (Tōkyō Daigaku Shuppankai, 2005), 363–
64, describes Akiko's use of the *genbun'itchi* style in her first translation of *Genji* as
"cross-dressing in a man's style" (*dansō no buntai*). This view strikes me as perverse: the
modern colloquial was no more masculine than it was feminine; both women and men
employed the style in their fiction.

Chapter Six:
A Genji of Her Own: Textual Malfeasance in *Shin'yaku Genji monogatari*

かたはらに源氏の君のそひぶしてあるを親見しいつぞやのこと
Katawara ni Genji no kimi no soibushite
aru o oya mishi itsu zo ya no koto. (2:176)
When was it that my father saw me
with Genji lying by my side?

君まさぬ端居やあまり数おほき星に夜寒をおぼえけるかな
Kimi masanu hashi-i ya amari kazu ōki
hoshi ni yosamu o oboekeru ka na. (1: 162)
You do not return; and reminded by the myriad stars of the many times
I waited on the verandah, a night chill comes over me.

The question bypassed in the previous chapter was unanswerable in its local context. None of the translation strategies that could be identified in the passage from 'Hahakigi' analyzed there offer the slightest clue why Akiko should suppress the long climactic scene of Genji's attempt to seduce Utsusemi. In an expanded compass of inquiry, however, this act of self-censorship emerges in a more revealing light.

Seeking an explanation for the major omission, one first of all recalls a series of minor omissions, all of which have one thing in common: Genji ignoring his wife while he charms the young ladies of her suite; his bawdy and only half-jesting suggestion that his host provide "shellfish" for his guests; his insomniac irritation at the waste of sleeping alone *(itazurabushi);* his delight in the sight of a woman in distress. All of these, like the suppressed climactic scene, diminish the image of Genji as the perfect lover; and all are omitted in Akiko's translation of 'Hahakigi.'

Further afield, a similar pattern can be detected in other chapters of her *Shin'yaku*. On the basis of this and other evidence to be reviewed in this chapter, I have come to the conclusion that these cuts are intentional (though most likely the intent is unconscious), and that Akiko has highly personal reasons for making them. Akiko's involvement with *Genji* is at times so total that she projects the facts of her own life back upon the source of her inspiration. Not only does she draw material from *Genji* into her own life and work; she sometimes turns the tables and refashions Murasaki Shikibu's text—and even Murasaki's life—to conform with events in her own life. This practice produces striking misrepresentations that to date have passed unnoticed, both in Japan and in the West. The trail of evidence that leads to an explanation of this complex transaction between life and art begins with a poem cited at the very beginning of this study:

> *Genji oba hitori to narite nochi ni kaku*
> > *Shijo toshi wakaku ware wa shikarazu.* (7:156)
> Writing Genji alone, left behind
> > Murasaki was young; I am not.

As we have seen, Akiko's identification with Murasaki Shikibu here is total: both women begin "writing *Genji*" after they have become widows. We have seen, too, that this view contradicts the conclusions of Akiko's own scholarship, in which she asserts that Murasaki may have begun writing *Genji* well before she was married. To maintain her sense of identity with Murasaki, Akiko must, at least for the purposes of this poem, repudiate her own construction of the facts of her paragon's life.

On first encounter, this discrepancy seems mildly interesting, but of no great significance. A poet is free to negotiate with reality, or ignore it completely. But then this is not just another poem. Murasaki Shikibu is an historical figure, and in Akiko's eyes a paragon to be studied, emulated, even adulated. In an essay written in 1915 she expresses her admiration in the following terms:

> Murasaki's learning is extensive and profound; her judgment is never prejudiced, nor is she insincere. No matter what her subject, she never adheres blindly to old beliefs, but will always put forward an astute opinion of her own. Discovering the staunch determination that lies behind her indirect turn of phrase, I feel as if I were gazing at an expanse of sea. (15:122)

It was not like Akiko to play fast and loose with the life of someone she respected so deeply. Nor could the alteration in Akiko's view of the inception of *Genji* be dismissed as pure accident.

The motives of this poem come more clearly into focus, however, in the light of two other texts, the one another poem by Akiko and the other her translation of a passage in *Genji*. Of the experience of the loss of her virginity, Akiko writes:

ふるさとを恋ふるそれよりやゝあつき涙ながれきその初めの日

Furusato o kouru sore yori yaya atsuki
    namida nagareki sono hajime no hi. (1:261)
Hotter still than those of homesickness
    the tears I shed that first day.

Given Akiko's reputation as a "poetess of passion," and her biographers' penchant for using her poems in the fictional reconstruction of her amours, it is hardly surprising that this poem has become a cornerstone in romantic accounts of Akiko's early life.[1] Yet so far no one seems to have noted that echoes of this very poem are clearly present in her first translation of *The Tale of Genji*. The passage in question describes the young Murasaki's behavior the morning after Genji deprives the child of her virginity. The key sentence of this passage in the 'Aoi' chapter reads as follows:

Kakaru migokoro owasuramu to wa kaketemo oboshiyorazarishi-kaba, nadote kō kokoroukarikeru migokoro o uranaku tanomo-shiki mono ni omoikikoekemu, to asamashū obosaru. (2:64; S 180)
Not even dreaming that he had such a thing in mind, she was appalled that she had trusted so completely one with such base intentions.

She is angry, she is dreadfully upset, she feels deceived—she may even have wept. But if she did, the author does not tell us about it. Nowhere

1. See, for example, Satō Haruo, *Akiko mandara* (Kōdansha, 1954), 134–35; Mori Fujiko, *Midaregami* (Rukkusha, 1967), 119; and, most recently, Watanabe Jun'ichi, *Kimi mo kokuriko ware mo kokuriko—Yosano Tekkan, Akiko fusai no shōgai* (Bungei Shunjū, 1996), I: 186–87.

in this sentence or anywhere else in the passage does Murasaki shed a single tear.

Now let us look at Akiko's translation of this sentence in her *Shin'yaku Genji monogatari:*

> *Konna kokoro ga aru to wa yume ni mo shiranaide tanomi ni omotte ita to omou to atsui namida ga harahara to ho o tsutau no de atta.* (194)
> Not even dreaming that he had this in mind, when she remembered how she had trusted him hot tears coursed down her cheeks.

Throughout most of the sentence, Akiko's translation is faithful, tending to condensation rather than expansion. *Kakaru migokoro owasuramu to wa* becomes *konna kokoro ga aru to wa,* a fairly straightforward rendition. *Kaketemo oboshiyorazarishikaba* is translated as *yume ni mo shiranaide,* a bit simpler in its modern inflections and idiom, but certainly adequate. *Nadote kō kokoroukarikeru migokoro o uranaku tanomoshiki mono ni omoikikoekemu* is severely contracted to *tanomi ni omotte ita to omou to,* which leaves both *nadote* and *kō kokoroukarikeru* unaccounted for, but at least does not distort. The last words of the sentence, however, are another matter. Where Murasaki Shikibu merely says that the child was appalled *(asamashū obosaru),* Akiko says that "hot tears coursed down her cheeks" *(atsui namida ga harahara to ho o tsutau no de atta).* The same hot tears, it would appear, as those of Akiko's own "first day."

Once alerted to such a propensity in an author/translator, one begins to suspect evidence of it in passages that might otherwise pass unnoticed. Consider, for example, the passage depicting Genji's unanticipated, and ultimately momentous, tryst with Oborozukiyo on the night of the Emperor's "Cherry Blossom Feast." The night grows late, the festivities end, the courtiers go their separate ways, the Emperor and Empress return to their quarters, and silence settles upon the palace. But the moon is bright, Genji is drunk, and he sets off in search of further pleasures. The original text reads:

> *Moshi sarinubeki hima mo ya aru to, Fujitsubo watari o, warinō shinobite ukagai arikedo, kataraubeki toguchi mo sashitekereba.*
> (1:426; S 151)

Thinking he might just find an advantageous opening, in great stealth he set out to reconnoiter the environs of the Fujitsubo; but all of the doors where he might have talked someone into something were locked tight.

Akiko translates:

> *Moshi suki ga atte chūgū ni hitokoto demo mono ga ieta nara to, konna koto o omotte Fujitsubo no soba o aruite mita ga to ga mina shimatte iru.* (162) '
> If there were an opening and he could have even just a word with the Empress—thinking thus, he walked around the Fujitsubo, but all of the doors were locked.

Only a suspicious eye would find fault with this translation. There is nothing in it that could be called mistaken, no "freedom" nor omission that could not be defended. And yet there is a curiously laundered quality about Akiko's version. Murasaki's vocabulary—her combination of *suki* (gap), *shinobite* (stealthily, clandestinely, secretly), *ukaga[u]* (spying or reconnoitering preliminary to an attack)—makes an almost military metaphor of her description of Genji's attempt to breach the defenses of the Wisteria Court. Akiko's Genji is altogether more placid in his approach. Most obviously, the element of stealth is elided; and instead of "spying" *(ukaga[u])* Genji simply "looks" *(mi[ru])*. And surely Akiko knows that an empress would not be anywhere near an outer door; and that *katarau* does not signify that he wants to have a brief chat with her.[2] Something is "off" here, and whatever it is seems motivated by a desire to make Genji appear to better advantage in translation than he does in the original. It is as if Akiko is protecting her hero from the possibility that her readers might think ill of him.

2. She certainly knows in her later *Shin-shin 'yaku* translation. Compare *"Moshi chūgū e sekkin suru kikai o hirō koto ga dekitara to omotte, Genji wa Fujitsubo no otodo o sotto ukagatte mita ga, nyōbō o yobidasu yō na toguchi mo mina tojite shimatte atta."* (Hoping that he might be able to seize an opportunity to approach the empress, Genji quietly called at the Fujitsubo, but all the doors where he might have summoned a lady-in-waiting were shut fast.) *Shinshin'yaku Genji monogatari* (1938–39; reprint, Nihonsha, 1948), I:264.

The notion at first seems far-fetched; yet the impression is strengthened in the next sentence where we see Genji's reaction to this frustrating situation:

> *Uchinagekite, nao araji ni, Kokiden no hosodono ni tachiyorita-maereba, san no kuchi akitari.* (1:426; S 151)
> He sighed, [thinking] "Now this will never do," and he went on to the gallery of the Kokiden, where the third door stood open.

Akiko translates:

> *Tansoku o shinagara Kokiden no goten no soto no hosorōka o tōru to san no kuchi ga aite ita.* (162)
> Sighing, he passed along the narrow corridor of the Kokiden, where the third door stood open.

In the original Genji is adamant: "this will never do" *(nao araji ni).* If he cannot sleep with Fujitsubo he must find *someone* to sleep with. Akiko allows her readers to hear him sigh and observe his movements; his somewhat less than admirable thought is suppressed. Even his movements seem less determined, substituting as she does *tōru* for *tachiyoru.*

Suspicion, of course, may feed upon itself; one must guard against overinterpretation. Yet as one reads further in this passage, what at first seemed suspicious and aberrant begins to look more like a distinct pattern. As Genji moves along the corridor, he hears and then sees an attractive young lady coming toward him. The original begins:

> *Oku no kururudo mo akite, hitooto mo sezu. Kayō nite yo no naka no ayamachi wa suru zo kashi to omoite, yaora noborite nozo-kitamau. Hito wa mina netarubeshi. Ito wakō okashige naru koe no, nabete no hito to wa kikoenu, "oborozukiyo ni niru mono zo naki" to, uchizunjite, konatazama ni wa kuru mono ka.* (1:426; S 151–52)
> The inner hinged door was open, and there was no sound of people. Thinking this just the way one goes wrong in affairs between men and women, [Genji] quietly stepped up, and peered inside. Everyone seemed to be asleep. [He heard] a very young and

beautiful voice, that did not sound like anyone of ordinary rank, chanting "naught to resemble a night of a misty moon;" and she was coming this way!

Akiko translates:

Oku no kururudo mo aite iru. Genji no Kimi wa sotto agatte naka o nozoite mita. Tatte iru Genji no Kimi no mimi ni wakai utsuku-shii onna no koe ga kikoete kita.

> *Teri mo sezu kumori mo hatenu haru no yo wa oborozukiyo ni shiku mono zo naki*

to, sore wa koka o utatte iru no de aru. Soshite sono hito wa kochira e aruite kita. (162)

The inner hinged door stood open. Genji quietly stepped up, and peered inside. As he stood there, Genji heard the young and beautiful voice of a woman.

"Neither shining brightly nor completely clouded: naught to compare with such a night in spring, a night of a misty moon." she said. It was an old poem she was chanting. And then that person walked this way.

Once the open door is noted, original and translation diverge sharply. Akiko omits to mention that there is no sign of life within. More significantly, however, she again launders Genji's thoughts, suppressing the line in which he muses that this is "just the way one goes wrong in affairs between men and women." Neither does Akiko allow Genji to make any mental notes about the social rank of the young woman.[3] Thereafter, the original continues:

3. Two aspects of Akiko's handling of this passage, though not germane to the present argument, are worth noting. One is Akiko's treatment of Oborozukiyo's chanted line of poetry. In the original, Murasaki Shikibu has her chant only the second hemistich of the poem by Ōe no Chisato (fl. ca. 900), which for Heian readers was sufficient to call to mind the whole. Akiko cannot assume this level of knowledge on the part of her readers: she quotes the entire poem, and then goes on to point out that "it was an old poem she was chanting." Akiko's source—or perhaps her memory—mistakes one syllable: *haru no yo wa* should read *haru no yo no.* Although later collected in the *Shinkokinshū* (no. 55; *NKBZ* 26:53), the poem is one of a number of *kudai waka* (Tapanese poems on lines from Chinese poems—in this case, by Po Chü-i) composed in 894 at the command of Emperor Uda.

Ito ureshikute, futo sode o toraetamau. Onna, osoroshi to omoeru keshiki nite, "Ana mukutsuke. Ko wa ta so" to notamaedo, "Nani ka utomashiki" tote,

*"Fukaki yo no aware o shiru mo iru tsuki no
oboroke naranu chigiri to zo omou"*

tote, yaora idakioroshite, to wa oshitatetsu. Asamashiki ni akiretaru sama, ito natsukashū okashige nari. Wananaku wananaku, "Koko ni, hito" to notamaedo, "Maro wa, minahito ni yurusaretareba, meshiyosetaritomo, nanjō koto ka aran. Tada shinobite koso" to notamau koe ni, kono kimi narikeri, to kikisadamete, isasaka nagusamekeri. (1:426–27; S 152–53)

Utterly delighted, he immediately grasped her sleeve. The woman, who appeared to feel frightened, said "Oh, horrors! Who is this?" "What's there to be upset about?" he said,

"One who knows the beauty of a late night appreciates this misted setting moon; and this far from misty bond."

He gently embraced her, lowered her, and shut the door. The sight of her, aghast with terror, was very fetching and pretty. Trembling, she said, "Come here, someone," but he said, "I am permitted what I please by everyone; so even if you summon someone, what is to come of it? Now just be quiet." At the sound of his voice, she determined that it was he, and took some small comfort in that.

Akiko's *Shin'yaku* reads:

Genji no Kimi wa ureshikute sono hito no sode o toraeta. Onna wa odoroite,

---

Second, her handling of the last phrase, *uchizunjite, konatazama ni wa kuru mono ka* ([she] chants [and Genji thinks] 'she is coming this way!'), in which the narrative point of view shifts from that of an external viewer of the scene to the internal thoughts of Genji between the first verb and the second, shows a clear awareness of the problem. After the chanting and her explanation of what was chanted, she places a full stop, thus dropping the viewpoint of the external narrator. Then, starting a new, she attempts to capture the interiority of the latter words with a shift in her own narrative stance, adopting (insofar as one can in modern Japanese) the viewpoint of Genji. "That person" *(sono hito)* walks "this way" *(kochira e)*. The language of this phrase is of that sort described by the Edo period scholar Nakajima Hirotari (1792–1864) as "shifting" *(utsurikotoba)*. See Akiyama Ken, "'Utsurikotoba' to iu koto," *Murasaki*, no. 21 (1984): 58–61; Ikeda Setsuko, "Utsurikotoba," in *Genji monogatari jiten*, ed. Akiyama Ken, Bessatsu kokubungaku series, no. 36 (Gakutōsha, 1989), 156–57; and Midorikawa Machiko, "Shifting Words from *Monogatari* to *Shōsetsu*: The Translation of Internal Speech in Japanese Literature," *Testo a Fronte*, no. 51 (2014): 131–46.

"Dare"
to koe o tateta.
"Watashi mo tsuki o mite ita hito desu."
to itte Genji no Kimi wa soko no to o shimete shimatta.
"Dare ka kite kudasai."
to onna wa furuenagara itta.
"Watashi wa mina ni shōchi sashite kita no da kara, anata ga o-yobi ni natte mo kuru mono ga nai deshō."
Genji no Kimi wa konna koto o itta. Onna wa ima no koe o kiite kono otoko ga Genji no Kimi de aru koto ni ki ga tsuita. Genji no Kimi de atta nara to iu ki ni mo natta. Tsuyoi hari mo nai onna de aru. (162–63)

Genji was overjoyed and took hold of that person's sleeve. The woman was startled.
"Who is it?" she said.
"I too am someone who was looking at the moon."
So saying, Genji shut the door to the place.
"Someone, please come!" said the woman, shaking.
"I come with everyone's consent, and so even if you call out there is nobody who will come."
Such were the things that Genji said. Hearing this voice, the woman realized that the man was Genji. She then felt that, "Well, if it's Genji... ."Shweas not a strong-willed woman.

Here the description of Genji's behavior seems quite systematically sanitized. Where in the original Oborozukiyo reacts in horror *(ana mukutsuke)*, in Akiko's translation she says only "who is it" *(dare)*. Genji is not allowed to ask "What's there to be upset about?" Nor does he continue his reply in poetry. He simply says, "I too am someone who was looking at the moon." There is no mention of a "bond" *(chigiri)*, an omission that elides the overtones of physical as well as karmic bonding that the word traditionally conveys. And when Genji takes physical possession of Oborozukiyo, Akiko omits to note that he "gently embraced her and lowered her" *(yaora idakioroshite);* she tells her readers only that "he shut the door." The *Genji* narrator's remark that "the sight of her, aghast with terror, was very fetching and pretty" is totally suppressed, as is Genji's own advice to the young lady that she should "just keep quiet."

By the end of this encounter, there seems little doubt that our initial suspicions have been entirely justified, that whatever other reasons might be offered in explanation of the departures and omissions in this passage, it is also informed by a private agenda. This agenda is epitomized with wonderful clarity in Akiko's translation of the famous description of the youthful Genji that introduces the 'Hahakigi' chapter:

> *Hikaru Genji, na nomi kotogotoshū, iiketaretamau toga ōka[n]naru ni, itodo, kakaru sukigotodomo o sue no yo ni mo kikitsutaete, karobitaru na o ya nagasamu to, shinobitamaikeru kakuroegoto o sae, kataritsutaekemu hito no mono iisaganasa yo. Saru wa, ito itaku yo o habakari, mamedachitamaikeru hodo, nayobika ni oka-shiki koto wa nakute, Katano no Shōshō ni wa, warawaretamai-kemu kashi. (1:129; S 20)*
>
> The Shining Genji! Grand though the name is, they say there were many transgressions for which he was criticized severely. And yet even those that he concealed with such great care, lest his amours be talked of even in ages to come and earn him a name for frivolity, have come down to us—thanks to the gossips of this world. In fact, however, he was so painfully discreet and righteous-seeming, and his life so bereft of romance and spice, that he would surely be the laughing stock of the Katano Lieutenant.

In Akiko's translation this rambling and richly nuanced characterization is distilled to a single confident claim:

> *Genji no Kimi wa seken ni takusan kata no aru kōshoku-otoko to wa chigatte ita. (21)*
> Genji was different from those libertines of the sort so numerous in this world.

Gone are Genji's transgressions, gone his care to conceal them and his concern for reputation, gone the "righteous-seeming" (*mameda[tsu]*) facade that hides both pretense and genuine discretion. Genji is simply "different," not like those other "libertines."

Yet if Akiko is indeed systematically altering the "facts" of Genji's life, masking his flaws and shielding him from the criticism of her readers, we must then ask: why? That a woman writer, steeped in *Genji* from childhood, should identify with Murasaki Shikibu, and even with the fictional Murasaki, seems natural enough. Though tampering

with the texts of these women's lives may not be sound scholarly practice, as a psychological phenomenon it is entirely explicable. But why
should Akiko tamper in the same way with the "facts" of the life of
Murasaki's male protagonist, the Shining Genji?

A clue of sorts—tenuous, but relevant—is to be found, I think,
in a letter from Akiko to Tekkan. The letter is dated Meiji 34.5.29/29
May 1901, less than a month before Akiko ran away from her home in
Sakai to join Tekkan in Tokyo. It reads in part as follows:

> Recalling *Genji* and what-not, who am I? Well certainly not the
> 'Yomogiu' lady, I should think. "The quick-witted and charming
> Gosechi dancer from Tsukushi came first to his mind."[4] Is that
> who I am? "Time and again she delighted him with unexpected
> letters, which he found fetching and touching. But in the end he
> made no overtures. His world was too circumscribed, he could not
> do as he liked, and when he moved on to other things, there were
> many who resented it."[5] When I think of such things as that—well,
> just don't you break your promises in this life the way Genji dis-
> appointed her! He faithfully promises everyone—beginning with
> Yūgao—that in the life to come, they will be reborn together on
> the same lotus. Yet even if he should have a lotus-seat at the upper-
> most of the nine levels, surely he couldn't get that many people
> on a single lotus flower? You see what I mean, Genji?—or is it

4. Quotation marks in original. Akiko's letter here reads: *"Kuchi togarishi kokoro nikukari-
shi Tsukushi no Gosechi nado saki omoiidetamau,"* loosely quoting (presumably from
memory) a passage from 'Hanachirusato' (The Orange Blossoms) which reads: *" 'Kayō
no kiwa ni, Tsukushi no Gosechi ga rōtage narishi wa ya' to mazu oboshiidezu."* ('Among
those of rank, yes, it is the Gosechi dancer from Tsukushi who is most fetching,' [Genji
mused], recalling [her] first of all.) See 2:147; S 217.
5. Akiko marks the opening of this citation-*cum*-summary with a quotation mark, the end
with a line break: *"Fumi tabitabi odorokasekoshi nado natsukashiku aware to obosedo
ima wa iwaji yo no naka sebakute migokoro ni makasezu yoso ni sugiitamau nimo
urameshige naru hito ōkari [.]"* Her words are, I think, loosely based on the final lines
of the 'Akashi' chapter, in which Genji replies to an unexpected letter and poem from
the Gosechi dancer. The narrator remarks: *"Akazu okashi to oboshishi nagori nareba,
odorokasaretamaite itodo oboshiizuredo, kono goro wa sayō no on-furumai sara ni tsut-
sumitamaumeri. Hanachirusato nado nimo, tada on-shōsoku nado bakari nite, obotsu-
kanaku, nakanaka urameshige nari."* (He found her endlessly attractive, and as he still
had a lingering affection for her, when he heard from her unexpectedly, he recalled her all
the more fondly. But it seems that of late he was behaving more discreetly in such matters. To Hanachirusato and some others he sent only letters, which they found unsettling
and, far from being pleased, were resentful.) See 2:265; S 270.

Narihira? In the next world, with your lotus-seat still unopened,
I ask you: just how many women can you get on it? In matters of
this sort, my love, in this life at least, pray let me be the only one
with whom you exchange sake cups.[6]

This is an elusive document, a playful, teasing letter written
in the excitement of a rather daring love affair. The lovers' repartee
is couched in pseudo-quotations; and in places it is so disjointed syntactically that it utterly defies anything like close translation. Under
careful scrutiny the letter nonetheless yields suggestive leads. In the
first place, it is the only surviving source in which Akiko explicitly
equates Tekkan to Genji and herself to a lover of Genji. And the manner in which the equation is made suggests that there is more to it than
romantic fantasy. Whatever his charms, Akiko's real-life "Genji" is a
man of philandering tendencies; and however great her infatuation, she
is not blind to his failing. In this sense the equation is highly appropriate, even realistic. "You are my Genji," she says, "but please don't be
too much of a Genji; in this life, at least, let me be your only love."

Against the backdrop of this conception of herself, her lover,
and their relationship, Akiko's liberties in her first translation of *The
Tale of Genji* begin to seem if not excusable, then at least explicable.
The wishful imagination that makes of a lover a paragon on the model
of the Shining Genji may also wish to eliminate the flaws that mar
the perfection of that paragon. In such a state of mind—and this letter
clearly shows Akiko's mind in such a state—it requires only a minimum of self-deception to deflect one's search for a solution from the
world of real life to the world of fiction. Texts are more amenable to
alteration than people.

What Akiko seems to be doing in her libertine rendering of the
'Hana no En' chapter I have described as "protecting Genji." But is it

6. Translated from the text given in Itsumi Kumi, "Yosano Akiko no *Genji monogatari*
kōgoyaku ni tsuite," *Kokugakuin zasshi* 94.1 (January 1993): 16–17, a new transcription
of a letter which first appeared in Satō Ryōyū, *Midaregami kō* (1956; reprint, *Kindai
sakka kenkyū sōsho*, vol. 104. Nihon Tosha Sentaa, 1990), 273–75. I am most grateful to
Professor Ichikawa Chihiro for providing me with a copy of her own transcription of this
letter, in which a number of misprints in the Itsumi text are corrected.

not possible that in "protecting" the fictional Genji, Akiko is actually attempting to protect herself against the disappointments of Tekkan, her own "real-life Genji?" Earlier we have observed her tampering with the facts of the fictional Murasaki's life to bring it into closer congruence with her own; then we saw her eliding those proclivities in Genji's character that detract from the Genji she is prepared to let her readers know. These are the very proclivities that we now see she once entreated the man himself to control in her letter to him. It is as if in obscuring Genji's fictional flaws, she is shielding herself from the very real flaws in her (by then) husband. She knew from the start that she would need a shield of some sort. Ten years and seven children later, at work on her *Shin'yaku Genji monogatari,* the Genji/Tekkan equation seen in her early letter seems still strong enough to provide it.

This is not an idea that can be pushed to extremes. Mental processes—of which even the subject herself may not always be aware—can never be proven beyond doubt. This one, however, is susceptible, if not of proof, at least of corroboration by a sort of documentary triangulation. Between June and September of 1913—which is to say, during the same months that Akiko completed her first translation of *Genji*—Akiko serialized in the *Tokyo Asahi shinbun* the only full-length novel she was ever to write. This work, subsequently revised and published as *Akarumi e* (Toward the Light), describes a difficult period in the marriage of two writers whose lives bear a striking resemblance to those of Akiko and Hiroshi—so much so, indeed, that scholars regard *Akarumi e* as a *roman à clef* of great "fidelity to fact."[7] Tōru, the husband, is subject to spells of lassitude and melancholy. His wife Kyōko suggests a trip to Europe to revitalize his flagging spirits, and with characteristic dispatch sets about making concrete arrangements for the journey—just as Akiko herself did in order to facilitate Hiroshi's departure for France in November 1911. The crucial matter of money was the most difficult to arrange. Kyōko writes first to her sister asking for a loan of 2,000 yen. She then visits her publisher and asks him to help her raise the money. Meanwhile, Tōru

7. The most recent edition of *Akarumi e* appears in a series entitled *Sakka no jiden,* that is, "Autobiographies of authors."

goes to Fukuoka to ask his elder brother for help. When he delays his return, and then writes to his wife that he has obtained the requisite funds, saying curtly that "further efforts on your part are unnecessary," his very success arouses jealous suspicions. She jumps to the conclusion that the money was obtained not from his brother at all, but from Sadano, a former lover of her husband with whom she is sure he is still in contact. Consumed with jealousy, Kyōko convinces herself not only that her husband has prevailed upon Sadano for a loan, but that he has never ceased to think about his former lover, that he prefers his son by her to any of his legitimate children, that he will find parting from Sadano more painful than parting from his wife, that Kyōko will grow old and ugly waiting for him to return.[8]

The rest of the novel describes how Kyōko discovers that none of this is true. But more importantly, as time passes she convinces herself that her husband's moodiness and ill treatment of her are *her own fault*. Her jealousy and anguish over a relationship that is over have been utterly unwarranted, in her own words, no more than *torikoshiguró*, worries that she might have spared herself. Writing to a friend in the last chapter of the novel, Kyōko confesses:

> And now at last I have come to understand the reason why he [Tōru] has been insufferably sarcastic and made me feel wretched, why at times he has treated me in a manner indescribable. I was intoxicated, irretrievably deluded in thinking him the thrall of a life-long passion [for Sadano]; how exasperating, how pitiful, how idiotic he must have found me![9]

What makes *Akarumi e* of particular interest to us here is that the relationship Akiko depicts between husband and wife in her novel has an exact parallel in her rendition of the relationship between Genji and Murasaki in her translation of the 'Maboroshi' (The Wizard) chapter of *Genji*. (We might note, too, that Akiko translated 'Maboroshi' after her return from the trip to Europe, the preparations for which

---

8. "Sadano" corresponds to Hayashi Takino. See the introduction, note 13.
9. Yosano Akiko, *Akarumi e* (1916; reprint, *Sakka na jiden* 3, Nihon Tosha Sentaa, 1994), 264–65 (page citations are to the reprint edition).

occupy a great deal of space in the novel. Hiroshi's self-confidence had been restored and it was a time when their relationship did indeed seem to be moving "toward the light.") Let us look first at 'Maboroshi' in the original.

After Murasaki's death, Genji withdraws from the world and in the year thereafter spends a great deal of time reflecting upon his loss and the life he had lived with her:

> *Nyōbō nado mo, toshigoro henikeru wa, sumizome no iro komay-aka nite kitsutsu, kanashisa mo aratamegataku omoisamasubeki yo naku koikikoyuru ni, taete on-katagata ni mo wataritamawazu, magirenaku mitatematsuru o nagusame nite, naretsukaumatsuru. Toshigoro, mameyaka ni migokoro todomete nado wa arazari-shikado, tokidoki wa mihanatanu yō ni oboshitaritsuru hitobito mo, nakanaka, kakaru sabishiki on-hitorine ni narite wa, ito ōzō ni motenashitamaite, yoru no on-tonoi nado ni mo, kore kare to amata o, omashi no atari hikisaketsutsu, saburawasetamau.* (4:508; S 723)

Her waiting ladies, too, especially those who had been with her for many years, went on wearing deep shades of mourning, yearning for her as if their sadness should never heal and there should never come a day when they might resign themselves [to her death]. But as he never went to visit any of his other ladies, they took comfort in being constantly with him as they waited upon him. Those women to whom over the years he had from time to time taken a fancy, though he had never been seriously interested in them, contrary to what one might expect on these lonely nights when he slept alone, he treated with no special regard; even for night duty he would summon this one and that one in great numbers, keeping them at a distance from his sleeping place.

Akiko translates:

> *Onnatachi mo Murasaki no Kimi ni nagaku tsukawarete ita mono wa, mina haru ni nattemo mada koi iro no mofuku o nuganaide iru. Sorera no hito wa Genji no Kimi ga dare no goten e mo oide ni narazu ni, itsumo koko ni oide ni naru no o sabishii kanashii naka no tanomi to mo shite iru rashii. Naka ni wa Genji no Kimi to shūjū no kankei igai no kankei no aru onna nado mo majitte ita ga, sono hitora e mo Genji no Kimi wa sappari to shita soburi*

o misete oide ni natta. Yoru mo darekare to ikunin mo ikunin mo o-nedoko ni chikai tokoro e hanashi no togi ni o-oki ni naru no de atta. (945–46)

None of the women who had served Murasaki for a long time, even though spring had come, removed their dark-colored mourning garments. As Genji did not visit anyone else's mansion, these people seemed to draw some strength in their loneliness and sadness from the fact that he was always there. Among them were some women who had a relationship with Genji other than the relationship of retainer to him. Even toward these people, Genji displayed the most scrupulous behavior. For even at night, he would station several of them, this one and that, at a place near his bed as conversation companions.

Here again, what might seem blemishes in Genji's character are touched up or glossed over. In Murasaki's text, Genji no longer visits "his other ladies" *(on-katagata),* whereas in Akiko's version it is "no one else's mansion" *(dare no goten e mo);* and the women "he had from time to time taken a fancy to" *(tokidoki wa mihanatanu yō ni oboshitarit-suru hitobito)* are transformed rather clumsily into "women who had a relationship with Genji other than the relationship of retainer to him" *(Genji no Kimi to shūjū no kankei igai no kankei no aru onna).* She seems at a loss, however, for a polite equivalent to the sort of loneliness Genji experiences now that he is sleeping alone *(sabishiki onhi-torine ni narite wa)* and simply cuts the reference to this condition. The description of Genji stationing his conversation partners "near his bed" *(o-nedoko ni chikai tokoro e)* seems only a careless error, for the original clearly indicates that he keeps them at a distance *(omashi no atari hikisaketsutsu saburawasetamau).* Thus far, however, she alters nothing more drastically than what we have seen in previous passages.

The original continues:

Tsurezure naru mama ni, inishie no monogatari nado shitamau oriori mo ari. Nagori naki on-hijirigokoro no fukaku nariyuku ni tsuketemo, sashimo arihatsumajikarikeru koto ni tsuketsutsu, nak-agoro monouramesyū oboshitaru keshiki no tokidoki mietamaishi nado o oboshiizuru ni, nadote, tawabure nitemo, mata mameyaka ni kokorogurushiki koto ni tsuketemo, sayō naru kokoro o mietate-matsuriken, nanigoto ni mo rōrōjiku owaseshi on-kokorobae narishikaba, hito no fukaki kokoro mo ito yō mishiritamainagara, enjihatetamau koto wa nakarishikado, hitowatari zutsu wa, ika naramu to suran, to oboshitarishi ni, sukoshi nitemo kokoro o midaritamaikemukoto no itōshū kuyashū oboetamau sama, mune yori mo amaru kokochi shitamau. Sono ori no koto no kokoro o mo shiri, ima mo chikō tsukōmatsuru hitobito wa, honobono kikoeizuru mo ari. (4:508–9; S 723–24)

Time and again, in his tedium, he would talk of the past. As he became, with no regrets, more and more deeply austere, and he recalled how at times in those days she had shown feelings of resentment over affairs he had no intention of pursuing to the end, he wondered why he had displayed such sentiments, whether frivolous or painfully amorous in a genuine way. Being a person of mature judgment in all things, she could see perfectly well what his deeper feelings were, and her anger never went to extremes; but on every such occasion she did worry how things would turn out. And the pity and regret he now felt for even the slightest distress [he had caused her] seemed more than his breast could contain. There were people who had known of his affairs on those occasions, and now waited upon him closely, who sometimes made veiled references to them.

Akiko's translation reads:

Seijin no yō na seikatsu ni ippo ippo haitte o-yuki ni naru ni tsukete, naki hito to gojishin to no koi ga kō made majime na mono de aru koto wa, mukashi mo kawari no nai shinjitsu de atta ga, ari no susabi ni suginai koi no tawamure de sono hito ni ōku uramareta to iu koto o tsukuzuku to o-kanji ni naru. Sono toki no gojishin no shiwaza mo kōkai sareru koto wa iu made mo nai ga, sono hito wa shinaidemo ii torikoshigurō o, dono onna no dono baai ni mo ichido zutsu fukaku fukaku suru hito de atta nado to mo o-omoi ni natta. Sonna baai o shitte, Murasaki no Kimi ni dōjō shite ita onnatachi wa, sonna hanashi o sore to naku mochidashi nado mo suru no de atta. (946–47)

As step by step he entered upon the life of a saintly ascetic, the constancy of his own love for the departed one remained, to the aforementioned extent, a fact unchanged from of old. Yet he was painfully aware that on account of his frivolous love affairs, which had never been more than passing fancies, he had been greatly resented by that person. That he regretted his deeds on those occasions goes without saying; still, it did seem to him that she had been one to search too deeply for worries—concerning each and every woman and affair—worries that she might well have spared herself. Women who knew of these affairs and sympathized with Murasaki would sometimes hint at such matters in an oblique way in conversation.

Akiko's protective tendencies here become positively reckless. In the original, Murasaki is described as "a person of mature judgment in all things" who "could see perfectly well what [Genji's] deeper feelings were" *(nanigoto ni mo rōrōjiku owaseshi on-kokorobae narishikaba, hito no fukaki kokoro mo ito yō mishiritamainagara)*. Even so, she could not but "worry how things would turn out" *(ika naramu to suran, to oboshitarishi)*, and Genji, in retrospect, regrets "even the slightest distress" *(sukoshi nitemo kokoro o midaritamaikemu koto)* he may have caused her on those occasions.

In her translation, Akiko alters this description in two highly significant particulars. She omits completely the reference to Murasaki's wisdom; and she recasts Genji's thoughts so that Murasaki becomes, in his view, not so much a woman wronged as "one to search too deeply for worries ... that she might well have spared herself" *(shinaidemo ii torikoshigurō o ... fukaku fukaku suru hito)*. Such extensive alterations cannot be the result of misinterpretation. In a manner that seems almost purposeful, Akiko shifts the weight of the blame for Murasaki's pain from Genji to Murasaki herself. Not only are the man's failings minimized, the anguish that they cause is dismissed as undue agitation on the woman's part. The emphasis of her translation thus stands in almost direct opposition to that of the original. Yet it coincides almost precisely with the attitude of the "Akiko" of *Akarumi e* toward her "Genji."

In *Akarumi e* we see Kyōko beset by fears that her husband is in love with another woman. Tōru's failings and Kyōko's anguish are vividly described, only to be undercut by his declaration of innocence, and Kyōko's subsequent realization that her apprehension has been misplaced. Her jealous imaginings turn out to have been no more than *torikoshigurō*, "worries that she might well have spared herself."[10]

10. Ibid., 151.

When we link these two texts back to the letter, there emerges what appears to be a triangular perspective upon a single concern: how to cope with a promiscuous spouse. The letter articulates the problem ("You won't do this, will you?"), the novel shows the woman making the psychological adjustments that will allow her to live with the problem ("You didn't do this, did you?"), and the translation elicits from the man assurances that those adjustments are entirely appropriate ("You know I never meant it, don't you?"). A real problem exists in the real world; a solution is sought in the world of a fiction. Proof positive is unattainable; but our conjecture, that Akiko's identification of Tekkan/Hiroshi with Genji may be the root cause of her libertine translations, no longer seems merely suppositious.

We must not ask too much of any of these texts. No one of them in isolation would point to such a conclusion. Some—the poems and the novel—however factual, reserve the right to fabricate without prior warning. And the translations cited here represent but a small sampling of the fifty-four chapters of *Genji*. Drawn into concatenation, however, these texts yield a pattern in which each successive addition meshes neatly with those already in place, and adds some new detail to the emerging design.

At the outset we are aware only of Akiko's avowal, reiterated throughout her career, of a strong identification with the writer Murasaki Shikibu and her art. We then notice extensions of that identification to Murasaki the widow and even to the fictional Murasaki. Yet such extensions seem hardly unnatural in a writer as steeped in the classics as Akiko was. But what of her repeated distortions of Murasaki's text, all seemingly directed to a single end, the obfuscation of Genji's flaws? Noting that her identification with *Genji* includes, naturally enough, identifying her husband with the Shining Genji, we begin to wonder if her minimizing the flaws of Murasaki's Genji might not be the result of a deflected urge to minimize the flaws of her own "Genji." The congruence of attitudes expressed in her novel and her translation of the passage from 'Maboroshi' seem strongly to corroborate this surmise. In the end we realize that the identification of which Akiko herself speaks so often touches many more aspects of her life than she mentions, that it is a negotiation between art and life of extreme complexity. We see, too, the degree to which this transforms the act of translation, for Akiko, from the mere transposition of words into something verging upon, as she herself put it, "writing *Genji*."

Nor does the complexity of the negotiation end here. One naturally wonders what form it might take in Akiko's second and final translation, her *Shin-shin'yaku Genji monogatari*. The answer is: there is no trace of it whatsoever. Every omission in the foregoing passages from 'Hahakigi,' 'Hana no En,' 'Aoi,' and 'Maboroshi' is fully and accurately filled, every distortion set right. Genji's attempted seduction of Utsusemi, his predatory meanderings following the Cherry Blossom Feast, his preemptory appropriation of the Oborozukiyo lady, his delight in her fear of him; and on the other hand his unmitigated remorse after the death of Murasaki—all are duly and explicitly reported. And the child Murasaki no longer weeps "hot tears" after her defloration. It is as if Akiko's elaborate and extended project of protecting Genji had been the work of an entirely different author.

Still one last question nags: How did someone who knew *The Tale of Genji* as well as Akiko did, indeed loved (and lived in) *Genji* as much as she did, bring herself to distort the novel as she did? The answer is almost certainly comprehended in the question. Seen strictly as a literary act, her tampering with the text she purports to translate must seem an act of infidelity to her author, a failure to keep faith with her readers, a disappointment to her admirers. Viewed in the context of a larger life, private as well as literary, these distortions appear in a different light. The poem cited as the first epigraph to this chapter acquires a whole new layer of meaning when read with an awareness of the strength of Akiko's identification with the women of *Genji*. No longer is it *only* a reader's recollection of that famous scene in which the Minister of the Right discovers his daughter in bed with Genji;[11] now one sees Akiko herself in it as well, savoring the memory of that exciting (and mortifying) situation as if she had experienced

11. In the 'Sakaki' (The Sacred Tree) chapter, 2:136–38; S 211–13.

it in person. And the second epigraph can have but a single subject, a woman with long and bitter experience of *her* Genji, who nonetheless has yet to abandon her fantasy.[12]

It is precisely this, I think, the totality with which she inhabited the world of *Genji* and the lives of its characters, that conduced so easily—probably even unconsciously—to her conflation of the worlds of fiction and fact. We gain a fuller understanding of Akiko, therefore, if we view her textual malfeasance in this translation not simply as lapses from literary fidelity, but as poignant evidence of the passion and pervasiveness of her involvement with *Genji*.

---

12. For an extended discussion of this poem, see Ichikawa Chihiro, "Yosano Akiko no kotenteki eihō ni tsuite," *Namiki no sato*, no. 46 (June 1997): 3–4.

Chapter Seven:
Akiko's Last *Genjis*

> I understand people are saying that I might become a lecturer at Nitobe-san's university [Tokyo Joshi Daigaku]; but of course I've declined the offer and devote all of my energy to writing .... For one thing, I expect that I shall be somewhat more highly regarded if I take up the lectureship after I have finished writing [my commentary on] *Genji*.
>
> (Letter to Kobayashi [Masaharu] and Yūko, 16 March 1918)

> Seven years ago, in the autumn, I suddenly resolved that come what may, I must make the time to fulfill my responsibility to retranslate *Genji*. I began writing immediately, and I continued writing; I hurried on lest what was left of my life be over before I should finish.
>
> ("Afterword," *Shin-shin'yaku Genji monogatari*, 1939)

Following the publication of her *Shin'yaku Genji monogatari* in 1912–13, Akiko's reputation as an authority on the Japanese classics continued to grow. This chapter will trace Akiko's professional engagement with *The Tale of Genji* through the remaining years of her life.

Unfortunately nothing further can be added to the brief account in chapter four of Akiko's modern versions of *Eiga monogatari, Murasaki Shikibu nikki*, and *Izumi Shikibu nikki*, which she translated immediately after completing the *Shin'yaku*. The corporate records of the Kanao family, containing all of Akiko's correspondence on these matters, were lost to floods in postwar Kyoto. Prior to this time, unfortunately, no scholar or biographer had been sufficiently interested in Akiko's work on *Genji* and the classics to consult them. And, although these projects must have occupied a great deal of her time, Akiko herself left little record of the work. In the afterword to her first translation she does note that

> [i]n order to read *The Tale of Genji*, it is necessary to understand the Heian court and the lives of the nobility which formed its

background. Therefore, following upon the present work, I have turned my attention to a new translation of *Eiga monogatari*, a realistic novel *(shajitsu shosetsu)* which takes the history of that period as its subject.[1]

But this is all we are told. The circumstances of the writing and marketing of these translations must therefore remain something of a mystery.

Throughout the Taishō period, Akiko continued to work on a *Genji* commentary she had begun in 1909 at the instigation of Kobayashi Masaharu, whose pen name was Tenmin (1877–1956). Tenmin and Hiroshi first met when the latter traveled to Osaka in the summer of 1900 to lecture to the Kansai Seinen Bungakkai (Kansai Young Men's Literary Association), of which Tenmin was a member. Although Tenmin seems not to have met Akiko until the autumn of the following year, just after her move to Tokyo, some of her earliest poetry had appeared in the literary magazines *Yoshiashigusa*, founded July 1897, and its successor *Kansai bungaku*, founded August 1900, both of which he had helped to edit and publish.[2] Like other "literary youths" of his time, he published several short stories, but the money for his patronage of the Yosanos was earned as a successful wholesaler of blankets, a business he founded in 1899 at Shinsaibashi in Osaka.[3] It was the fortuitous removal of his residence to Kyoto in the spring of 1923 that saved the letters Hiroshi and Akiko had written him from almost certain destruction in the American bombing raids of World War II, thus preserving the primary source for any account of his relationship with the Yosanos.

Tenmin had helped to make up the losses incurred in publishing *Myōjō* since its inception.[4] Casting about for a way to continue his

---

1. Yosano Akiko, "Shin'yaku Genji monogatari no nochi ni," in *Shin'yaku Genji monogatari* (Kanao Bun'endō, 1912–13), 4:6.
2. Ueda Ayako and Itsumi Kumi, eds., *Yosano Hiroshi Akiko shokanshū: Tenmin bunko zō* (Yagi Shoten, 1983), i–ii. Hereafter, page numbers are cited in the text.
3. Fujita Fukuo, "Shinshisha no patoron Kobayashi Tenmin," *Kokubungaku: kaishaku to kyōzai no kenkyū* 9.15 (December 1964): 137.
4. Ibid., 135. Miyamoto Masaaki, "'Maboroshi no Akiko Genji' to Tenmin Kobayashi Masaharu," *Ube kokubun kenkyū*, no. 24 (August 1993): 2, 5.

support of the Yosanos after the magazine ceased publication in 1908, he hit upon the idea of commissioning a commentary on *Genji*. Having obtained their agreement, he arranged to send a sum of money each month, nominally in payment for installments of Akiko's commentary.[5]

In her initial letter of September 1909 discussing the terms of the sponsorship, Akiko herself seems unsure how best to describe the work, calling it a "commentary or an exposition of *Genji*" *(Genji no chūshaku nari ya kōgi nari ya)*. She explains her conception of the project and her finances as follows:

> Firstly, for a good deal of the present *kana* text of *Genji*, (many) Chinese characters would be substituted to make it easier to read; and the many mistakes in punctuation would be put right (both of these would be done by Hiroshi).[6]
>
> To it, we would add a commentary many times larger than Mr. Ochiai's in the *Complete Works;*[7] and together with this, illustrations would be inserted to complete the book. If it were to be something along these lines, I believe I could undertake the job at the remuneration and within the time period you graciously suggest. ...
>
> At this point I shall explain our finances frankly. Every month we require one hundred and thirty yen (including monthly installment payments). Our regular income is about seventy yen.[8] I do work for the *Manchō*, the *Niroku [shinpō]* the *Miyako [shinbun]*, *Chūgakusekai, Shōjo no tomo, Joshi bundan, Ōsaka Mainichi*, and *Tōkyō Mainichi*,[9] but if I cannot find about another twenty-five yen's worth of work every month we cannot make ends meet, and

5. Kobayashi Tenmin, "Akiko *Genji* ni tsuite," *Uzu* 4.2 (February 1956): 1–3. I am grateful to the anonymous employee of Kuramadera who kindly sent me this issue of *Uzu*.
6. Akiko indicates here that Hiroshi will shoulder some of the work, but the actual extent of his involvement is unclear. While he was often the one who wrote to apologize for delays, he usually referred to the project as that of his wife.
7. The five volume edition of *Genji* edited by Hagino Yoshiyuki, Ochiai Naobumi, and Konakamura Yoshikata and published 1890–91 by Hakubunkan in their *Nihon bungaku zensho*.
8. At this time primary school teachers began on a salary of ten yen per month and first-year civil servants earned a minimum of fifty yen per month. A small free-standing house in Tokyo's Itabashi ward cost around three yen a month to rent. Source: *Nedanshi nenpyō: Meiji, Taishō, Shōwa*, ed. *Shūkan Asahi* (Asahi Shinbunsha, 1988).
9. For details of this work, see the notes in Ueda and Itsumi, *Yosano Hiroshi Akiko shokanshū*, 22–23.

so I have to write extra fiction *(shōsetsu)*, essays, children's stories and such. I can do the regular work in about twelve days. The other eighteen days I should have to give over entirely to the *[Genji]* commentary. Therefore, I would like to set the amount of the sponsorship you have kindly offered at twenty yen per installment.

I wish to undertake this project on the assumption that it will be my whole life's work *(watakushi isshō no jigyō)*. Be that as it may, since we have decided that the time period will be one hundred months, that will mean, I think, a fee of 2000 yen for the manuscript. (20–21)

For a time, then, Akiko worked simultaneously on both the commentary and the 1912–13 *Shin'yaku*. Since Akiko notes in her afterword to the *Shin'yaku* that she had begun working on the translation in January 1911, and since her letter accepting the terms of Tenmin's proposal was written in September 1909, we must assume that when Kanao came to her with Uchida Roan's suggestion for a modern translation of *Genji*, she was *already* engaged in work on the *Genji* commentary. There is also the evidence of Hiroshi's letter to Tenmin dated 9 August [1910] which concludes with a frankness that borders on the brutal:

Akiko sends her regards. She will be able to send last month's installment of the *Genji* commentary tomorrow. She has been undergoing treatment for caries, and since she has had eighteen teeth extracted, she is exhausted and is running late with the fair copy. (24)

Neither Akiko nor Hiroshi ever mention the *Shin'yaku* translation—neither its progress nor its eventual publication—to Tenmin. That she decided to take on the project regardless of her previous commitment to Tenmin is one indication of how desperately she needed whatever income the translation might bring in.[10]

---

10. Akiko's desire that Kanao spend money advertising the *Shin'yaku* rather than buying her a lavish kimono, noted in chapter four, p. 80, suggests that she was paid not by the page, nor a lump sum for the manuscript, but a percentage of whatever profits the *Shin'yaku* produced.

Akiko had firm ideas about the quality of existing commentaries on *Genji,* and was determined that hers would be superior. In a short piece she wrote for *Waseda bungaku* in 1910, she mentions Tenmin's sponsorship of her work and then fairly explodes with indignation:

> Just how many readers have been misled by earlier commentaries on *The Tale of Genji* I have no idea! The present printed edition of *Kogetsushō* draws extensively from the annotations of other works; but every one of these annotations is as much as eighty-percent mistaken. There mustn't have been any scholars in the past fully capable of reading *Genji.* Even the scrupulous commentary in the venerable Motoori Norinaga's *Tama no ogushi* is about twenty-percent mistaken. Notwithstanding the plethora of historical data that they cite, all of it irrelevant to the novel *The Tale of Genji [shōsetsu de aru Genji monogatari],* these earlier scholars are shockingly ignorant of the facts of the Heian period.... Moreover, when it comes to misinterpretation of the text, I discover at least thirty or forty cases per chapter.... In recent years I have been advising everyone to stay away from misleading commentaries and recommending that they read unannotated editions of *Genji.* (14:46–47)

It would seem that Akiko meant her commentary to be the one annotated text of *Genji* she could confidently recommend to others.

Tenmin proved a generous and forbearing friend. Their correspondence reveals that although he paid in advance, more often than not Akiko was late with an installment, or unable to do any work at all on the project for months at a time. By March 1918 the hundred months was up but the commentary was only half finished (199). In the eight years since she had begun work on the commentary she had given birth six times: in 1910, 1911, 1913, 1915, 1916, and 1917. After the complicated delivery of twins in February 1911 she had confessed to Tenmin, "I cannot but pray that next year at least, there shall be no birth" (37). During these same eight years, she also published eight collections of poetry, eight volumes of essays, three collections of children's stories, her *novel Akarumi e,* a collection of short stories and, of course, her modern language translations of *Eiga monogatari, Murasaki Shikibu nikki* and *Izumi Shikibu nikki,* and *Tsurezuregusa.*

But Akiko would not—could not—give up the project. Nitobe Inazō (1862–1933), founding principal of Tokyo Women's Christian University (Tokyo Joshi Daigaku), had invited her to become a lecturer at the school, but as she wrote to Tenmin, she had "of course" declined, because she wanted to concentrate on the *Genji* commentary, and because she felt that as a lecturer she would be better recognized if she "finished writing *Genji* first" (203–4). Hiroshi estimated that Akiko would need another four or five years to complete the work (202). Then Akiko wrote to say that henceforward she would prepare double the number of manuscript pages each month (206). Tenmin responded by increasing his sponsorship from twenty to fifty yen per installment (210).

Anxious to revise what she had completed so far, Akiko had asked Tenmin to bring her a year's worth of manuscript whenever he came up to Tokyo. Somehow she would find the time to rewrite it, over and above the regular monthly installment (199). Tenmin complied with her request; and so it happened that the entire manuscript was in Tokyo, stored at the Bunka Gakuin, when fires engulfed the city after the earthquakes of 1 September 1923.

Three days later, on 4 September, Hiroshi wrote to Tenmin and told him what had transpired. The letter begins with an *ottegaki*, a postscript traditionally added in the space at the right-hand edge of the paper before the letter proper begins.

> Kanda, Nihonbashi, Kyōbashi, eighty percent of Kōjimachi, Asakusa, Shitaya, Honjo, Fukagawa and elsewhere has burnt to the ground. My wife's *Genji* manuscript, having caused you nothing but trouble, was completely burnt along with the Bunka Gakuin. (361)

The work of fourteen years had been reduced to ashes. This essential information imparted, Hiroshi's letter continues with a poignant appeal for help:

> Greetings
> Owing to the conflagration which followed upon the great earthquake, seventy percent of the entire city of Tokyo is scorched

earth; fifty or sixty thousand people are said to have died in the disaster. Fortunately for my family, the wind changed direction about half a *chō* [approximately fifty-four meters] from our house and we were spared from the fire. None of us was injured; two nights we took refuge on the embankment of the moat at Ushigome....

At the moment it is difficult to obtain goods without ready cash and we are short of food, candles and such. All the banks have burnt down and so it is impossible to make withdrawals. Thus we have no financial recourse in Tokyo. I am sorry to trouble you, but in view of the above, would you be so kind as to send about three hundred [yen] in cash in order to get us through this desperate situation? If it is not possible to send it by postal transfer, might I ask you to send someone from Nagoya to Nagano and thence in on the Shin'etsu line?[11]

Postal service having just now resumed, for the moment I beg of you the foregoing.

In haste ... (361–62)

Curiously, Akiko herself wrote nothing to Tenmin about the loss of her manuscript. Perhaps there was nothing she could say. Instead, she described her devastation in the two poems translated below:

十余年わが書きためし草稿の跡あるべしや学院の灰

Jūyonen waga kakitameshi sōkō no
    ato arubeshi ya gakuin no hai. (5:40)

My manuscript, the accumulated writing of more than ten years:
    is there no trace of it to be found in the ashes of the school?

失ひし一万枚の草稿の女となりて来たりなげく夜

Ushinaishi ichimanmai no sōkō no
    onna to narite kitari nageku yo. (4:574)

Ten thousand pages of manuscript lost.
    Such a woman have I become, I lament through the night.

For the time being, Akiko's lectures on *Genji* at the Bunka Gakuin would have to compensate for the loss of her commentary. "At the very least I want to offer [these lectures] to Murasaki Shikibu as a token of my gratitude" (19:258), she wrote in 1926.

11. The Shin'etsu line ran from Takasaki in Gunma prefecture through Nagano to Niigata. Hiroshi presumably meant to go out to Takasaki and collect the money.

One often reads that Akiko translated *Genji* three times, but if the single page of her commentary that has come down to us is representative of the rest of the manuscript, her "second translation," as this lost work is usually described, would seem not to have been a translation at all. This page survives only because she forgot to include it in an installment she sent to Tenmin in April or May of 1914. When she later discovered it she enclosed it in a letter of 11 May 1914 to Tenmin's wife Yūko. It seems not to have been placed with the manuscript itself but remained with her letter.[12] The page consists of extremely short quotations *(shō)* from the text of *Genji*, each marked by a circle, and followed by Akiko's commentary. The quotations are from the section of the 'Usugumo' (A Rack of Cloud) chapter in which Genji's return to the Nijō-in with the Akashi princess and her nurse is described (2:425; S 334), and Akiko's comments include, for example, the following sentence:

> *Tada sae sabishiki sansō ni ite, aisuru ko ni wakaretaru hito no kono goro no kanashimi wa ika bakari naran to, saru kokoromochi ni nariitamau toki wa kurushimi o mo Genji wa mune ni oboeitamaedo, mainichi kanete yori no risō no gotoku ni hime o kyōiku nashiyukitamau koto wa, sōai no hito to tomo ni aru ue ni sara ni kōfuku no atsumari kitarishi kan no nasaruru koto naru beshi to iu nari. (109)*
>
> The passage says: how sad must she be now, all alone in an isolated mountain villa, parted from her beloved child, and when he realized this, Genji was filled with pain; but inasmuch as he might now devote his days to educating the Princess according to his long-cherished ideals, and, moreover, be with the person who loved him as he loved her [i.e. Murasaki no ue], his happiness could only increase.

Apart from a sprinkling of recently coined nouns *(risō, sōai),* her extant comments are in a language that can only be called classical. Just as she had adopted the *genbun'itchi* style for her *shōsetsu* version of *Genji*, so, for her commentary, a classical style seemed the appropriate choice. The extant fragment reveals a work that is part paraphrase, part summary;

---

12. A photograph of this page appears at the beginning of *Shokanshū*. The text is printed and discussed in Ueda and Itsumi, *Yosano Hiroshi Akiko shokanshū*, 108–9.

but of course we shall never know how she would have molded this into a "commentary," as she always called it.

Akiko also continued to receive poetic commissions. In his memoir *En naki tokei* (A Doomed Timepiece) Yosano Shigeru recalls how Takita Choin (1882–1925), editor of *Chūō kōron*, came to the family house late in 1918 or 1919 and commissioned a set of poems that Akiko later published under the title *Genji monogatari raisan* (In Praise of The Tale of Genji).[13] The *Raisan* poems did not appear in print until 1922, but following their first publication Akiko was able to raise 350 yen for the running expenses of *Myōjō,* relaunched in November 1921, through the sale of an album of the *Raisan* poems in her own hand.[14] Akiko later added twenty-one poems on topics from *Eiga monogatari* and five more on topics from *Heike monogatari;* and under the title "Emaki no tame ni" (For a Picture-scroll) she included them all in her poetry collection *Ryūsei no michi* (Path of a Shooting Star, 1924).[15] In later years, the *Raisan* poems were also sold as scrolls and *tanzaku.*[16]

We might note in passing that the sale of *tanzaku* seems to have been an important source of income for the Yosano family. The day before she gave birth, in her forty-first year, to their thirteenth and as it turned out their last child Fujiko,[17] Akiko prepared no less than three hundred *tanzaku* of her poems. A month later she explained:

13. Yosano Shigeru, *En naki tokei* (Saika Shobō, 1948), 210–13. For a fuller account of the *Raisan* poems, see G. G. Rowley, "Yosano Akiko's Poems 'In Praise of The Tale of Genji'," *Monumenta Nipponica* 56.4 (2001): 439–86.

14. Shinma Shin'ichi, "Yosano Akiko to *Genji monogatari*," in *Genji monogatari to sono eikyō: kenkyū to shiryō—kodai bungaku ronsō dairokushū,* ed. Murasaki Shikibu Gakkai (Musashino Shoin, 1978), 277. *Genji monogatari raisan* was first published in *Myōjō,* 2d ser., 1.3 (January 1922): 3–8.

15. For a detailed discussion of the *Eiga* poems, see Satō Motoko, *"Eiga monogatari* to Yosano Akiko—'saiwa' toshite no 'Emaki no tame ni' shūsai tanka—," *Shitennōji Kokusai Bukkyō Daigaku Bungakubu kiyō,* no. 15 (1982): 47–66.

16. See the photographs in *Sumi,* no. 78 (May–June 1989): 22, 23, 32. *Tanzaku* are long, narrow pieces of stiff paper on which poems are inscribed.

17. Fujiko was born on 31 March 1919. Only in 1939 did she discover that she was not named after Fujitsubo, as she had thought, but after Murasaki Shikibu herself. "'You didn't know?' Mother's face said. 'Well, at first, Murasaki Shikibu was known as Tō [the *fuji* of Fujiwara] Shikibu, so that's why.'" Mori Fujiko, *Midaregami* (Rukkusha, 1967), 249.

> I feel a responsibility to prepare for [each] birth by building up some material security with my own efforts. I am also aware that I may die in childbirth, and so with that risk uppermost in my mind, even a woman as weak as myself feels a tension of body and soul that enables her to work with heightened efficiency. (18:69)

There is something close to appalling in the starkness of her explanation and her uncomplaining acceptance of the reasons for her phenomenal capacity to produce. But of course she could not afford to be otherwise: she had to cope with the daily demands of children and deadlines, leaving Hiroshi with time to brood over what might have been.

After the complete destruction of Akiko's *Genji* commentary in September 1923, it was nearly a decade before she was able to summon the strength to begin a second translation of *Genji*. In the meantime she was, as ever, far from idle. At some point, most likely during the period of 1915–27, Akiko composed a seventy-page digest of *The Tale of Genji* that has only recently been printed.[18] The manuscript is undated, but clearly it was intended for publication, as *furigana* readings are given for each *kanji*. Ikeda Toshio, the scholar who first revealed the existence of the manuscript, attempts to date it in various ways. In that the handwriting does not appear to be that of a young person, the work would seem to be a product of Akiko's latter years; yet comparison of the vocabulary of the digest with her first and second translations of *Genji* suggests the opposite, for the digest more closely resembles the *Shin'yaku*. In the end, it is the paper on which the digest is written that provides the most reliable evidence. Ikeda traces the squared manuscript paper to a stationer in Kagurazaka, only a short distance from where the Yosanos lived at Fujimi-chō in Tokyo's Kōjimachi ward from 1915 until 1927. As it seems unlikely that Akiko

---

18. That is, seventy pages of 400-character *genkōyōshi* (squared manuscript paper). It has been published as *Kōgai Genji monogatari* (Yokohama: Tsurumi Daigaku, 1993). For details of the physical appearance of the digest and a discussion of the contents of the work together with illustrative examples, see Ikeda Toshio's "Kaisetsu" to the foregoing, a revised version of his "Yosano Akiko no sōko nidai," *Tsurumi Daigaku kiyō*, no. 21 (February 1984): 131–46.

would have continued to patronize the Kagurazaka stationer after their move west to Ogikubo in September 1927, Ikeda's tentative conclusion is that the digest is a product of the Fujimi-chō years.[19]

The style of the digest is confidently terse: Akiko is principally concerned with events, rarely pausing to comment on emotions. Translation of one of the shorter chapters may convey something of the effect of her reduction of *Genji* to pure plot. Her summary of the 'Hana no En' chapter is as follows:

> *Genji no Kimi hatachi no haru no nigatsu nijūikunichi ni Shishinden de kō'ō [sic] no gyoen ga atta. Sakushi no asobi ni oite tensai Genji no Kimi no shi ga kōsai o hanachi, Shun'ōden no mai ni Genji no Kimi no myōgi wa hito o ewashimeta. En ga owatte hitobito wa taisan shita no de aru ga, Genji no Kimi wa eigokochi ni, moshi ya kikai ga jibun o shite koishii hito ni awaseru no de wa nai ka to iu yō na koto o omotte Fujitsubo no soto made itta no de aru ga, mono o ii-ireru yō na to no sukima mo nakatta. Kokiden no chikaku e itte miru to nyogo [sic] wa Seiryōden no o-tonoi ni agatta rusu-rashikute shizuka de atta. Nobotte itte aita san no kuchi to iu tokoro kara naka o nozoite iru to, wakakute utsukushii kifujin da to Genji no Kimi ga chokkaku de kanjiru yō na hito ga "Oborozukiyo ni shiku mono zo naki" to kuchizusaminagara dete kita. Sode o toraeta toki ni odoroita onna wa, ma mo naku aite no nanibito de aru ka o satotta. Soshite onna wa mi ni sashisematte iru aru unmei o nikumu kokoro ni wa narenakatta. Jōjintachi wa wakareru toki ni na mo iwazu ni ōgi dake o torikaeta no de aru ga, onna wa Udaijin no musume no Roku no Kimi de, Kokiden no nyogo [sic] no imōto de atte, Tōgū no kōkyū ni hairu hazu no hito de atta.*[20]

In the spring of Genji's twentieth year, sometime after the twentieth of the second month, there was a cherry blossom viewing feast at the Shishinden. In the composing of Chinese poems, the poem of the talented Genji radiated brilliance; and in the dancing of the Spring Warbler, the consummate performance of Genji bewitched his audience.

19. Ikeda Toshio, "Kaisetsu," 4, 12–15. The stationer is the Sōmaya Genshirō Shōten on the Kagurazaka Slope, http://www.soumaya.co.jp.

20. *Kōgai Genji monogatari*, 17–19 (photographic reproduction), 6 (transcription).

The feast ended, and people went their separate ways; but Genji, being intoxicated, and thinking that chance might allow him to meet the woman he loved, went as far as the outside of the Fujitsubo, but there was not so much as a crack of an opening in a door through which he might send in a message. When he passed near the Kokiden, it was quiet, as it appeared that the consort was spending the night in the Seiryōden and was not present. When he mounted the stairs, and peered in from the open third door, a person whom Genji sensed intuitively to be a beautiful young noblewoman appeared, chanting, "naught to compare with a night of a misty moon." The woman, who was shocked when he took her sleeve, realized immediately who her partner was. Nor could this woman bring herself to resent the fate that now beset her.

When the lovers parted, they did not speak their names, but only exchanged fans. The woman was the sixth daughter of the Minister of the Right and a younger sister of the Kokiden consort; it was she who was to enter the women's quarters of the Crown Prince.

The entire second half of 'Hana no En' is reduced to a single sentence. Akiko is certainly not concerned to provide a comprehensive account of *Genji* in the digest. The summary of the 'Maboroshi' chapter, to mention a further example, consists of no more than four poems—Genji's seasonal meditations on loss—and a single-sentence explanation of his preparations to leave the world. Ichikawa Chihiro suggests in a recent study that the digest is similar in intent to Akiko's *Genji monogatari raisan* poems, in which each chapter of *Genji* is pared down to the events and emotions that most appeal to her.[21] The 'Hana no En' summary cited above certainly corroborates Ichikawa's observation. Her suggestion also points to a major difference between the digest and the *Raisan* poems. Compare, for example, Akiko's 'Hana no En' poem from the *Raisan* collection:

春の夜の靄に酔ひたる月ならん手枕かしぬわが假臥に
Haru no yo no moya ni yoitaru tsuki naran
  tamakura kashinu waga karibushi ni. (4:324)
It must have been the moon, drunken in the spring night mist,
  that lent me its arm to pillow my head as I lay dozing.

21. Ichikawa Chihiro, "Yosano Akiko to *Genji monogatari—sono* gyōseki to 'kako ni asobu' Akiko—," in *Kindai no kyōju to kaigai to no kōryū*, ed. Imai Takuji et al., vol. 9 of Genji monogatari kōza series (Benseisha, 1992): 47–48.

Whereas the *Raisan* poems tend to highlight some emotional aspect of each chapter, it is precisely the *absence* of feeling from the digest which is so very striking, giving the work something of the character of an *aide-mémoire.*

Despite the concision, however, Akiko maintains a consciousness of rank that borders on the punctilious. Her attention to titles is apparent not only in the passage quoted above, but throughout the digest. As in her translations of *Genji,* she is also careful to distinguish members of the imperial family from other characters with polite language: when Genji sends Fujitsubo a poem in the 'Momiji no Ga' chapter, the verb is *o-okuri shita,* but after he is made Jun-Daijō Tennō in 'Fuji no Uraba,' his poems are *on-uta,* and all of his actions are described with deferential forms. Occasionally this concern with distinctions leads to some odd locutions. In her summary of the 'Wakana jō' (New Herbs: Part One) chapter, for example, she writes: *Shujakuin [sic] ni wa o-yokata no himemiya ga o-ari ni natta* (the retired emperor Suzaku had four princesses),[22] and: *Sono aida ni Kiritsubo no Miyasudokoro wa Tōgū no miko o ikunin ka o-umi shita* (during that time, the Akashi princess bore the Crown Prince several children).[23]

In her hitherto published writings, Akiko herself gives no clue as to why the digest is as it is and for whom it was written. We can only hope that her correspondence, an edition of which is currently in preparation, may provide answers to some of the many questions that surround this work.[24]

Akiko's participation in two other projects during the early years of the Shōwa period provides further evidence of the respect she now commanded as an authority on *The Tale of Genji.* The first was her work as editor of the *Nihon koten zenshū* series; the second, her

22. Yosano, *Kōgai Genji monogatari,* 75, 26.
23. Ibid., 78, 27. The event described is actually narrated in the 'Wakana ge' (New Herbs: Part Two) chapter (4:158; S 592).
24. So far as I can determine, there is no reference to the digest in Akiko's collected correspondence, *Yosano Hiroshi Akiko shokan shūsei,* 4 vols., ed Itsumi Kumi (Yagi Shoten, 2001-3.

provision of a preface for a monograph on *Genji* by a scholar from the National Literature world.

In October 1925, Akiko and Hiroshi joined Masamune Atsuo (1881–1958) in editing the *Nihon koten zenshū* series.[25] Sold by subscription, the series seems to have attracted considerable interest. Following the appearance of advertisements in *Myōjō* and other publications late in 1925, the editors were swamped with more than three times the number of applications they had anticipated. The popularity of the series gave the Yosanos financial leeway such as they had never before enjoyed. By September of 1927 they had been able to put together enough money to rent a plot of land in Ogikubo, where they built a house of their own to Akiko's design.[26] With such success came a workload that was daunting. Akiko wrote:

> What with collating and correcting, every month my husband and I check a thousand pages of text at least four times. In December, therefore, we were frequently busy with our brushes until three in the morning. Moreover, on top of this I have duties at school [the Bunka Gakuin], duties concerning *Myōjō*, as well as other things to write.[27]

Shinma suggests that one reason the Yosanos were keen to launch the series despite the work it entailed may have been Hiroshi's desire to take up where his teacher Ochiai Naobumi had left off years before. Naobumi, as noted in chapter three, was one of the editors of Hakubunkan's mid-Meiji *Nihon bungaku zensho*. Like many contemporary scholars of National Literature, Naobumi also wrote

25. The following account is based on Shinma Shin'ichi, "Hiroshi, Akiko to *Nihon koten zenshū.*," *Nihon kosho tsūshin* 41.10 (October 1976): 2–3; and the Yosanos' correspondence with Tenmin, collected in *Shokanshū.*. Although Tenmin was not directly involved in the *Nihon koten zenshū*. project, the Yosanos continued to seek his advice (see, for example, Hiroshi's letter to Tenmin in Ueda and Itsumi, *Yosano Hiroshi Akiko shokanshū.*, 412–13) and financial support. On the Yosanos' involvement with the *Nihon koten zenshū* series, see also Kōuchi Nobuko, *Yosano Akiko to shūhen no hitobito* (Sōjusha, 1998), 281–318.

26. Mori, *Midaregami*, 242; Yosano Hikaru, *Akiko to Hiroshi no omoide* (Kyoto: Shibunkaku Shuppan, 1991), 139.

27. Cited in Shinma, "Hiroshi, Akiko to *Nihon koten zenshū*," 2.

poetry, and was a member of the Shinseisha (Society of New Voices) group which, under the direction of Mori Ōgai, published *Omokage* (Vestiges, 1889), a collection of poems translated into Japanese from Western languages. In 1893 Naobumi formed the Asakasha group (the "Faint Scent Society," but named for the district of Tokyo in which Naobumi lived), dedicated to the reform of poetry, and Hiroshi became a member. Although he went on to found his own coterie of poets, the Shinshisha, in 1899, Hiroshi remained a faithful disciple and was present at Naobumi's deathbed in 1903. Akiko herself was sufficiently moved to compose poems lamenting Naobumi's passing.[28] So it may have been this link with one of the pioneers of the Meiji period National Literature world that inspired the Yosanos to embark upon the *Nihon koten zenshū* project.

Their involvement was, however, brief. For reasons that remain unclear, they resigned from the editorial team in 1928, midway through publication of the second series.[29] Perhaps, in the end, the workload was beyond them—certainly for a time the series fell behind schedule—or perhaps it was a clash over editorial policy that led to the Yosanos' resignation. Whatever the reasons, their departure was final: once Hiroshi and Akiko left the editorial team, their names were removed even from the title pages and the colophons of volumes they had helped to produce, whenever these volumes were reprinted.

Nevertheless, by the time of their resignation, together they had edited more than fifty volumes of the classical canon, broadly defined.[30] Their selection was obviously influenced by Akiko's conviction, expressed in her afterword to the *Shin'yaku*, that in order to understand the world of *The Tale of Genji*, one must read the collateral literature of that period. Thus their "canon" included not only all Heian

28. Fukuda Kiyoto and Hamana Hiroko, *Yosano Akiko,* Hito to sakuhin series (Shimizu Shoin, 1968), 65–66.
29. A total of 264 volumes in six series were published by the Nihon Koten Zenshū Kankōkai between 1925 and 1944. A complete list of the contents of each volume can be found in Shoshi Kenkyū Konwakai, ed., *Zenshū sōsho sōran: shinteiban* (Yagi Shoten, 1983), 629–31.
30. See Yosano Hiroshi, Masamune Atsuo, and Yosano Akiko, *"Nihon koten zenshū* kankō shushi," *Myōjō,* 2d ser., 7.3 (September 1925): 130–31, for a twelve-point statement outlining the editors' aims and their conception of the series.

period works by women, both major and minor, but also the tenth century manual of herbal medicine *Honzō wamyō* (918), and Fujiwara Michinaga's *kanbun* diary *Midō kanpaku ki* (completed before 1027), which to this day has yet to be included in any canon compiled by National Literature scholars. Furthermore, the unsigned introductions to the volumes containing *Genji monogatari*, *Eiga monogatari*, and *Midō kanpaku ki* were almost certainly written by Akiko.[31] At the end of the introduction to the *Genji* volumes, an essay that was to be entitled "Genji monogatari zakkō" (Miscellaneous thoughts on *The Tale of Genji)* and would discuss the authorship and compilation of *Genji*, was promised for inclusion in the final volume.[32] By the time this volume appeared in July 1928, however, the Yosanos were no longer part of the *Nihon koten zenshū* editorial team and, though Akiko may have channeled the results of whatever research she had done for the piece into other work, the essay was never written.

Late in 1927, just before their departure from the *Nihon koten zenshū* project, Akiko was asked to provide a preface for a different sort of work: Fujita Tokutarō's *Genji monogatari kōyō*, a "companion guide" to *Genji* containing detailed summaries of each chapter; translations of sample passages into modern Japanese; a history of the development of prose writing in the Heian period; a chronology; a list of characters; and a bibliography. Her introduction to this solid accumulation of scholarship from the National Literature world stands alongside another shorter preface, by none other than Tokyo University lecturer Sasaki Nobutsuna. Although Sasaki refers to the author, his former student, as "Fujita-kun," Akiko—perhaps because she had not enjoyed the benefit of higher education—prefers the humility of "Fujita Sensei," or "Fujita Bungakushi" (B.A.). In all other respects, however, she and Sasaki here stand as equals in their endorsement of the work of the younger scholar.

---

31. The essays for the *Eiga monogatari* and the *Midō kanpaku ki* volumes are reprinted in *Akiko koten kanshō*, Yosano Akiko senshū series, vol. 4, ed. Yosano Hikaru and Shinma Shin'ichi (Shunshūsha, 1967).

32. Unsigned "Kaidai," in *Genji monogatari I,* Nihon koten zenshū series, ed. Yosano Hiroshi, Masamune Atsuo, and Yosano Akiko (Nihon Katen Zenshū Kankōkai, 1926), 8. Mention of the proposed piece is also made in essays of Akiko's dated 1928 and 1935, where it is called simply "Genji monogatari kō."

In the course of this piece, Akiko, with weary resignation, makes mention of her own work on *Genji:*

> Earlier, during the Taishō period, I began writing a complete commentary *[zenkōhon]* on *Genji*. After ten years' work I had got as far as the Uji chapters, but as the manuscript was burnt in the Fires, I was disinclined to take up my brush again and gave up.[33]

And at the very end of her preface she cannot resist adding the following abrupt comment:

> I put Murasaki Shikibu's death at about Chōwa 4 [1015]. Therefore, I divide *The Tale of Genji* into two parts. In my opinion, the first part, up to and including the 'Fuji no Uraba' chapter, was written by Murasaki Shikibu, and the remaining second part is the work of someone else. The author of the second part was Murasaki Shikibu's only daughter, who frequented the Uji villa of Regent [Fujiwara no] Yorimichi (992–1074) and went by the name of Daini no Sanmi. This is a view which differs from that of Fujita Sensei, but whether there was one author or two does not make a great difference to an appreciation of the text of *Genji*.[34]

That *The Tale of Genji* divides into two parts was an opinion Akiko held firmly throughout her career and her first published statement of this theory is found in her afterword to the *Shin'yaku*. Only later did she come to believe that these two parts represented the work of two different authors of *Genji*, that the chapters from 'Kiritsubo' to 'Fuji no Uraba' were by Murasaki Shikibu, and that the succeeding chapters—from 'Wakana' to 'Yume no Ukihashi' (The Floating Bridge of Dreams)—were written by her daughter Daini no Sanmi. Akiko does not say just when—or why—she was so persuaded, but she notes her change of opinion in the afterword to her second translation.[35]

---

33. Yosano Akiko, "Genji monogatari kōyō jo," in Fujita Tokutarō, *Genji monogatari kōyō* (Furōkaku Shobō, 1928), 6–7. The same resignation is evident in an account of the loss of the commentary in "Dokusho, mushiboshi, zōsho," (1926, 19:258).

34. Yosano, "Genji monogatari kōyō jo," 9.

35. Yosano Akiko, "Shin-shin'yaku Genji monogatari atogaki," reprinted in *Akiko koten kanshō*, vol. 4 of *Yosano Akiko senshū*, ed. Yosano Hikaru and Shinma Shin'ichi (Shinshūsha, 1967), 37–39. The complete afterword is translated in Appendix B.

The summary of these ideas in her preface to Fujita's mono graph, dated New Year, Shōwa 3 (1928), coincides precisely with the detailed exposition of her arguments in the "epoch-making"[36] essay "Murasaki Shikibu shinkō" (A New Study of Murasaki Shikibu) published in the January and February 1928 issues of *Taiyō*.

This essay, Akiko's most famous work as a scholar of *Genji*, is the culmination of more than fifteen years of research and rewriting. The development of her ideas and the growing precision of her argument may be traced through essays from 1912 onward.[37] When she began writing about Murasaki Shikibu, Akiko was especially concerned to counter the notion put forward in the genealogy *Sonpibunmyaku*, repeated in the *Kogetsushō*, and propounded in her own time by Sassa Seisetsu, that Murasaki was amorously involved with her patron Michinaga.[38] A short piece entitled "Murasaki Shikibu no teisō ni tsuite" (Concerning Murasaki Shikibu's Virtue) that she wrote in 1917 begins on a note of outrage:

> When I read that Dr. Sassa had cast doubt on Murasaki Shikibu's virtue in a certain journal, for Murasaki Shikibu's sake I was unable to do other than protest this slander. It is rude of me to say so, but I am of the opinion that Dr. Sassa's argument is utterly without foundation. The primary sources for Murasaki Shikibu's biography are the *Murasaki Shikibu shū* and the *Murasaki Shikibu nikki*. If Dr. Sassa had read these two works carefully, he would, on the contrary, be unable to do other than affirm Murasaki Shikibu's virtue. (16:370)[39]

36. Mitani Kuniaki, "Kaisetsu," *Genji monogatari I,* Nihon bungaku kenkyū shiryō sōsho series (Yūseidō, 1969), 329.
37. See the list in Appendix A, beginning with "Genji monogatari ni arawaretaru hitobito," *Shinchō* 16.5 (May 1912): 92–97. "Murasaki Shikibu shinkō" can also be found in *Akiko koten kanshō,* 5–31, supplemented by many useful notes not to be found elsewhere.
38. In *Sonpibunmyaku, Shintei zōho Kokushi taikei* edition, ed. Kuroita Katsumi (Yoshikawa Kōbunkan, 1980), 2:54, Murasaki is described as the "mistress of Regent Michinaga" *(Midō kanpaku Michinaga no mekake).* A similar description is given in the genealogy cited in "Hattan," the first chapter of the *Kogetsushō.*
39. Sassa "cast doubt" on Murasaki Shikibu's virtue in "Genji monogatari ni egakareta onna," *Jogaku sekai* 14.3 (February 1914): 12, when he wrote that in the Heian period, people preferred to do what was beautiful rather than what was right, that men and women exchanged love poems without embarrassment, and that some of these exchanges, such as the one between Fujiwara no Michinaga and Murasaki Shikibu, were included in imperially commissioned collections of poetry. "If we are talking about the chastity of

Over the years, the desire to defend Murasaki's "virtue" led Akiko to marshal a wealth of biographical sources relating to the woman she most admired. Oka Kazuo (1900–81), for one, explicitly acknowledges his debt to this body of scholarship. In the preface to his own "Basic Study of *The Tale of Genji*," he writes, "concerning the biography of Murasaki Shikibu, my research has, from the outset, owed much to the venerable Andō Tameakira and Mrs. Yosano Akiko."[40]

In "Murasaki Shikibu shinkō," Akiko's case for dual authorship of *The Tale of Genji* is made on the basis of both biographical and internal evidence. Teramoto Naohiko (1912–90) has suggested that she was probably the first reader of *Genji* to recognize the existence of a major break *(kugiri)* in the narrative at the end of the 'Fuji no Uraba' chapter.[41] As mentioned above, this break, in Akiko's opinion, marked the point at which Murasaki's *Genji* ended and Daini no Sanmi's began. She also maintained that 'Hahakigi' was the first chapter of *Genji* to be written and that 'Kiritsubo' was added at a later stage. The essay is still valued as a pioneering work of modern scholarship on Murasaki Shikibu, in which several of the critical approaches of twentieth-century *Genji* studies are foreshadowed. Mitani Kuniaki (a student of Oka Kazuo) explains his decision to place "Murasaki Shikibu shinkō" at the head of a selection of outstanding studies of *Genji* in the following terms:

> While on the one hand noting its value as the greatest advance in the study of Murasaki Shikibu since Andō Tameakira's *Shijo shichiron* [1703], I wish also to draw attention to the modern critical sensibility with which this essay seems to pulsate, that very individual appreciation which informs the whole of Akiko's work on the *Shin'yaku Genji monogatari*. As regards critical methodology,

---

women, it is a fact that there were very few examples at the Heian court," he states. Nonetheless, Sassa's short piece is not a critique of Murasaki Shikibu or her female characters; but rather a plea that they be judged by the standards that prevailed in their own day rather than in later ages.

40. Oka Kazuo, "Chogen," (Preface) *Genji monogatari no kisoteki kenkyū*, rev. ed. (Tōkyōdō, 1966), 3. Andō Tameakira is the author of the *Genji* commentary *Shika shichiron* (also known as *Shijo shichiron),* completed 1703.

41. Conversation, 18 October 1986.

all of the critical approaches that we now term modern—the empiricist, the socio-historical method; the cultural-historical method; the aesthetic method and so on—are to be found in germinal form, bolstered by Akiko's own intellectual appreciation and critical spirit, in this essay. For this reason, among others, the essay seemed an appropriate one with which to grace the beginning of the present collection of studies.[42]

One wishes Mitani had been more precise in connecting Akiko's scholarship with the critical approaches of modern *Genji* studies, but with a bit of speculation one can perhaps reconstruct his meaning. As we have seen, in biographical studies of Murasaki Shikibu, Oka Kazuo drew the lines of scholarly lineage from Andō Tameakira directly to Akiko, and thence to his own work in the field. Modern studies of the structure of *Genji,* according to Teramoto Naohiko, began with Akiko's designation of a sharp structural break following 'Fuji no Uraba.' Building upon this observation, Ikeda Kikan developed his thesis of a tripartite *Genji* and his hypothetical reconstruction of the order in which the component chapters were composed. In all of these fields of *Genji* studies, Akiko is recognized by post-war scholars as an important pioneer. Her writings, however, also touch upon many other subjects such as classical poetry, Heian period literary salons, the Heian period woman's "education," and Japanese women's writing in general. The sources upon which she bases her consideration of these matters range not only over the entire corpus of Heian writing in Japanese *(wabun),* but also a considerable body of writing in Chinese, such as the *Midō kanpaku ki, Shōyūki,* and *Honchōreisō* (c. 1010).

Inevitably Akiko was drawn to translate *Genji* a second time. She had never been happy with her first, much abbreviated, version, and she felt that only a complete translation would suffice to thank Ueda Bin and Mori Ōgai for the prefaces they had written for her, and Nakazawa Hiromitsu for the illustrations that had made the *Shin'yaku* such a glittering publication.[43] In the autumn of 1932, aged fifty-four,

42. Mitani, "Kaisetsu," 329–30.
43. *Shin'yaku Genji monogatari* is discussed, for example, in Okano Takao, *Kindai Nihon meicho kaidai* (Yūmei Shobō, 1962), 121. For Akiko's view of her first translation, see her "Shinshin'yaku Genji monogatari atogaki," 37.

she began work. In her afterword to the *Shin-shin'yaku Genji monoga-tari,* as this final version was to be entitled, Akiko describes how she was suddenly overcome with the desire to retranslate *Genji:*

> Seven years ago, in the autumn, I suddenly resolved that come what may, I must make the time to fulfill my responsibility to retranslate *Genji.* I began writing immediately, and I continued writing; I hurried on lest what was left of my life be over before I should finish. But in the spring of 1935 I lost my husband. Needless to say, the chores I had to do as sole support of the family increased. On the other hand, I also felt that I had not the strength in my crushed heart to do more than compose poems. By that time, including the work done during my husband's illness, I had gone as far as the 'Hashihime' chapter. I had not even made a fair copy of the chapters after 'Wakana.' I wasted two years staring at the *Shin-shin'yaku* manuscript, piled up like a wall.[44]

Sometime during those two years, Akiko participated in perhaps the most far-fetched activity of her *Genji* career: the recording of a musical suite *(kumikyoku)* entitled *Genji monogatari* and consisting of three movements: "Fujitsubo" (The Wisteria Court/Consort), "Kosuzume" (Baby Sparrows) and "Wakakusa" (Young Grasses). To my knowledge, the only surviving evidence of her involvement with the project is a captioned photograph of Akiko standing before a microphone at the Koronbiya [Columbia] recording studios which appeared in the *Fujo shinbun* of 8 November 1936. She was there to read the original text of *Genji,* which became side one of the first record. The remaining five sides were composed of various combinations of vocal and instrumental music. *Fujo shinbun* commented:

> Even though the piece is based upon forms of composition used in Western music [duets, string quartets etc.], it is informed by *gagaku-style* melodies that are completely Japanese and this evokes the classical emotional atmosphere *(kotenteki jōcho)* of *The Tale of Genji.*[45]

---

44. Yosano, "Shin-shin'yaku Genji monogatari atogaki," 37.
45. "Kumikyoku *Genji monogatari* no fukikomi," *Fujo shinbun,* no. 1900 (8 November 1936): 3. A 1936 recording of the musical suite, including Akiko's recitation of the opening section of the 'Kiritsubo' chapter, has survived, and may be heard on *The Legendary of* [sic] *Suzuki*

During the summer of 1937, Akiko prepared a translation of *Kagerō nikki*. This was first published the following year in the "Heianchō joryū nikki" volume of Hibonkaku's *Gendaigoyaku kokubungaku zenshū* series, together with reprints of her 1916 translations of *Murasaki Shikibu nikki* and *Izumi Shikibu nikki*.[46]

A fortunate meeting with Kanao in the autumn of 1937 spurred Akiko to finish her new translation of *Genji*.[47] Her disciple Yuasa Mitsuo (1903–89) describes visiting her after she resumed work:

> At that time Sensei was busy with the modern translation of *Genji*. It was a relief not to be treated formally as a guest. After two or three words of greeting, Sensei quickly took up the *Nihon koten zenshū* edition of *Genji* and her pen raced across the paper. Saying nothing we sat there stiffly by the desk gazing in admiration at the awesome figure intent on the translation.[48]

By the time the *Shin-shin'yaku* manuscript was ready for checking, Akiko could no longer read small print and her youngest

---

Quartet, with Suzuki Shin'ichi (1898–1998, devisor of the "Suzuki method," first violin), Suzuki Kikuo (second violin), Suzuki Akira (viola), and Suzuki Fumio (cello), Quartett Haus Japan QHJ-1003, 2008, compact disc. The suite is just under twenty minutes long and was composed by Suzuki Fumio. Heartfelt thanks to Margaret Mehl of Copenhagen University for locating this CD. The section of the recording that features Akiko's recitation of *Genji* can also be heard on *Yomigaeru jisaku rōdoku no sekai*, Columbia Music Entertainment COCP-33360, no date, compact disc. My thanks to Kannotō Akio for alerting me to the existence of this CD and identifying the text Akiko recites: "Yosano Akiko no rōdoku shita *Genji monogatari* no tekisuto wa nani ka: *Shin-shin'yaku Genji monogatari* no shūhen," *Heianchō bungaku kenkyū*, 2nd series, no. 16 (2008): 39–41.

46. Yosano Akiko, trans., *Heianchō joryū nikki*, vol. 9 of *Gendaigoyaku kokubungaku zenshū* (Hibonkaku, 1938).

47. Yosano, "Shin-shin'yaku Genji monogatari atogaki," 37. Kanao Tanejirō, "Akiko fujin to Genji monogatari," *Dokusho to bunken* 2.8 (August 1942): 9.

48. Yuasa Mitsuo, "Akiko *Genji* to Kanao Bun'endō," *Nihon kosho tsūshin* 39.2 (February 1974): 5. Yuasa's identification of the text upon which the *Shin-shin'yaku* translation was based is important, for no scholarly comparison with her earlier *Shin'yaku* translation can begin until such fundamentals have been established. It has usually been assumed that the *Shinshin'yaku* translation was made from Akiko's own thirty volume woodblock printed edition of *Genji*, without colophon, now held by Kuramadera. The *Nihon koten zenshū* text that she actually used is based upon an unannotated edition of *Genji* printed with wooden movable type *(kikatsuji)*, also without colophon, but thought to date from the Genna period (1615–24). Details of the text are provided in the "Kaidai" to the first volume of *Genji* in the *Nihon koten zenshū* series.

child Fujiko was called in to help. She recalls that as they worked through the height of summer Akiko would say, red pen in hand, "Only the Uji chapters to go now!" or "Only so many pages before it's finished!"[49] The six volumes of *Shin-shin'yaku Genji monogatari* were published, again by Kanao Bun'endō, between October 1938 and September 1939. Fujiko records the following anecdote to illustrate the profound sense of elation her mother felt at finally completing her "whole life's work":

> Meaning to congratulate, someone once kindly suggested, "It must be a great relief to you that all of your children are married with families of their own." My mother replied, "Not at all. Children grow up by themselves. The sort of joy one feels when children get married is nothing compared to the joy I felt when I finished translating *Genji*."[50]

The *Shin-shin'yaku* does not seem to have attracted the notice that had greeted the publication of the *Shin'yaku* a quarter of a century earlier; I have been unable to track down any reviews from the period. Although the *Shin-shin'yaku* was illustrated with over fifty woodcuts by Masamune Tokusaburō (1883–1962), it was a modest production in comparison with the 1912–13 *Shin'yaku*. Kanao could not afford to advertise extensively, and it was apparently taken by some to be merely a reprint of the earlier work.[51]

A further reason for the apparent lack of attention may be that Akiko's translation had a powerful competitor in *Jun'ichirō yaku Genji monogatari*, Tanizaki Jun'ichirō's first modern translation of *Genji*, which began to appear in January 1939. He enjoyed the backing of the major publishing house Chūō Kōronsha, which lavished considerable financial support upon the presentation and advertising

---

49. Mori Fujiko, "Haha Yosano Akiko (4)," *Fujin kōron* 28.5 (May 1943): 61.
50. Ibid.
51. Yuasa, "Akiko *Genji* to Kanao Bun'endō," 6. Further evidence that the first edition of the *Shin-shin'yaku* was a commercial failure is cited by Kawazoe Fusae, *Genji monogatari jikūron* (Tokyo Daigaku Shuppankai, 2005), 378, and includes Yosano Shigeru's remark, in a lecture given in 1968, that "my mother's *Tale of Genji* didn't sell even a thousand copies."

of the twenty-six volume work. Akiko certainly saw Tanizaki's effort as detracting from her own accomplishment, but she was confident that the recognition that she felt was her due would come with time. Tenmin reports the following conversation:

> Akiko said to me, "[A]lthough the book won't appear to great fanfare, it is something into which I have poured body and soul; I am sure that fifty years, a hundred years hence, there will come a time when I will be recognized by all those of good sense."[52]

To Masamune Atsuo, her former colleague on the *Nihon koten zenshū* project, she wrote:

> I am much indebted to Tokusaburō-sama [youngest of the three Masamune brothers and illustrator of the *Shin-shin'yaku*] for his assistance with *Genji*. Moreover, I heard from Arai-sama [?] that Hakuchō-sama [eldest of the brothers] kindly said that the Yosano *Genji* is better than the Tanizaki *Genji* because it is livelier.... It is all because of my relationship with you that he is kind enough to support me.[53]

The publicity attending the appearance of Tanizaki's translation as well as the importance the military regime attached to exercising control over his publisher Chūō Kōronsha may have worked against him, however. For as is well known, Tanizaki's first translation of *Genji* was heavily expurgated: the sections describing Genji's tryst with Oborozukiyo; his liaison with Fujitsubo; and Fujitsubo's horror at the resulting pregnancy were excised in their entirety, without the usual *fuseji* to indicate the deletions.[54] Akiko's *Shin-shin'yaku* suffered

---

52. Kobayashi [i.e. Tenmin], "Akiko *Genji* ni tsuite," 3.
53. Letter dated 20 July 1939, cited in Itsumi Kumi, "Yosano Akiko no *Genji monogatari* kōgoyaku ni tsuite," *Kokugakuin zasshi* 94.1 (January 1993): 34.
54. For a more detailed discussion of Tanizaki's translations of *Genji*, see Ibuki Kazuko and G. G. Rowley, " 'The Tanizaki *Genji*': Inception, Process, and Afterthoughts," with translations by Thomas Harper of Tanizaki Jun'ichirō's "On Translating *The Tale of Genji* into Modern Japanese" (1938) and "Some Malicious Remarks" (1965), in *The Grand Old Man and the Great Tradition: Essays on Tanizaki Jun'ichirō in Honor of Adriana*

no such fate and was published without cuts. And there is nothing vague about her version of these events. Ōmyōbu gathering up Genji's outer clothing and removing them from the "bedroom" the morning after; Fujitsubo's reluctant realization that she is pregnant; the terror they both feel, though Genji's fear is tempered by a (rather modern) delight in his potency; Fujitsubo's expanding girth and her morning sickness—all the details are there.[55] More detailed comparisons of the *Shin-shin'yaku* with Tanizaki's first translation will be drawn in the next chapter.

On 3 October 1939, a banquet was held at the Seiyōken Restaurant in Ueno to celebrate the publication of the *Shin-shin'yaku*. Fortunately, a photograph survives that preserves something of the atmosphere of the occasion.[56] The great dining room of Tokyo's premier Western-style restaurant, with its high, decorated ceilings, floorlength curtains, and crystal chandeliers, is filled with some 170 people from all over Japan, each with a sprig of *aoi* pinned to his or her costume. Here they sit in long rows, facing tables spread with starched linen, spread with a full panoply of china and silver, and adorned with long-stemmed flowers in thin-stemmed vases. Hardly a Heian atmosphere, but certainly appropriate to the celebration of a project of modernity. At the banquet, congratulatory speeches were made by a number of men from the literary world, almost all of whom had at one time been associated with the Shinshisha. They included Arishima Ikuma (1882–1974), Kinoshita Mokutarō (1885–1945), Takamura Kōtarō (1883–1956), Satō Haruo (1892–1964), and Horiguchi Daigaku (1892–1981). All the speeches were subsequently printed in a special issue of the coterie magazine *Tōhaku,* successor to *Myōjō,* founded in 1930 and run by Yosano disciples.[57] The issue

Boscaro, edited by Luisa Bienati and Bonaventura Ruperti (Center for Japanese Studies, The University of Michigan, 2009), 25–52.

55. Yosano Akiko, *Shin-shin'yaku Genji monogatari* (1938; reprint, Nihonsha, 1948), 1:169–72; cf. *NKBZ* 1:305–9.

56. Shioda Ryōhei, ed., *Yosano Akiko,* vol. 16 of *Nihon bungaku arubamu* (Chikuma Shobō, 1955), 49.

57. *Tōhaku* 10.10 (October 1939).

also included a set of commemorative *tanka* by Koganei Kimiko, who was not merely congratulatory but so extravagant in her praise as to suggest that Akiko's *Shin-shin'yaku* had rendered even the work of Motoori Norinaga superfluous:

たをたをともつれし筋のなきものを玉の小櫛は今何かせん

Taotao to motsureshi suji no naki mono o
Tama no ogushi wa ima nani ka sen.[58]

With no more entangling complications to impede us,
what need have we now for *Tama no ogushi?*

The high point of the evening was a short address by Akiko herself. She used the opportunity not to talk about her translation, but rather to reiterate her theory of the dual authorship of *Genji.* Satō Haruo later recalled how she seemed to glow with youth and beauty as she spoke, invigorated, as ever, by her subject.[59]

It is tempting to speculate that by this time Akiko at last felt confidently enough in possession of *Genji* to take on the mantle—quite literally, even—of the Murasaki Shikibu of her day. For her neighbor and colleague at Bunka Gakuin, the novelist and critic Abe Tomoji (1903–73), recalled that when he and Akiko rode the train to school together, he to lecture on English literature, she to lecture on *Genji,* she often wore a kimono and *haori* of a deep purple— *koi murasaki.* "In the garden of my present home in Setagaya," he continues, "there is a shrub called the Murasaki Shikibu, which in autumn fairly glows with small berries of a rich purple; it sometimes sets me to thinking of Akiko."[60]

58. Koganei Kimiko, "Genji kyōen," *Tōhaku* 10.10 (October 1939), 58. The poem clearly refers to Norinaga's epigraph to *Genji monogatari Tama no ogushi:*

Sono kami no kokoro tazunete midaretaru
suji tokiwakuru tama no ogushi zo.

To untangle the tangled strands, to search
the minds of ages past: this little bejeweled comb.

59. Cited in Shinma, "Yosano Akiko to *Genji monogatari,*" 268.

60. Abe Tomoji, "Yosano Akiko no omoide," *Nihon no koten geppō,* no. 2 (Kawade Shobō Shinsha, 1971), no page numbers.

The *Shin-shin'yaku* translation, Akiko's last *Genji*, was her last major work of prose. Apart from some obituaries, during the remainder of her life she reserved her energies for poetry. She died at home on 29 May 1942. According to Fujiko, Akiko's only regret was that she had been unable to publish in any detail the results of her research into the authorship of *Genji*.[61]

61. Mori, "Haha Yosano Akiko (4)," 62; Mori, *Midaregami,* 251. As Janine Beichman noted in her review of my book in *Journal of Asian Studies* 61.1 (2002): 263, Akiko published several hundred poems during the last few years of her life, and the posthumous collection *Hakuōshū* (White Cherry Blossoms, 1942), "is now considered to be one of Akiko's major works...its poems even appear[ing] in some high school *kokugo* textbooks."

Chapter Eight:
The Tale of Genji: "My Whole Life's Work"

われも見る源氏の作者をさなくて父と眺めし越前の山
Ware mo miru Genji no sakusha osanakute
    chichi to nagameshi Echizen no yama. (7:18)
Now I too see them: the mountains of Echizen that the author of *Genji*
    in her youth gazed upon with her father.

Genji monogatari wa wagakuni no koten no naka de jibun ga mot-
tomo aidoku shita sho de aru. Shōjiki ni ieba, kono shōsetsu o mikai
suru ten ni tsuite jibun wa ikka no nukigatai jishin o motte iru.
The Tale of Genji is my favorite book among the classics of our
country. To be honest, when it comes to the understanding and
appreciation of this novel, I have the unshakable confidence of a
master.

"After Shin'yaku Genji monogatari" (1913)

In the foregoing chapters we have noted two tendencies in
Akiko's work with *The Tale of Genji* that may appear to stand in opposition to each other. On the one hand, her first translation extricated
Murasaki's fiction from the realm of the classics and their guardians,
the scholars of National Literature. Akiko rewrote *Genji* in the colloquial style of the Meiji novelist, transforming it from a classic that
had to be studied with the aid of commentary into a novel that could be
read cover to cover without interruption. Her subsequent work, on the
other hand, showed a steadily stronger scholarly bent. In the course of
composing her own commentary on *Genji,* editing a series of canonical
texts, and documenting the biographical details of Murasaki Shikibu's
life, Akiko herself became a recognized member of that community of
classicists from whom she once wrested the *Genji.* Accustomed as we
are to the sharp separation of writer and scholar in the world of modern
Japanese letters, the question naturally arises how Akiko might have
bridged this gap. I suspect, however, that in her own mind there was no

gap to bridge, that she sensed no opposition between these two aspects of her work.

In the poem above, for example, we see how easily the persona of the scholar reconstructing the life of her author blends with the persona of the poet "on tour,"[1] while the prose epigraph suggests that within Akiko's conception of *Genji*, ".classic" *(koten)* and "novel" *(shōsetsu)* could be virtual synonyms. More cogent still is the evidence of the language of her last, complete translation of *Genji*, the *Shinshin'yaku Genji monogatari*. For here, I think, in this linguistic blend of the creative writer and the scholar, is where we may find some clue to the reasons Akiko was able to effect so great a change in the style of *Genji* translating, while at the same time shifting the center of gravity of her work steadily closer to the world of those scholars who had failed to develop such a style.

Evidence of this sort does not lie on the surface of the text, but must be teased out of it. For this reason a mode of analysis different from that applied to the *Shin'yaku* has been used. Rather than examining longish passages in comparison with the original, I examine Akiko's translations of the immediate contexts of several occurrences of a single word. Her translations are compared with the modern rendition given beneath the text in the *Nihon koten bungaku zenshū* edition of *Genji*, and the first of Tanizaki Jun'ichirō's three translations, his *Jun'ichirō yaku Genji monogatari* of 1939–41.[2] The *NKBZ* version provides a contrast with a highly learned style of translating employed

1. The poem is one of a number Akiko wrote during a trip to Fukui Prefecture in the autumn of 1933. Hiroshi and Akiko were often invited to visit provincial cities and towns. As Kōuchi Nobuko explains, this was one of the ways the Yosanos made their living: they would be scheduled to give lectures; meet with local educators, poets, fans, and the press; and of course compose poetry, which would be presented to local admirers in the form of *tanzaku*, poetry cards *(shikishi)*, and the like. See Kōuchi Nobuko, *Yosano Akiko—Shōwaki o chūshin ni—*(Domesu Shuppan, 1993), esp. 155–60.
2. The first Tanizaki translation has been chosen because it is the near contemporary of Akiko's *Shin-shin'yaku*. In second translation of 1951–54, Tanizaki makes only one small alteration to his original translations of the passages quoted below. His third translation of 1964–65 differs from his second version only in orthography: "historical" *kana* spellings are replaced with postwar spellings, and a few words previously written in *kanji* are written in *kana*. For a more detailed but highly idiosyncratic account of the differences between the three Tanizaki translations, see Roy Andrew Miller, "Levels of Speech *(keigo)* and the Japanese Linguistic Response to Modernization," in *Tradition and Modernization in Japanese Culture*, ed. Donald H. Shively (Princeton: Princeton University Press, 1971), 651–62.

specifically as an aid to readers of the original text. It serves also as a reliable control when questions of interpretation arise. Tanizaki's translation offers the opportunity to identify a few specific points in which Akiko's work contrasts with that of her younger contemporary, who presumably writes for the same audience.[3] Obviously the scope of such a comparison is too limited to serve as a basis for judging the overall merits of either translation, but such is not the intention of the present exercise. The aim of this analysis is to determine, to the extent that the text allows, Akiko's sense of the nuance of the original occurrence; how this understanding is expressed; and the techniques that are used to incorporate this understanding into the larger context of the sentence that conveys it.

The single word examined here is *uretashi,* a Heian word for which there is no precise modern equivalent, unlike, for example, *tsurashi,* for which there is the modern Japanese *tsurai* (hard to bear, painful). *Uretashi* must therefore be actively dealt with and not just replaced by a standard equivalent. For present purposes, it has also to recommend it the fact that it is used only ten times in *Genji*; every occurrence can be examined, thus avoiding an unintentionally biased selection.

A sampling of dictionary definitions suffices to suggest the variety of possibilities open to the translator—and the difficulty of choosing among them. *Iwanami kogo jiten* defines *uretashi* as follows:

> A contraction of *ura (=kokoro)* and *itashi.* 1. One's treatment (by another person) is angering *(ikidōroshiku)* or irritating *(imaimashii).*

3. I have consulted, but in the present discussion do not draw upon, the following comparisons of Akiko and Tanizaki's translations of *Genji:* Ikeda Kikan, "Genji monogatari no gendaigoyaku—Yosano, Kubota, Igarashi, Tanizaki, Funabashi shi no rōsaku—," in *Hana o oru* (Chūō Kōronsha, 1959), 337–41; Hidaka Hachirō, "Futatsu no Yosano Genji," *Tosho shinbun,* no. 720 (24 August 1963): 8; Fukunaga Takehiko, "Gendai no *Genji monogatari,*" *Asahi shinbun,* 20 December 1964, 18; Nomura Seiichi, "Yosano Genji to Tanizaki Genji," in *Genji monogatari no sōzō* (Ōfūsha, 1969), 336–49; Kuwahara Satoshi, "Tanizaki Genji no tokusei," *Heian bungaku kenkyū,* no. 77 (May 1987): 148–56; Kitamura Yuika, *"Genji monogatari* no saisei—gendaigoyaku ron," *Bungaku* 3.1 (Winter 1992): 44–53; Hiranuma Megumi and Igarashi Masataka, *"Genji monogatari* gendaigoyaku no nagare—Yosano Akiko kara Hashimoto Osamu made—," *Kokubungaku: kaishaku to kanshō* 59.3 (March 1994): 159–65.

2. One is hurt by an unfeeling *(mujō na)* act or attitude, in response to which one wishes to state one's grievance *(fuhei)* or dissatisfaction *(fuman)*.[4]

Koga daijiten offers a wider range of meanings, some of them expressing rather stronger feelings:

1. A state of violent mental reaction *(kokoro ga hageshiku nami-datsu sama)* [which is manifested] in abhorrence *(zōo)*, indignation *(fungai)*, or the like. Angering *(haradatashii)*. Irritating *(imaimashii)*. Offensive *(shaku ni sawaru)*. 2. Embittering *(shingai de aru)*. Resentful *(urameshii)*. 3. Odious *(kimi ga warui)*. Repulsive *(itowashii)*.[5]

Kitayama Keita quotes six of the ten occurrences in *Genji* and offers four potential equivalents thereof:

Irritating *(imaimashi)*. Detestably resentful *(nikuku urameshi)*. Angering *(haradatashi)*. Embittering *(shingai nari)*.[6]

Nihon kokugo daijiten adds an historical dimension:

In ancient times [*uretashi*] was most often used with reference to acts of another person that conflicted with one's own desires. From the Heian period forward it came to express feelings of dissatisfaction toward other situations in general. Resentful *(urameshii)*. Detestable *(nikui)*. Offensive *(shaku ni sawaru)*. Embittering *(shingai de aru)*. Lamentable *(nagekawashii)*. Disagreeable *(iya da)*.[7]

Insofar as they can be determined by lexicographical means, then, the semantic givens of the comparison may be summarized as follows: In early usage, *uretashi* denotes the bitterness of betrayal. A person you

---

4. Ōno Susumu, Satake Akihiro, and Maeda Kingorō, eds., *Iwanami kogo jiten,* rev. ed. (Iwanami Shoten, 1990), 198c.
5. Nakada Norio, Wada Toshimasa, and Kitahara Yasuo, eds., *Kogo daijiten* (Shōgakukan, 1983), 234b.
6. Kitayama Keita, *Genji monogatari jiten* (Heibonsha, 1957), 124b.
7. *Nihon kokugo daijiten* (Shōgakukan, 1972–76), 3:90c.

took to be your friend, or at least an ally, to your astonishment, treats you badly. The shock and pain of the experience, as well as the anger and resentment toward the person who caused it, are described as *uretashi*. As time passes the edge of the word's bitterness is dulled and the specificity of its reference becomes blurred, so that it comes to be used to describe unfortunate situations that are not the fault of any particular individual.

Upon encountering the word *uretashi,* the translator must therefore answer a number of questions concerning that particular occurrence. Does the word refer to the doer of the deed, the deed itself, or the reaction of the person to whom it is done? Or does it refer to some generalized situation, the perpetrator of which either is not known or not stated? Where do the speaker's feelings lie on the scale that ranges from regret to irritation to indignation to outrage? For the translator of *Genji,* the possibilities are not so numerous: every occurrence of *uretashi* in this text expresses the speaker's resentment toward a particular person for a particular attitude or act. It is also interesting to note that nine out of the ten occurrences describe a man's resentment toward a woman whom he imagines has mistreated him. In Murasaki Shikibu's vocabulary, *uretashi* retains much of the barbed specificity of its earliest senses.

What, then, are the resources available to the translator of this difficult word? As the foregoing definitions indicate, there are any number of terms that might serve as modern equivalents for *uretashi*. The translations compared below show a decided preference for three: *imaimashii, shingai na/da,* and *nasakenai* (heartless). None of the equivalents appear to cover quite the same denotational ground as the original, however.[8] (It will be apparent from the translations below that English, too, lacks a precise equivalent for *uretashi.*) The instinctual recoil from the source of one's affliction is conveyed well by *imaimashii;* but it cannot qualify as an exact substitute, as it evolves from a word that originally described abhorrence rather than enmity. The shock of unexpected betrayal is vividly present in *shingai;* but the

---

8. These remarks are based upon definitions given in *Nihon kokugo daijiten* and Kindaichi Kyōsuke, et al., eds., *Shin-meikai kokugo jiten,* 4th ed. (Sanseidō, 1989).

betrayer may as well be a situation as a person. A human betrayer is certainly implied by *nasakenai;* but the emphasis of the word seems to lie more heavily upon the inhumanity of that person than upon the anguish of the betrayed. The same is true of its Sino-Japanese counterpart *mujō na.*

Replacement by a single word is by no means the only way to translate *uretashi.* The syntactic deployment of whatever word the translator may choose can affect the overall sense of the sentence as much as the denotational meaning of that word. The translator may also choose to distribute the sense of the original word throughout the immediate context, rather than opt for translation by substitution. In comparing the way Murasaki's translators have rendered *uretashi,* we must therefore attend not only to the words chosen, but also to their syntactical relationship to surrounding words, as well as any other strategies the translators may have employed to replicate the sense of the original.[9]

With these observations and cautions in mind, let us look at Akiko's translations of *uretashi* in comparison with those of the *NKBZ* translators and of Tanizaki. The first occurrence is in the 'Utsusemi' (The Shell of the Locust) chapter:

> *Kogimi ni, "ito tsurō mo uretō mo oboyuru ni, shiite omoikaesedo, kokoro ni shimo shitagawazu kurushiki o, sarinubeki ori mite taime(n) subeku tabakare" to, notamaiwatareba* ... (1:192; S 49)
> He [Genji] was always telling Kogimi that "This is so painful and irritating that I've tried to force myself to give up on her [Utsusemi]; yet agonizing though it is, it just doesn't work. You must watch for a good opportunity and arrange for me to meet her ... "

9. For a more detailed discussion of the translation of classical Japanese into modern (i.e. eighteenth-century) Japanese, see Motoori Norinaga's preface to *Kokinshū tōkagami,* ed. Ōkubo Tadashi, vol. 3 of *Motoori Norinaga zenshū* (Chikuma Shobō, 1969); and T.J. Harper, "Norinaga on the Translation of *Waka:* His Preface to *A Kokinshū Telescope,*" in *The Distant Isle: Studies and Translations of Japanese Literature in Honor of Robert H. Brower,* ed. Thomas Hare, Robert Borgen, and Sharalyn Orbaugh, Michigan Monograph Series in Japanese Studies, no. 15 (Ann Arbor: Center for Japanese Studies, The University of Michigan, 1996), 205–30.

[NKBZ] Kogimi ni, "mattaku hidoi to mo, <u>imaimashii</u> to mo omou
ni tsuke, muri ni mo omoinaosō to suru keredo, jibun no omoidōri
ni mo ikazu … "
[T] "Anmari tsuraku <u>kanashii</u> kara, muri ni mo wasureyō to shite
iru keredomo,jibun no kokoro ga jibun de dō ni mo naranai no da."
(1:137/1:88/1:82)[10]
[A] "Anna mujō na <u>urameshii</u> hito wa nai to watashi wa omotte,
wasureyō to shite mo jibun no kokoro ga jibun no omou yō ni naranai kara kurushinde iru no da yo." (1:77)[11]

Toward the end of the previous chapter, 'Hahakigi,' Genji's first
attempts to seduce Utsusemi end disastrously in repeated rejection. To
someone so "unused to being detested" this comes as a great shock,
and he "realizes for the first time how cruel life can be." He is "shamed
and doubts he can go on living" (1:191; S 49)—and is bitterly resentful
toward the woman who has done all this to him: ito tsurō mo uretō mo
oboyuru ni …

NKBZ renders this as imaimashii. It also drops the adverbial
inflection of the original and casts the word as a pure adjective, bringing it into association with the verb using the quotative particle to.
Instead of "thinking/feeling resentfully," Genji "thinks/feels 'this is
irritating.'"

Tanizaki retains the adverbial tsuraku, but omits to translate
oboyu; kanashii, his substitute for uretashi, would seem to lie outside
the range of emotions denoted by this word, for it conveys none of
Genji's resentment of Utsusemi's cold treatment of him. "Sad" (among
other things) he may be, but he blames neither himself nor the situation
for his condition. His discontent is directed at a particular person, and
it is more bitter than sad.

Akiko translates the pair of adjectives tsurashi and uretashi
with mujō na and urameshii. She too drops the adverbial form and,

---

10. Volume and page numbers refer respectively to Tanizaki Jun'ichirō's Jun'ichirō yaku
    Genji monogatari, 26 vols. (Chūō Kōronsha, 1939–41); Shin'yaku Genji monogatari
    fukyūban, 6 vols. (Chūō Kōronsha, 1956–58); and Shin-shin'yaku Genji monogatari,
    10 vols. (Chūō Kōronsha, 1964–65).
11. Page numbers refer to the six-volume reprint of Akiko's Shin-shin'yaku Genji monogatari
    in the Nihon bunko series (Nihonsha, 1948–49).

as in the *Shin'yaku,* chooses to clarify, in this case by adding *hito,* the unstated doer of the resented deed. " 'Never was there so unfeeling and resentful a person,' I thought."

The second instance of *uretashi* also occurs in the 'Utsusemi' chapter. Genji, having decided that after all he will go on living, makes a further attempt upon Utsusemi, only to discover that she has anticipated his approach and fled the room. He is thus forced to pretend that he has come in quest of her companion, Nokiba no Ogi; all of the old anger and resentment that come flooding back is again described as *uretashi,* this time in its attributive form, pointing directly at *hito,* that is, Utsusemi:

> *Nikushi to wa nakeredo, migokoro tomarubeki yue mo naki kokochi shite, nao kano uretaki hito no kokoro o imijiku obosu.* (1:200; S 54)
>
> He [Genji] did not find her [Nokiba no Ogi] off-putting, yet neither did he feel there was any reason to be attracted to her; and what that other hateful person [Utsusemi] must be thinking of it all was too dreadful to contemplate.
>
> [NKBZ] *Nikuge wa nai mono no, o-suki ni naru dake no tokoro mo nai ki ga shite, yahari ano imaimashii onna no kimochi o, hidoi to o-omoi ni naru.*
>
> [T] *Kimi wa o-kirai na no de wa nai ga, ki ni iru hazu mo nai yō na kokochi ga nasutte, hitoshio ano hakujō na hito no shiuchi o urameshii to oboshimesu.* (1:147/1:96/1:90)
>
> [A] *Nikuku wa nakutemo kokoro no hikareru ten no nai ki ga shite, kono toki de sae Genji no kokoro wa mujō na hito no koishisa de ippai datta.* (1:83)

NKBZ again chooses *imaimashii,* and retains the syntactical structure of the original. Tanizaki, too, retains the syntax of the original, but substitutes *hakujō na* "unfeeling" for *uretashi.* This describes Genji's assessment of Utsusemi well enough, but—like Tanizaki's previous translation *kanashii*—conveys none of Genji's own bitterness.

Akiko also retains the syntax of the original, this time using *mujō na* to render *uretashi.* Curiously, both Tanizaki and Akiko seem to stray from the original in the latter clause. Both agree that "he did not find her off-putting, yet neither did he feel there was any reason to be attracted to her...." Thereafter, however, Akiko goes on to say that "even at that time Genji's heart was filled with longing for that heartless person;" whereas Tanizaki says, "he felt utterly resentful of his treatment by that unfeeling person." Tanizaki is certainly closer to the original, yet in his version, Genji's resentment is directed not toward Utsusemi's thoughts/feelings, but her treatment of him. Whether these departures are the result of mistaken interpretation or translator's license is impossible to say.

In the third occurrence, yet another woman who proves impervious to Genji's charms, Princess Asagao, is the object of his vexation. But the emotional nuances are quite different from those in the attempt upon Utsusemi. The princess has seen from the experience of the Rokujō lady what pain a liaison with Genji can bring, and she is determined not to subject herself to this sort of agony (2:13; S 159). She bears Genji no ill will, and does her best not to hurt his feelings; but her rebuff is firm and unbending. Genji, for his part, dares not take umbrage to such an extent as before. Asagao is the daughter of a prince and not the second wife of a provincial governor. Besides which, he is fifteen years older, and (in some ways) more mature:

> *Otodo wa, anagachi ni oboshiiraruru ni shimo aranedo, tsure-naki onkeshiki no* <u>uretaki</u> *ni, makete yaminamu mo kuchioshiku* ... (2:478; S 356)
> The minister [Genji] was by no means angry with her [Asagao]; still he would have regretted to give up in defeat to the <u>vexation</u> of her cold demeanor.
> [NKBZ] *Genji no otodo wa, sō hitori katte ni iradatte orareru wake de wa nai ga, himegimi no tsurenai go-yōsu ga* <u>imaimashii</u> *ue ni, maketa mama de owaru no mo zannen da shi* ...
> [T] *Kimi mo hontō wa sō hitamuki na go-shiishin to iu no de mo nai ga, tsumetai o-shiuchi ga* <u>shingai na</u> *no de, makete o-shimai ni naru no mo imaimashiku* ... (8:26/2:339/4:52)
> [A] *Genji wa anagachi ni asette kekkon 'ga shitai no de wa nakatta ga koibito no reitan na no ni makete shimau no ga* <u>zannen</u> *de naranakatta.* (2:295)

NKBZ once again substitutes *imaimashii* for *uretashi.* Tanizaki opts for *shingai na;* for him, however, the subject of the clause is no generalized manner *(on-keshiki)*, but quite specifically the princess's treatment *(o-shiuchi)* of Genji.

At first glance, Akiko's translation seems a bit out of focus. None of the lexicographers cited above suggests *zannen* as a potential equivalent for *uretashi*. There are, however, depths to *zannen* that ordinary conversational usage does not often draw upon. *Nihon kokugo daijiten* defines these as follows:

> To feel resentful *(kuyashiku omou koto)* of being outdone by another person or suffering defeat in competition. Or the state thereof. Mortification *(munen)*. (9:293b)

Taken in this sense it seems the perfect word to render Genji's more composed, more mature resentment of a woman's refusal. Perhaps the final *naranakatta* may be meant to convey something of the sense of irritation that is lacking in *zannen?* In any case, Akiko's version probably comes closest to reproducing the emotional quality of the original.[12]

The fourth occurrence of *uretashi* is in the 'Fuji no Uraba' chapter. Tō no Chūjō, having at long last decided that Yūgiri would make an acceptable husband for his daughter Kumoinokari, is shocked to find Yūgiri so unresponsive to hints of his change of heart. In the end he must lower himself to inviting Yūgiri to his home, where, under the pretext of drunkenness, he can make the offer more obvious. His resentment at being forced into the position of petitioner is expressed in his use of *uretashi:*

> *Murasaki ni kagoto wa kakemu fuji no hana*
> *matsu yori sugite* <u>*uretakeredomo.*</u> (3:43O; S 527)
> Let us blame its purple hue; <u>vexing</u> though it was to wait for the wisteria to overgrow the pine.
> [NKBZ] *Fuji no hana no uramurasaki ni uramigoto wa matte yukimashō. Fuji no hana ga matsu no kozue o koete nikurashii to*

---

12. What appear to be differing interpretations of the first half of the sentence are the results of textual variants. Akiko and Tanizaki follow an alternate reading of the text which gives *oboshi iraruru* as "to be overwhelmed with passion," rather than "to be angry or upset," as in the *NKBZ* text. Cf. *NKBT edition of Genjt*, 2:264.

omou keredomo—machidōshii omoi o saseta anata o <u>*imaimashii*</u>
to omou ga, sono guchi wa musume no hō ni mōshimashō....
[T][Tanizaki gives the original poem, without any explanatory
note in his first translation; in his second translation it is glossed
as follows:]
Hyōmen no i wa, "fuji no hana ga matsu yori sakikosu no wa <u>*shin-*</u>
<u>*gai da*</u> *keredomo, sono murasaki no iro ni koto yosete menjimashō"*
de aru ga, kokoro wa, "anata kara no o-mōshikomi o matte ita no
ni, munashiku tsukihi ga sugite, tōtō konata kara orete deru no wa
nagekawashii shidai da keredomo, sore mo musume no en ni koto
yosete shinbō shimashō" to iu koto. (ll:134/3:348-49/5:198-99)
[A] [Akiko quotes the original poem, without explication; 3:313]

NKBZ again substitutes *imaimashii* for *uretashi,* and makes
the syntactical adjustments needed to compensate for inflections no
longer available in modern Japanese. Tanizaki again prefers *shingai
da,* which in his explication he rephrases as *nagekawashii.* In contrast
to the varied approach Akiko adopted to the poetry of *Genji* in her first
translation, in her second translation she consistently gives only the
original text of a poem, with no exegetical note. She seems to assume,
optimistically, that her readers are as competent at deciphering Heian
verse as she herself is.

The fifth example of *uretashi* occurs in the 'Wakana jō' chapter.
It is Genji's fortieth year, and Tamakazura arranges a gala celebration.
Here Genji expresses his "resentment" toward her for calling attention
to his age. The word must be placed in quotation marks, because in
this case it is susceptible of multiple interpretation. Genji is genuinely
grateful to Tamakazura for remembering him and showing concern for
him. He expresses his gratitude with a touch of humor ("How could you
be so cruel as to remind me of how old I am?") that in itself constitutes
an intimacy. Yet at the same time, the reminder really does hurt, especially coming from Tamakazura, who has rejected him as a lover with
the reminder that he was, after all, supposed to be her "parent" (3:206; S
438). He has never really forgiven her, and a veiled hint of this lingering
resentment of her previous "counting" of his age may well be carried in
his use of *uretashi.* The translator is thus faced with the formidable task
of rendering a complexly subtle use of an obsolete word:

*Hito yori koto ni kazoetoritamaikeru kyō no ne no hi koso, nao
<u>uretakere</u>.* (4:50–51; S 551)
This Day of the Rat, which you [Tamakazura] took the trouble to
calculate before anyone else, I [Genji] nonetheless <u>regret</u>.
*[NKBZ] Anata ga dare yori mo saki ni watashi no toshi o kazoete
oiwai shite kudasatta kyō none no hi wa, kaette yahari <u>urameshii</u>
kimochi desu.* (4:49-50)
*[T] Watashi ga yonjū ni narimashita koto o, dare yori saki ni o-
yomitori ni natte, iwatte kudasaimashita kyō none no hi ga, ureshii
nagara <u>kanashiku</u> nai koto mo arimasenu.* (12:53/4:3116:32)
*[A] Anata ga dare yori mo saki ni kazoete kudasutte nenrei no iwai
o shite kudasaru ne no hi mo, sukoshi no <u>urameshiku</u> nai koto wa
nai.* (4:31-32)

NKBZ and Akiko agree upon *urameshii*. And all translators
seem to agree that the emphasis of the *koso-izenkei* construction must
some-how be accounted for. *NKBZ* has Genji say that "contrary to what
one might expect I feel resentful." Tanizaki's *kanashii* again seems to
overlook the element of resentment in *uretashi*: Genji is "delighted but
not without a certain sadness." Akiko's "not without a touch of resentment" conveys the state of mind more accurately.

The sixth occurrence of *uretashi* is in the 'Wakana ge' chapter. Kashiwagi is smitten by his first glimpse of Genji's neglected
child bride Onnasannomiya and sends her a poem alluding to the
incident. The princess's waiting lady Kojijū replies in her stead, urg-
ing Kashiwagi not to let on that this has happened. He cannot but see
the justice of her warning, but neither is it the sort of reply he had
hoped for:

Kotowari to wa omoedomo, "<u>uretaku</u> mo ieru kana ... "
(4:145; S 587)
   True enough, he [Kashiwagi] thought; and yet how <u>maddening</u>
that she [Kojijū] should say so.
*[NKBZ] Naruhodo sore mo sono tōri to wa omou keredomo,
"<u>imaimashiku</u> mo itte yokoshita mono da ... "*
*[T] Kotowari to wa omou keredomo, <u>tsurenai</u> iikata o suru
mono kana
... (13:1/4:105/6:107)*

[A] *Kojijū ga kaite kita koto wa dōri ni chigai nai ga mata* <u>rokotsu na hidoi</u> *kotoba da to mo Emon no Kami ni wa omowareta.* (4:100)

NKBZ yet again chooses *imaimashii,* retaining the syntactical structure of the original: Kojijū "speaks vexingly." Tanizaki alters the syntax with *tsurenai:* she replies in a "heartless manner of speaking." Akiko too uses the attributive form, but expands the single word *uretashi* into two, *rokotsu na* and *hidoi,* both of which modify *kotoba:* "these are brusque, harsh words." There is no danger that *her* readers will underestimate the force of the blow to Kashiwagi's expectations.

In the seventh example, also from 'Wakana ge,' *uretashi* is called upon to bear a greater weight of shock, anger, and resentment than in any other instance in *Genji.* Genji has only recently learnt that Onnasannomiya has been unfaithful, and the pain of his discovery is still too great to discuss other than obliquely. This pain is the object of reference in this occurrence of *uretashi.*

> *Mata, ima wa, koyonaku sadasuginitaru arisama mo, anazurawa-shiku menarete nomi minashitamauramu mo, katagata ni kuchio-shiku mo,* <u>uretaku</u> *mo oboyuru o …* (4:259-60; S 629-30)
> And now that I've [Genji] grown so old and ugly, I suppose that to you [Onnasannomiya] I seem despicable and boring—which for me is not only regrettable but <u>hurtful</u>.
> [NKBZ] *Sore ni mata ima de wa, sukkari toshiyori ni natte shi-matta watashi no sugata mo, toru ni tarazu kawaribae mo shinai to bakari kimete irassharu no deshō kara, are ni tsuke kore ni tsuke zannen ni mo* <u>nasakenaku</u> *mo omowaremasu ga …* (4:260)
> [T] *Mata kono goro no yō ni kō toshi o totte shimaimashite wa, anazurawashū furukusaku mo o-omoi ni narimashō shi, sore ya kore ya o kangaemasu to, kuchioshiku* <u>nasakenai</u> *ki ga suru no desu ga …* (13:148/4:191/6:97)
> [A] *Mata anata to wa nenrei no sa no hanahadashii otto o keibetsu shitaku mo naru deshō keredo, watashi toshite sore o zannen ni omowanai wake wa arimasen ga …* (4:181)

NKBZ and Tanizaki both render *uretaku* with *nasakenaku* (heartless). If, as seems likely, Akiko intends *zannen ni* to translate *kuchioshiku,* then there is no word in her translation that corresponds even indirectly to *uretaku.* Or perhaps her intention was to subsume the meaning of both adjectives of the original in the single phrase *zannen ni omowanai wake de wa arimasen ga* (As for me, I cannot but resent this [your disdain for me]). This method at least has the virtue of identifying pointedly the person betrayed and his betrayer, which may in itself have seemed to account for the pointedness of *uretashi. NKBZ* and Tanizaki follow the syntax of the original precisely. Akiko, too, although she omits to translate *uretashi* directly, renders its partner in an adverbial inflection.

In the eighth instance, an interesting contrast to the previous example, Genji's son Yūgiri directs the same charge of contempt for an aging husband against his wife Kumoinokari. Here, too, there is a hidden agenda. But this time it is the husband himself who is the transgressor. Yūgiri's accusation is a desperate but feeble attempt to deflect his wife's resentment at his taking a second partner. The force of *uretashi* only serves to emphasize the hollowness of his allegation:

> *Nengetsu ni soete itō anazuritamau koso <u>uretakere</u>.* (4:414; S 688)
> Your [Kumoinokari's] terrible contempt for me [Yūgiri] the older I get—that is <u>painful</u>.
> *[NKBZ] Nengetsu ga tatsu ni tsurete hidoku kono watashi o naigashiro ni nasaru yo ni narareta no ga <u>nasakenai</u>.* (4:415)
> *[T] Dandan nengetsu ga tatsu ni tsurete, hito o naigashiro ni nasaru no wa <u>shingai</u> desu.* (15:45/4:31717:110)
> *[A] Nengetsu ni sotte watashi o anadoru koto ga hidoku naru no wa <u>komatta mono da</u>.* (4:294)

NKBZ again substitutes *nasakenai* for *uretashi.* Tanizaki does likewise with *shingai.* Akiko does more than merely substitute; she translates *uretashi* with the phrase *komatta mono da* (that you disdain me all the more the older I get *is vexing indeea).* In doing so she again departs from the repertoire of dictionary definitions, choosing a phrase that not only expresses Yūgiri's frustration but exposes his disingenuousness as well. Here, as elsewhere, she seems more inclined than either *NKBZ* or Tanizaki to take into account the context in which *uretashi* occurs and to vary her translation accordingly. Whatever its lack of precision as a substitute for the Heian word, the virtue of *komatta mono da* is that it rises out of the situation rather than simply functioning as a synonym. Although all three translations follow the original syntax, *NKBZ* and Akiko attempt to render the stress of the *koso-izenkei* construction, the former with *hidoku* and the latter with *mono da,* whereas Tanizaki seems to ignore it.

The ninth occurrence of *uretashi* is in the 'Takekawa' (Bamboo River) chapter. Kaoru pays a New Year's visit to Tamakazura. While he awaits her emergence, her waiting ladies make no secret of their admiration for him, and flirt quite openly with him. His enjoyment of their attentions is rudely extinguished, however, when their mistress Tamakazura enters the room and upbraids the young ladies for behaving so outrageously in the presence of this "most proper young gentleman" (5:63; S 755). The irritation that the name causes, and his resentment toward Tamakazura for calling attention to it, are here expressed in *uretashi:*

> *Jijū no kimi, mamebito no na o* <u>*uretashi*</u> *to omoikereba ...* (5:64; S 756)
> The chamberlain [Kaoru] found his nickname, "that proper young gentleman," most <u>irritating</u>.
> *[NKBZ] Jijū no kimi wa, mamebito to iu adana o hidoku* <u>*nasakenai*</u> *to omotta no de ...* (5 :63)
> *[T] Sore o go-tōnin mo o-kikitsuke nasarete, "mamebito" to wa* <u>*nasakenai*</u> *na o tsukerareta mono yo to o-omoi ni naru.* (16:145- 46/5:103/8:28)
> *[A] Gen no jijū wa kimajime-otoko to iwareta koto o* <u>*zannengatte*</u> *... (5:122)*

Both *NKBZ* and Tanizaki again choose *nasakenai;* Akiko translates *uretashi* as *zannengatte* (gives the appearance of resenting). Both of these choices convey an important element of Kaoru's resentment—the self-pity, the irritation, the mortification. *NKBZ* follows the original syntax, but Akiko replaces the *to omou* construction with the affix-*garu,* a subtly effective touch which, almost visibly, renders the "directedness" of *uretashi* that has been lost in most of its modern equivalents.

The tenth and final example of *uretashi* occurs in the 'Azumaya' (The Eastern Cottage) chapter. Even after Nakanokimi's marriage to his rival Niou, Kaoru cannot bring himself completely to abandon his designs on her. She attempts diplomatically to divert his advances by mentioning the presence of an "image" (Ukifune) to which he might transfer his affections, and he, with equal indirection, but no ambiguity, makes clear his resentment at her kind rebuff:

> *"Tsui ni yoru se wa, saranari ya. Ito <u>uretaki</u> yō naru, mizu no awa ni mo arasoi haberu kana...."* (6:47; S 951)
> "Yes, of course, I [Kaoru] shall ultimately 'come to rest upon some shoal.' But how <u>maddening</u> it is as one jostles, as it were, with the foam upon the waters ...."
> [*NKBZ*] *"Tsui ni yoru se wa aru to iimasu ga, imasara sore wa mōsu made mo nai koto desu yo. Mattaku <u>nasakenai</u> o-shiuchi no tsurasa wa, hakanai mizu no awa ni hariau yō na mono de gozaimasu ne ...."* (6:47-48)
> [T] *" 'Tsui ni yoru se' wa doko ni aru no ka, mōsu made mo nai de wa arimasen ka. Sore ni tsuketemo, toritome no nai mizu no awa to hakanasa o arasou mi nano deshō ka ...."* (20:52-53/6:128/ 9:153-54)[13]
> [A] *" 'Tsui ni yoru se' (Onusa to na ni koso tatere nagaretemo tsui no yoru se wa arikeru mono o) wa doko de aru to watashi ga omotte iru koto wa anata ni dake wa o-wakari ni naru hazu desu shi, sono hanashi no hō no wa hakanai mizu no awa to arasotte nagareru nademono de shika nai no desu kara, anata no o-kotoba no yō ni taishita kōka o watashi ni motarashite kure mo shinai deshō."* (6:146)
> "You alone ought to know just where I think the 'shoal upon which I [Kaoru) shall ultimately come to rest' is; and since *that* [the "image" Nakanokimi has mentioned] is no more than a *nademono* doll which jostles and flows with the evanescent foam upon the waters; it is likely to do as little for me as your words."

An allusive comment of this sort is a translator's nightmare, so it is hardly a wonder that the three renditions cited here differ so. *NKBZ* again substitutes *nasakenai* for *uretashi* and may in addition intend that *tsurasa* work in combination with it. It manages to remain syntactically faithful by identifying the *yō* of the original as *o-shiuchi no tsurasa* (the pain of your actions), while relegating explanatory

---

13. The only change Tanizaki made to his versions of the passages quoted here was to omit the phrase *sore ni tsuketemo* from his second and third translations.

material to the headnotes. Tanizaki is fairly restrained in eking out the implicit meanings of the allusions in the translation itself; this he is able to do because he employs headnotes throughout, though not to the extent of an edition such as *NKBZ*.[14] In Akiko's highly exegetical translation, the feeling of *uretaki* is spread throughout the latter half of the sentence, but with no particular word(s) or phrase corresponding directly to it. Lacking the benefit of notes to bolster her translation (though in this case she resorts to the bracketed inclusion of the poem alluded to), Akiko almost totally replaces Kaoru's cryptic complaint with an exposition of its implied meanings.

We have seen that Murasaki Shikibu, whether she employs *uretashi* for jocular effect, or to express the deepest sort of resentment, seems never to use the word in disregard of its sharp edges and pointed reference. What, then, do the renditions examined above reveal of the translators' understanding of her use of the word, and the strategies they employ to render it into modern Japanese?

NKBZ is the most mechanical of the three translations in its handling of *uretashi*. In five cases it simply substitutes *imaimashii,* and in four cases *nasakenai.* In one case it departs from this pattern to use *urameshii. NKBZ* is also the most syntactically faithful of the three. Given the purposes of the translation—to help the reader follow the original text printed immediately above it—the rather rigid strategies of synonym substitution and syntactic fidelity are by no means flaws. To the student, a literal translation may be of more use than the imaginative art of a writer/translator.

Tanizaki's rendition also reveals a high degree of syntactic fidelity. He tends, too, to favor the synonym-substitution method of translation, using *shingai na/da* three times and *nasakenai/tsurenai* a further three times. In two other instances, however, he seems to miss the fundamental emotion of resentment in *uretashi,* translating it as *kanashii.* His, we might say, is the translation of a talented reader who comes to the text as an adult and thus lacks the confidence of the scholar or native speaker of the original language.

14. In his headnote to this passage, Tanizaki provides both text and gloss of the *Ise monogatari* poem alluded to by Kaoru.

Akiko, by contrast, commands a repertoire of translation strategies that is decidedly more various than those of the other translators. She never translates *uretashi* in the same way twice. As a result, her translations can be more finely tuned to the individual quality of the situations in which each instance of *uretashi* occurs. Her "take" on the text is spontaneous and broad of reach rather than considered and narrowly focused; she is translating sentence-by-sentence, not word-by-word; she is translating style as well as meaning. Nowhere, to be sure, does she claim such an aim for her translation; but the following remark, apparently a response to Masamune Hakuchō's famous paean to Arthur Waley's English version of *Genji*,[15] does suggest that such would be her approach:

> A work of literature in translation is not identical to the original work; it is a new creation that mimics the original in another language. And being written in another language, it goes without saying that it never can be the same, even if it happens to be translated by the writer of the original.
>
> For this reason, the gentleman who says that he recently read the translation of *The Tale of Genji* by the Englishman Waley, and because it was so beautifully written felt that for the first time he could understand the original *Genji*, is quite mistaken. Literature is not to be read for meaning alone; it must be read as well for its own unique language *(tokushu na gengo)*. *The Tale of Genji*, therefore, does not exist independently of the beauty of Murasaki Shikibu's language. Waley's translation no doubt has its own freshness and value as English literature; and in this sense it is only proper to praise and appreciate Waley. But *The Tale of Genji* itself can be criticized only on the basis of reading the original text.[16]

And although as a non-native speaker of Japanese one must be sceptical of one's own judgments on matters of language, Akiko seems, at

15. Masamune Hakuchō, "Saikin no shūkaku–Eiyaku *Genji monogatari* sono ta—," in *Masamune Hakuchō zenshū* (Shinchōsha, 1967), 7:184–88.

16. Excerpt from "Tōihakutei zakki" (1934), in *Akiko koten kanshō*, vol. 4 of *Yosano Akiko senshū*, ed. Yosano Hikaru and Shinma Shin'ichi (Shinshūsha, 1967), 144. Kawazoe Fusae, *Genji monogatari jikūron* (Tōkyō Daigaku Shuppankai, 2005), 342, traces the first appearance of Akiko's response to Waley's translation to an essay entitled "Saikin no kansō," *Yokohama bōeki shinpō*, 17 December 1933.

least in this small sampling, the most sensitive reader of the situations here depicted and the style in which they are couched; and the most versatile in adapting the modern language to them. In a few cases her translations are not simply sensitive and versatile but ingenious—as in her use of *zannen* to describe Genji's controlled but nonetheless raw resentment toward a woman who has refused him; her *sukoshi no urameshiku nai koto wa nai* for Genji's double-edged feelings of gratitude and mortification; her *komatta mono da* for Yūgiri's hollow protestations of persecution. None of these translations would have been possible without departing from the standard repertoire of lexicographers and the strategies of synonym-substitution.

How, then, does the evidence of this brief analysis bear upon the questions posed at the beginning of the chapter? In chapter five it was noted how drastic a departure from the practice of her immediate predecessors Akiko's adoption of the colloquial style in her translation was. In chapter seven, we followed the subsequent development of a more scholarly interest in *Genji,* an interest that led to the production of a commentary (written, it would appear, in a decidedly classical style), an edition of the text of *Genji,* and a pioneering biography of Murasaki Shikibu. In the present chapter, we have seen evidence of the continuation of both tendencies in her last translation of *Genji,* the *Shin-shin'yaku.* Here the more scholarly Akiko is no longer willing to cut and rewrite as she did in her first translation, and close scrutiny of her new translations shows them to be incisively precise; yet the language of those translations remains as thoroughly colloquial as ever. In short, her adoption of the colloquial, the *genbun'itchi* of the novelist, remains the central, constant feature of her translation style; and it is in no way vitiated by her steadily growing scholarly bent. We must return, therefore, to the question of how she was able to effect so radical a change in translation style in the first place if we are to understand how that style retained its vitality throughout a career that changed so much in other ways. Unfortunately, the question of the origins of Akiko's translation style is all but totally ignored by scholars of her work, and she herself is silent on the matter. Yet one need only recall the extremity of her departure, and the tone of wonder with which it was received—even by as austere a figure as Ōgai—to realize that the question remains unanswered.

Although we lack any direct attempt by scholars of Japanese literature to come to terms with this question, we are not without hints to possible approaches. One of these is Mitani Kuniaki's comment that Akiko's first colloquial translation "shows clearly" that she has made use of Kigin's *Kogetsushō*.[17] Mitani does not explicitly link the *Kogetsushō* with the development of Akiko's translation style, but the suggestion bears further investigation, for Kigin's work is of some importance in the early history of the translation of the Japanese classics. As is well known, the *Kogetsushō* is not merely a commentary. Although its frequent interlinear glosses are normally regarded as commentarial devices, they can also be seen as precursors to vernacular translation. It may be well, therefore, to examine the critical apparatus of the *Kogetsushō* as a possible source of Akiko's phraseology.

Apart from headnotes that consist mainly of quotations from earlier commentaries, the *Kogetsushō* provides readers with four sorts of aids: *furi-kanji*, *furigana*, identification of subjects, and interlinear glosses translating into the colloquial of his day phrases that Kigin thinks may be unclear. Only the last of these need concern us here. To take a couple of examples from the 'Hana no En' chapter, in the sentence *Yo itō fukete namu, koto hatekeru* (The night grew late, and it came to an end, 1:425) *koto hatekeru* is glossed *hana no en hateshi nari* (the cherry blossom festival ended). Genji's *meshiyosetaritomo, nanjō koto ka aran* (even if you summon someone, what is to come of it? 1:427) is glossed *hito o yobitamautomo nanigoto ka aran to nari* (this means even if you call someone it would be of no avail). In this way the interlinear notes frequently translate for the reader whole phrases or even short sentences.

Comparing Akiko's *Shin'yaku* versions of 'Hana no En' and 'Maboroshi' with the *Kogetsushō* texts of these chapters, however, one finds no evidence that she has borrowed her phraseology from Kigin or the commentators he cites. On the other hand, it is not impossible

17. Specifically, the 1890–91 edition of *Kogetsushō* edited by Inokuma Natsuki. "This version of the text of *Genji* determined the Meiji period reading [of *Genjī*]; many [published] lecture notes, as well as ... [Sassa et al.'s] *Shinshaku Genji monogatari* and Yosano Akiko's colloquial translation show clearly that this *Kogetsushō* text has been used." Mitani Kuniaki, "Meiji-ki no *Genji monogatari* kenkyū," *Knkubungaku: kaishaku to kanshō* 48.10 (July 1983): 53.

that she has taken matters of detail from the *Kogetsushō:* like Kigin, she identifies the Naden with the Shinshinden; similarly, the *haru no uguisu saezuru to iu mai* is identified as the dance otherwise known as the Shun'ōten. Indeed, it is difficult to imagine where else she might have come by information of this sort. Akiko was certainly familiar with Kigin's work, because in her afterword to the *Shin'yaku* she stoutly denies its usefulness:

> Needless to say, I do not hold in high regard any of the exist-
> ing commentaries on *The Tale of Genji.* In particular, I find the
> *Kogetsushō* a careless work that misinterprets the original.[18]

On the basis of this partial examination, however, it seems unlikely that the *style* of her first translation is based upon the *Kogetsushō.*

Another hint as to the sources of Akiko's language is Shinma's observation that when she began work on the *Shin'yaku,* she had already accumulated a good deal of experience in the writing of colloquial prose in the form of short pieces of drama and fiction, and that this practice probably contributed materially to her style. Shinma's further suggestion that her style in the *Shin'yaku* may have been inspired by the current vogue for "naturalist literature" *(shizenshugi bun-gaku)* thus raises the possibility that her choice of language was in part "political." Shinma pursues the idea no further, but it is well known that the vernacularization of literature was debated vigorously by Akiko's older contemporaries, and that writers' views on this matter could affect profoundly the language of their writings.[19] Might not the same be true of Akiko herself? If her style were intended as a "statement," a position taken in opposition to another that she rejects, we might expect to find some evidence, or even an exposition of this position, elsewhere in her oeuvre. Yet as far as I have been able to ascertain, she gives no indication in any of her writings that she ever pondered the use of other styles, as Ozaki Kōyō did, or that she placed herself consciously under the

18. Yosano Akiko, "Shin'yaku Genji monogatari no nochi ni," in *Shin'yaku Genji monogatari* (Kanao Bun'endō, 1912–13), 4:3.
19. See, for example, P. F. Kornicki, "The Novels of Ozaki Kōyō," (D. Phil diss., University of Oxford, 1979), 170–82; Nanette Twine, *Language and the Modern State: The Reform of Written Japanese* (London: Routledge, 1991), 132–62.

influence of any philosophy of style, as the Ken'yūsha coterie of writers did. The most we can conclude from her silence is that the stylistic trends of her day may well have worked as an enabling factor, in conjunction with more direct causes, in the determination of her translation style.

In the absence of the evidence needed to elevate the foregoing conjectures to the level of working hypotheses, I would venture a third suggestion, no less speculative, but based at least upon fragments of Akiko's own testimony. Repeated reference has been made to Akiko's reticence to speak of her work on *Genji* and her silence on the matter of her translation style. In one sense, however, this silence is only seeming. One sets out in search of evidence of the influence of Kigin and/or the political concerns of her day—and finds none. Yet again and again Akiko herself points to the influence of Murasaki Shikibu:

> From the age of eleven or twelve, Murasaki Shikibu has been my teacher. I have no idea how many times I read through *The Tale of Genji* before I turned twenty. Her writing captivated me that much. I was entirely self-taught; Murasaki Shikibu and I faced one another with no intermediary, just the two of us; and so I feel that I have had *The Tale of Genji* from the very mouth of this great woman of letters. (19:258)

As a result Akiko was, as we have seen, virtually bilingual in classical and modern Japanese:

> That I was early able to understand what Japanese literature is about is because Murasaki Shikibu was my teacher. Moreover, because of this, as a young girl the strength of my memory and my powers of comprehension were developed, and as a result, after I had read *Genji* I didn't find reading other classical works in the least bit difficult. To this day I know much of *Genji* by heart; I remember the representative literary and historical works from each period in great detail; and I am able to lecture to students—all because at the beginning I had the good fortune to read Murasaki Shikibu carefully. (19:258)

The effect of this "bilingualism" upon her work on the *Shinshin'yaku* is vividly described by her disciple Yuasa Mitsuo, who sat in her study and watched her "pen race across the page" as she took in the original with a glance to the left, and with barely a pause, re-cast what she had read as modern Japanese with her right hand.[20] This is not so much "translation" as simultaneous interpretation with a pen. No pauses to ponder what the right word might be, or how the words might best be ordered. Hardly any intervention of discursive thought. Apparently no stopping to look up anything in the dictionary. Might not this relationship to her work—and her author—offer a key to the style of her translation and the radical break with her predecessors that it represents? The evidence of the foregoing analysis of her *Shinshin'yaku* tends to support such a view.

C. S. Lewis, in describing how he "learned rather laboriously from [his] own reading some things that could have been learned more quickly from the *N.E.D.*," has this to say of the process:

> One understands a word much better if one has met it alive, in its native habitat. So far as is possible our knowledge should be checked and supplemented, not derived, from the dictionary.[21]

Lewis's phrase describes perfectly Akiko's encounter with *Genji*. She "met it alive," in almost the same "native habitat" as the *Sarashina* diarist did. As a young woman she had read the text many times over "with no intermediary," that is, without the help of teachers, dictionaries, or commentaries. In this, her "meeting" with the text stands in direct contrast with those of her immediate predecessors, for whom, it appears, *Genji* had always been an object of study. For them, *Genji* was *koten,* a venerated classic, written in an ancient language and explicated in a learned language. It is hardly to their discredit that, thus disposed, they should think a translation in the *genbun'itchi* style would be "too modern," that "the elegance of the original would be lost," that in the end their translation strategies should be commentarial strategies in disguise. For Akiko, however, *Genji* was also a *shōsetsu,* a novel, written

---

20. Yuasa Mitsuo, "Akiko *Genji* to Kanao Bun'endō," *Nihon kosho tsūshin* 39.2 (February 1974): 5; see chapter seven, p. 152.
21. C. S. Lewis, *Studies in Words,* 2d. ed. (1967; reprint, Cambridge: Cambridge University Press/Canto, 1990), 2.

in the *genbun'itchi* of its author's day. What could be more natural than to translate it into the *genbun'itchi* of Akiko's own day? For her, this was neither a radical departure from tradition nor a political declaration; it was simply a form of faithfulness to her author. As something like a "native speaker" of Heian Japanese, she had no need to consult commentaries (as the *NKBZ* translators do frequently) or seek the assistance of specialist scholars (as Tanizaki did from Yamada Yoshio). Her translations, therefore, display not so much consistent responses to recurrent words as varied versions of individual situations. It is a mark of how naturally her style came to her that she herself never called it *genbun'itchi* or *kōgo*. As we have seen, she speaks simply of "writing *Genji*."

As Akiko develops a more scholarly interest in *Genji*, this work too is characterized by the same flexibility. The evidence is scant, but it seems certain that she wrote her massive commentary not in the modern colloquial style of her translations, but in the learned language of her scholarly predecessors.[22] We have seen, too, how her last translation shows much more of a scholar's concern for the integrity of the text. Yet the language of her last *Genji* is not a whit less colloquial than that of her first. Freedom of rendition is combined with a fine sense of nuance. Far from sensing a conflict between the two *"Genji-worlds"* that she now inhabits, she credits the lessons she learnt in the one for her success in the other. Her "unshakable confidence" in her philological grasp of *Genji*, acquired in the course of countless readings of *Genji* the (women's) romance, was the indispensable precondition of her work on *Genji* the (men's) classic.

Akiko, we might conclude, was decidedly a modern, but one with a private vision; a writer of her age, but by no means typical of her age. Fortunately it was an age in which her emulation of the life and work of a paragon of a millennium past struck her contemporaries (and many of our own) as the very height of both literary and academic modernity.

22. See chapter seven, p. 139.

Epilogue

On 6 May 1940 Akiko suffered a cerebral hemorrhage that left her an invalid for the remainder of her life. Appropriately enough, it would seem that thoughts of *Genji* occupied her mind almost until the very end. This we know from no less a witness than Ikeda Kikan (1896–1956), one of the twentieth century's most eminent scholars of *Genji*. On 5 May, the day before she collapsed, Ikeda visited Akiko at her home in Ogikubo. Ten years later, he recalled the visit in the following account:

> I had urgent business and unannounced I visited her house in Ogikubo.... . That day Akiko seemed livelier than usual. After we had dealt with our business, as ever our talk turned to *Genji*. I have no objection to her positing a structural break between 'Fuji no Uraba' and 'Wakana jō,' but I was unable to accept her opinion that Daini no Sanmi had written all of the chapters from 'Wakana' on. She was a person who stated her opinions gently, but never would she retreat from them. And so I began to feel "What's with this woman!" *(Nani o kono obasan.')* For more than thirty minutes we argued fiercely; then suddenly she got up and went off into her study. When at length she returned, she held two beautiful sheets of tinted card *(shikishi)* in her hand, one a faint green and the other pale crimson. She handed them to me with a smile saying, "Something to remember this by." On the two tinted cards were the following poems, beautifully written.

須磨の山藤もさくらも幼なй
Suma no yama fuji mo sakura mo osanakere
   kyō no runin no kozo ueshigoto.[1]

---

1. Not collected in *TYAZ*.

Mere saplings both, the wisteria and the cherry in the mountains of Suma,
    planted last year by the exile from the capital.
花見れば大宮のへのこひしきと源氏にかける須磨ざくらさく
Hana mireba ōmiya no he no koishiki to
    Genji ni kakeru Sumazakura saku. (7:456)[2]
The Suma cherries described in *Genji* bloom, those of which Genji
    says "Whenever I see the blossoms I long for the palace."

I was overwhelmed. I felt ashamed of the harsh things I had
said. Of course I had no regrets for the myriad of manuscripts I had
collated, the commentary I had contributed, for my studies of the
structure [of *Genji*], nor even for my for youth, every day of which
for the past twenty years I had given over to *Genji*. But as far as
my life being touched by the classics was concerned, I was far
the inferior of this lone, elderly woman. Was my scholarship then
destined to rot away? I was depressed.

As I left, the red of the azaleas, heartlessly it seemed, forced
itself upon my perception, and I realize now that this was the last
day in this present world that I was to discuss *Genji* with my worthy opponent, so deserving of respect. The next day, the sixth,
she collapsed of a cerebral hemorrhage, and although she made
a brief recovery, in the end she was unable to stand again and she
passed away.

I wonder if this year too the red azaleas bloom in the garden
of that house in Ogikubo where their mistress no longer lives?[3]

As ever, we are left with as many questions as answers. What
was Ikeda's "urgent business" with Akiko? Did it concern their work
with the classics? How long, and in what circumstances, had Ikeda
and Akiko been meeting to discuss—and argue over—*Genji*? One
thing at least is clear, however: Ikeda the *Genji* scholar could see the
degree to which Akiko's had been a life "touched by the classics."
Her one book, *The Tale of Genji*, had been, quite literally, her "whole
life's work."

2. In both of these poems Akiko refers to a scene from the 'Suma' chapter of *Genji*: "The New
    Year came to Suma, the days were longer, and time went by slowly. The sapling cherry
    Genji had planted the year before sent out a scattering of blossoms, the air was soft and
    warm, and memories flooded back, bringing him often to tears" (Seidensticker's transla-
    tion, 2:204; S 243). There is no mention of wisteria *(fuji)* in the chapter.
3. Ikeda Kikan, *Hana o oru* (Chūō Kōronsha, 1959), 186–88.

Appendix A:
Akiko's Publications on the Japanese Classics

What follows is as full a list as I have been able to prepare of Akiko's publications on *The Tale of Genji* and other Japanese classics, arranged in order of appearance. In the case of some of Akiko's essays, where I have been unable to verify place of first publication, I have noted instead the name and date of the collection of Akiko's essays in which the piece later appeared. A page reference to *Teihon Yosano Akiko zenshū* (*TYAZ*) is provided for those works which are collected there.

"Ise monogatari hyōwa." *Myōjō*, no. 14 (August 1901): 21–26 [with Ochiai Naobumi, Yosano Tekkan and three others]; no. 15 (September 1901): 60–63 [with other members of the Shinshisha].

Review of *Kokubungaku zenshi: Heianchōhen*, by Fujioka Sakutarō. *Myōjō* 6.11 (November 1905): 111.

Review of *Eiga monogatari shōkai*, by Wada Hidematsu and Satō Kyū. *Myōjō* 8.5 (May 1907): 104–6.

"Te no ue no kōri." *Joshi bundan* 4.5 (April 1908): 5–8.

"Sei Shōnagon no kotodomo." In *Hitosumi yori*. Kanao Bun'endō, 1911; *TYAZ* 14:56–65.

"Genji Tamakazura." *Mitsukoshi* 1.9 (October 1911). A draft of the 'Tamakazura' chapter from *Shin'yaku Genji monogatari*. Unseen.

"Genji Sekiya." *Subaru* 4.1 (January 1912): 169–72. A draft of the 'Sekiya' chapter from *Shin'yaku Genji monogatari*.

"*Genji monogatari* ni arawaretaru hitobito." *Shinchō* 16.5 (May 1912): 92–97.

Shin'yaku Genji monogatari. 4 vols. Kanao Bun'endō, 1912–13.

Shin'yaku Eiga monogatari. 3 vols. Kanao Bun'endō, 1914–15. Reprinted in *Koten Nihon bungaku zenshū* 9. Chikuma Shobō, 1962.

Tokugawa jidai joryū bungaku: Reijo shōsetsushū. 2 vols. Fuzanbō, 1915. Akiko edited this collection of *"shōsetsu"* (in this case *yomihon)* by Arakida Rei (1732–1806). Volume one includes two introductory essays by Akiko: "Reijo shōsetsushū o yo ni susumeru ni tsuite," and "Arakida Reiko [sic] shōden."

"Murasaki Shikibu no kotodomo." In *Hito oyobi onna toshite.* Tengendō Shobō, 1916; *TYAZ* 15:117–26.

"Murasaki Shikibu to sono jidai." In *Hito oyobi onna toshite; TYAZ* 15:127–29.

"Heian-chō no koi." In *Hito oyobi onna toshite; TYAZ* 15:153–59.

Shin'yaku Murasaki Shikibu nikki shin'yaku Izumi Shikibu nikki. Kanao Bun'endō, 1916.

Shin'yaku Tsurezuregusa. Oranda Shobō, 1916. Includes a preface, "Shin'yaku Tsurezuregusa no hajime ni," pp. 1–18. Reprinted 1922.

"Murasaki Shikibu no kōshō." In *Warera nani o motomuru ka.* Tengendō Shobō, 1917; *TYAZ* 15:418–19.

"Murasaki Shikibu no nikki ni kansuru watakushi no hakken." In *Ai, risei oyobi yūki.* Oranda Shobō, 1917; *TYAZ* 16:49–61.

"Murasaki Shikibu no teisō ni tsuite." In *Wakaki tomo e.* Hakusuisha, 1918; *TYAZ* 16:370–71.

"Izumi Shikibu kashū." In *Meicho hyōron bunshū* 1. Kōbunkan, 1919 [with Hiroshi]. This edition appears to be a reprint of *Meicho kōgai oyobi hyōron sōsho* 11. Meicho Hyōronsha, 1915. I have not seen the 1915 publication. Reprinted 1936.

"Genji monogatari raisan." *Myōjō,* 2nd ser. 1.3 (January 1922): 3–8; *TYAZ* 4:323–31.

"Emaki no tame ni," set of eighty *tanka* consisting of the fifty-four 'Genji monogatari raisan' poems, twenty-one poems on topics from *Eiga monogatari,* and five poems on topics from *Heike monogatari.* In *Ryūsei no michi.* Shinchōsha, 1924; *TYAZ* 4:323–36.

"Heian-chō no josei." *Josei kaizō* 3.9 (September 1924): 64–69.

"Koten no kenkyū." *Myōjō,* 2nd ser., 6.2 (February 1925): 148–51; *TYAZ* 19:84–86.

"Nihon koten zenshū kankō shushi." *Myōjō,* 2nd ser., 7.3 (September 1925): 130–31 [with Hiroshi and Masamune Atsuo].

"Genji monogatari kaidai." In *Genji monogatari.* 5 vols. Nihon koten zenshū series. Nihon Koten Zenshū Kankōkai, 1926, 1:1–8.

"Eiga monogatari jōkan kaidai," and "Eiga monogatari gekan kaidai." In *Eiga monogatari.* 3 vols. Nihon koten zenshū series. Nihon Koten Zenshū Kankōkai, 1926, 1:1–12 and 3:1–9. Reprinted in *Rekishi monogatari I.* Edited by Masubuchi Katsuichi, Nihon bungaku kenkyū shiryō sōsho series. Yūseidō, 1971, 31–40.

"Midō kanpaku ki kaidai," and "Midō kanpaku kashū no nochi ni." In *Midō kanpaku ki.* 2 vols. Nihon koten zenshū series. Nihon Katen Zenshū Kankōkai, 1926, 1:1–12 and 2:1–4 at end of volume.

"Genji monogatari kōyō jo." In *Genji monogatari kōyō,* by Fujita Tokutarō. Furōkaku Shobō, 1928, 1–9.

"Murasaki Shikibu shinkō." *Taiyō* (January, February 1928). Reprinted in *Genji monogatari I.* Edited by Mitani Kuniaki, Nihon bungaku kenkyū shiryō sōsho series. Yūseidō, 1969, 1–16. *TYAZ* 12:478–508.

"Izumi Shikibu shinkō." In *TYAZ* 12:509–51. The essay is a revised version of the three earlier essays "Onna shijin Izumi Shikibu (jō)," *Josei* 13.1 (January 1928): 209–16; "Onna shijin Izumi Shikibu (chū)," *Josei* 13.2 (February 1928): 119–29; and "Onna shijin Izumi Shikibu (ge)," *Josei* 13.3 (March 1928): 98–115.

"Izumi Shikibu no uta." In *Tanka kōza* 8. Kaizōsha, 1932, 75–88.

"Murasaki Shikibu—Nihon josei retsuden." *Fujin kōron* 20.9 (September 1935): 214–17.

Heianchō joryū nikki. Gendaigoyaku kokubungaku zenshū series 9. Hibonkaku, 1938, containing Akiko's translation of *Kagerō nikki,* as well as reprints of *Shin'yaku Izumi Shikibu nikki* and *Shin'yaku Murasaki Shikibu nikki.*

"Sawarabi Genji." *Tōhaku* 10.3 (March 1939): 38–49. A draft of the 'Sawarabi' chapter from *Shin-shin'yaku Genji monogatari.*

"Ukifune." *Tōhaku* 10.5 (May 1939): 51–59; 10.7 (July 1939): 10–19; 10.8 (August 1939): 57–66; 10.9 (September 1939): 42–45; and 10.10 (October 1939): 48–53. A serialization of the 'Ukifune' chapter, also from *Shin-shin'yaku Genji monogatari.*

Shin-shin'yaku Genji monogatari. 6 vols. Kanao Bun'endō, 1938–39.
Kashū Izumi Shikibu. Naigai Shuppansha, 1939 [with Hiroshi].
    Unseen, but almost certainly a reprint of "Izumi Shikibu kashū."
    Meicho hyōronshū 1. Kōbunkan, 1919.
[Kōgai] Genji monogatari. Edited by Tsurumi Daigaku Bungakubu.
Yokohama: Tsurumi Daigaku, 1993.

Appendix B:
Selected Translations

I: "AFTER *SHIN'YAKU GENJI MONOGATARI*"

I began writing the present work in January of Meiji 44 [1911], and by October of Taishō 2 [1913] I had completed it. During these few short years, I was unable to spend all of my time preparing the translation. I was perpetually pushed to the limit by the pressure of work, both with my family and in my study. During this time I traveled to Europe and I was twice confined; one of these confinements was a difficult birth in which my life was at risk.[1] Nonetheless, sustained by the interest that I have had in the original work since I was twelve or so, the translation has been the core of my work for the past three years, and by dint of these meager efforts, I have been able to complete it earlier than we had initially planned. In retrospect, I am not without a feeling of relief that I have managed to accomplish this feat.

The Tale of Genji is my favorite book among the classics [*koten*] of our country. To be frank, when it comes to the understanding and appreciation of this novel [*shōsetsu*], I have the stubborn confidence of a master.

As regards my approach to the translation process, in the same way that in painting circles beginners may venture free renditions in order to emulate masterpieces from earlier ages, I eliminated those fine points which, being alien to modern life, we have no sympathy with nor interest in, and the excessive nicety of which needlessly puts [readers] off; my principal endeavor was to delineate the spirit of the original using the instrument of the modern language. I endeavoured

1. See chapter four, p. 80, n. 23.

to be both scrupulous and bold. I did not always adhere to the expressions of the original author; I did not always translate literally. Having made the spirit of the original my own, I then ventured a free translation.

Needless to say, I do not hold in high regard any of the existing commentaries on *The Tale of Genji*. In particular, I find *Kogetsushō* a careless work that misinterprets the original.

For the reason that I did not feel that any more was necessary, I have attempted a somewhat abbreviated translation of the chapters following the first chapter 'Kiritsubo,' as these are chapters which have long been widely read and offer few difficulties. From the second volume of the present work, however, for the benefit of those who might find it difficult to read the original, I paid careful attention to the meaning and adopted the method of virtually complete translation.

The Tale of Genji can be divided into two large parts: the part in which Hikari [sic] and Murasaki are the main characters, and the part in which Kaoru and Ukifune are the main characters. When we reach the ten Uji chapters in the second part, the extreme glitter and refinement of the exquisite narrative of the first part give way to simpler descriptive passages. This air of freshness, this sense of rejuvenation, is the product of Murasaki Shikibu's genius, ever vigorous, at which one can only marvel. If there are those who do not go as far as the ten Uji chapters when reading *The Tale of Genji,* they cannot be called people who have read the whole of Murasaki Shikibu.

None of the principal characters in *The Tale of Genji,* neither men nor women, is given a name. Therefore, past readers have borrowed words from poems with which the characters are associated, using them as nicknames. For the sake of convenience, I have followed these customary appellations in the present work.

At the outset, when the first volume of the present work was published, Mori [Ōgai] Sensei and Ueda [Bin] Sensei—whom I have held in high regard since the time when I read *Mesamashigusa* and *Bungakkai*—*both* Doctors of Letters, were good enough to bestow upon this witless author prefaces she did not deserve. Such encouragement I shall ever esteem. Nor I alone; the author's descendants shall likewise long regard it an honor.

I am grateful, too, to the master artist Nakazawa,[2] who from beginning to end, and always consulting the author's wishes, has devoted enormous effort to the illustrations and decoration of the book. His great talents have brought to life the tremendous diversity of scenes contained in the fifty-four chapters, giving the book a striking luster. There are not a few illustrated scrolls of *The Tale of Genji* in existence, but this master's illustrations are the first to develop a new approach in the European style.

In order to read *The Tale of Genji*, it is necessary to understand the Heian court and the lives of the nobility that formed its background. Therefore, following upon the present work, I have turned my attention to a new translation of *Eiga monogatari*, a realistic novel [*shajitsu shōsetsu*] that takes the history of that period as its subject.

In conclusion, I wish to add that in the summer of last year, in Paris, I personally presented copies of the first two volumes of this work to the sculptor Auguste Rodin Sensei, and the poet Henri de Régnier Sensei.[3] Rodin Sensei looked through the illustrations and, exclaiming all the while over the beauty of the Japan se woodblock prints, he said:

> The number of people in France and in Japan studying the language and thought of our two countries will gradually increase. I bitterly regret being unable to read Japanese, but I trust that one day in the future I shall be able to appreciate the thought of this book by means of a friend's translation.

The memory of his words is still fresh in my mind.

Taishō 2 [1913], October
Yosano Akiko[4]

II: "AFTERWORD," *SHIN-SHIN'YAKU GENJI MONOGATARI*

At this point in history there is no need to explain the value of the vast *Tale of Genji*, that immortal shining light of Oriental literature.

---

2. "Nakazawa Gahaku," that is, Nakazawa Hiromitsu (1874–1964).
3. Henri de Régnier (1864–1936) was a French writer associated with the Symbolist movement.
4. Yosano Akiko, "Shin'yaku Genji monogatari no nochi ni," in *Shin'yaku Genji monogatari* (Kanao Bun'endō, 1912–13), 4:1–7 at end of volume.

Twenty years ago, at the behest of the owner of Kanao Bun'endō, I translated *The Tale of Genji* in abbreviated form. This was the *Shin'yaku Genji monogatari*. Included were prefaces by the two Doctors of Letters, Mori Rintarō and Ueda Bin, and illustrations by the master artist, Nakazawa Hiromitsu. For the past twenty-some years I have felt ashamed of my crude translation, which is a sin against these three Sensei. It has been my hope that as an apology to the three Sensei, I might one day be able to rewrite it as a complete version, but the realization of this was difficult. Seven years ago, in the autumn [of 1932], I suddenly resolved that come what may, I had to make the time to fulfill my responsibility to retranslate *Genji*. I began writing immediately, and I continued writing; I hurried on lest what was left of my life be over before I should finish. But in the spring of 1935 I lost my husband. Needless to say, the chores I had to do as sole support of the family increased. On the other hand, I also felt that I had not the strength in my crushed heart to do more than compose poems. By that time, including the work done during my husband's illness, I had gone as far as the 'Hashihime' chapter. I had not even made a fair copy of the chapters after 'Wakana.' I wasted two years staring at the *Shin-shin'yaku* manuscript piled up like a wall. It was then that in Kyoto I met the head of Bun'endō, who had moved his business to Osaka some years previously. He is a man who has been good enough to favor me with his patronage ever since my earliest collections of poetry. When I heard that he wanted to open up a branch in Tokyo again, I told him of what I had done of *Shin-shin'yaku Genji monogatari*, and we agreed that it would be good if that should provide him with the opportunity of reopening in Tokyo. He was delighted. He even went to pay his respects to a Kannon in which he places great faith. He did not doubt that I had developed in the twentyeight years since I had handed over to him my first feeble efforts. Now that at last the book has been published, I join my hands in prayer to the Gods and Buddhas who have forgiven me the mortal sins of my [earlier] methods.

I believe that *The Tale of Genji* is a work in two parts by two authors, but I am unable to set forth my research on the matter in detail here. It has long been said that the ten Uji chapters are the work of Murasaki Shikibu's daughter Daini no Sanmi. Many Tokugawa period scholars of National Learning denied this. Formerly I too was so persuaded. In the Meiji period, when Dr. Kume Kunitake (1839–1931) wrote in a Noh journal that *Genji* appears to have been written by several people, I did not at all believe him, thinking that although Dr. Kume was a first-rate scholar of history he was no scholar of literature.[5] It was some years before I began work on the *Shin-shin'yaku* that I realized that there were two authors of *Genji*. The work of the first author ends at 'Fuji no Uraba'—everything is very auspicious, and after Genji becomes *Daijō Tennō* everything is tinted in gold. Undaunted, the second author begins to write about Genji facing a turn in his fortunes. The woman he loved best, the lady Murasaki, dies; and there is also Nyosan no Miya's [Onnasannomiya's] indiscretion. In preparation for the birth of Kaoru, the main character of the latter part, the court in the reign of the retired Emperor Suzaku is suddenly introduced. Suzaku's pathetic fondness for Nyosan no Miya prepares the way for the bounty of Kaoru; the skill with which the novel is here structured surpasses that of the first part.

If one reads the original with care, one ought to notice that from 'Wakana' on the style *(bunshō)* is different. What had without fail been *kandachime, tenjōbito* becomes *shodayū, tenjōbito, kandachime*. This should be immediately apparent to those who read a recent movable type edition rather than an old manuscript or woodblock-printed edition. The style is bad, and poems are fewer. Moreover, great poems are exceedingly scarce. The first part, written by Murasaki Shikibu, abounds in superb poems. Not that there are none whatsoever in the second part:

> *Me ni chikaku utsureba kawaru yo no naka o*
> *yukusue tōku tanomikeru kana.*[6]
> Before my very eyes it changes, this bond between us;
>   and I trusted it to last for ever and ever.
>
> *Obotsukana tare ni towamashi ika ni shite*
> *hajime mo hate mo shiranu waga mi zo.*[7]
> This uncertainty: whom might I ask; and why is it so?
>   I know nothing of whence I come or whither I shall go.

5. The essay by Kume Kunitake that Akiko mentions here is "*Genji monogatari* no sakusha oyobi sono setsu," *Nōgaku* 7.5 (1909): 1–7.
6. The lady Murasaki to Genji in 'Wakana jō,' 4:58; S 555. Translation by T.J. Harper, "More *Genji* Gossip," in *Journal of the Association of Teachers of Japanese* 28.2 (November 1994): 180.
7. Kaoru in 'Niau' (His Perfumed Highness), 5:18; S 737. Translation in Harper, "More *Genji* Gossip," 181.

These superb poems closely resemble the first poem in the autumn section of the *Goshūishū* [completed 1086], by Daini no Sanmi:

> *Harukanaru morokoshi made mo yuku mono wa*
> *aki no nezame no kokoro narikeri.*[8]
> Waking, in the autumn,
>   it is as if one travels even to distant Cathay.

At the beginning of the 'Takekawa' chapter, which is couched as a tale told by an elderly serving woman who had worked in the household of the late Chancellor [Higekuro], it is written, *"Murasaki no yukari koyonaki niwa nizameredo."*[9] This passage means: "what follows will not be of the same quality as the previous chapters written by Murasaki Shikibu," and it is wrong of commentators to interpret it as referring to the [character] lady Murasaki. It would be strange, would it not, to draw a comparison between the descendants (*yukari*) of the lady Murasaki, who had no children, and those of another household.

'When I was doing this research in the past, I calculated twenty-six years as the period between the writing of the first part [of *Genji*] and the writing of the second part. The era of the Heian court had already given way to an era in which provincial administrators using military force were beginning to gain power. One such is the rich man who, having been governor of Michinoku, becomes vice-governor of Hitachi.[10]

It is still possible to see a plaque in the hand of Emperor Go-Reizei in the temple next door to the Byōdō-in. In Chinese diaries kept by men of the period, it is written that when Go-Reizei was Crown Prince, he often went to visit the mansion of Yorimichi in Uji.[11] Daini no Sanmi was Emperor Go-Reizei's wet-nurse; in his entourage she went often to Uji and came to know the place well.

---

8. The poem is actually the first in the second of the autumn chapters of the *Senzaiwakashū* (completed 1187). *Shinpen Kokka taikan,* 1:191c, no. 302.
9. Cf. 5:53. S 751 gives "[i]t may not seem entirely in keeping with the story of Murasaki."
10. Ukifune's stepfather; see 5:448; S 920–21.
11. Fujiwara Yorimichi (992–1074), eldest son of Michinaga, and Regent for fifty-two years during the reigns of Emperor Go-Ichijō (r. 1016–36), Go-Suzaku (r. 1036–45), and Go Reizei (r. 1045–68).

As for the poems, they are not as good as those of the author of the first part, but neither are they ordinary. As a masterly novel in the hand of one who had distinguished herself as a poet at that time, I have searched high and low for Daini no Sanmi's personal poetry collection (*Daini no Sanmi no ie no shū*), but it is no longer extant. I carefully examined the *Daini shū,* which is listed in the catalogue of Kōgakukan in Ise, but it is the work of Sanmi's daughter, the woman known [also] as Sanmi who served Go-Reizei's consort; and the compositions are far inferior to her mother's poems, let alone her grandmother's.

By the time of the *Sarashina nikki,* Ukifune was already the subject of conversation, but because the *Sarashina nikki,* which begins with an account of the author's younger days, was written in her later years, it is possible that she does not always remember correctly. Although in my estimate of twenty-six years I took into account the year in which the Sarashina diarist returned to the capital [c. 1020], I may have overestimated this period.

The author whose style and narrative technique in 'Wakana' is rough, has by 'Kashiwagi,' by 'Yūgiri,' become a splendid writer. I say this because the content [of these chapters] so abounds with genius. From 'Azumaya' on, her technique, quite as the content, is magnificent. The author of the first part, Murasaki Shikibu, was extraordinary as a novelist (*shōsetsu sakka*) and as a poet (*kajin*); Daini no Sanmi, who wrote the second part, was in my opinion a great general practitioner of literature (*bungakusha*). It is a shame that I do not have the time to explain this in more detail.

I am very happy that the artist with whom I am on the closest terms, Masamune Tokusaburō, has been good enough to design the frontispiece and the bindings.

Shōwa 14 [1939]
Yosano Akiko[12]

---

12. Yosano Akiko, "Shin-shin'yaku Genji monogatari atogaki," translated from the reprint in *Akiko koten kanshō,* 37–39.

List of Characters

Abe Tomoji　阿部知二
Akarumi e　明るみへ
Akebono Joshi　曙女史
Amayo monogatari damikotoba
　　雨夜物語だみことば
Andō Tameakira　安藤為章
Ansei　安政
aoi　葵
Arakida Rei　荒木田麗
Arishima Ikuma　有島生馬
Arishima Takeo　有島武郎
Arisugawa no Miya　有栖川宮
Asada Sada　浅田サダ／信
Asahi shinbun　朝日新聞
Asakasha　浅香社
Asakusa　浅草
Azumakagami　吾妻鑑
Ban Kōkei　伴蒿蹊
Bashō　芭蕉
Bungakkai　文学界
Bungei kurabu　文藝倶楽部
bungo　文語
Bunka Gakuin　文化学院
bushidō　武士道

Byōdōin　平等院
Chikuhakuen　竹柏園
Chikuhakuen Joshi　竹柏園女史
Chikuhakukai　竹柏会
chō　町
Chōbunsai Eishi　鳥文斎栄之
Chō Tsuratsune　長連恒
Chōwa　長和
Chūgaku sekai　中学世界
Chūō kōron　中央公論
Chūō Kōronsha　中央公論社
Daini no Sanmi　大弐三位
Dokusō　毒草
Eiga monogatari　栄華物語
Eiga monogatari shōkai　栄華物
　　語詳解
Ehon tsūzoku sangokushi　絵本通
　　俗三国志
Emaki no tame ni　絵巻のために
En naki tokei　縁なき時計
Fujii Shiei　藤井紫影
Fujimi-chō　富士見町
Fujita Tokutarō　藤田徳太郎
Fujiwara Kintō　藤原公任

Fujiwara Koreyuki　藤原伊行

Fujiwara Michinaga　藤原道長

Fujiwara Nobutaka　藤原宣孝

Fujiwara Sanesuke　藤原実資

Fujiwara Shunzei　藤原俊成

Fujiwara Tametoki　藤原為時

Fujiwara Teika　藤原定家

Fujiwara Yorimichi
　　藤原頼通

Fujiwara Yukinari　藤原行成

Fujo no kagami　婦女の鑑

Fujo shinbun　婦女新聞

Fukagawa　深川

furigana　振り仮名

furi-kanji　振り漢字

Fūryūbutsu　風流仏

Furyū Genji monogatari
　　風流源氏物語

fuseji　伏字

gabuntai　雅文体

gagaku　雅楽

geijutsu　芸術

genbun'itchi　言文一致

gendaigoyaku　現代語訳

Genji kokagami　源氏小鏡

Genji monogatari　源氏物語

Genji monogatari kōgai
　　源氏物語梗概

Genji monogatari kōyō
　　源氏物語綱要

Genji monogatari raisan
　　源氏物語礼讃

Genji monogatari tai'i
　　源氏物語大意

Genji nannyo shōzokushō
　　源氏男女装束抄

Genji shaku　源氏釈

Genpei seisuiki　源平盛衰記

gidayū　義太夫

gōkanbon　合巻本

Gonki　権記

Go-Reizei Tennō　後冷泉天皇

Goshūiwakashū　後拾遺和歌集

Gotō Shōko　後藤祥子

Haginoya　萩の舎

Hagiwara Hiromichi　萩原広道

haikai　俳諧

haibun　俳文

Hakubunkanbon　博文館本

Hana no ran　華の乱

Hatsukoi　初恋

Hayashi Takino　林滝野

Heike monogatari　平家物語

Higuchi Ichiyō　樋口一葉

Hiratsuka Raichō　平塚らいてう

Hinata [Hayashi] Kimu
　　日向[林]きむ

hōben　方便

hon'an　翻案

Honchōreisō　本朝麗藻

Honjo　本所

Horiguchi Daigaku　堀口大学

Hō Shizu　鳳志津

Hō Shō　鳳志よう／晶

hoshūka　補習科

Hō Sōshichi　鳳宗七

Hō Tsune　鳳津祢

Hō Zenshichi　鳳善七

Honzō wamyō　本草和名

Ichijō Kaneyoshi　一条兼良

Ichijō Tennō　一条天皇

Ichikawa Chihiro　市川千尋

Iga no taome　伊賀ノ太乎女

Ihara Saikaku　井原西鶴

Ikeda Kikan　池田亀鑑

Ikeda Toshio　池田利夫

Imakagami　今鏡

lmameki no chūjō　今様ノ中将

Inō Kōken　稲生恒軒

Ise　伊勢

Ise monogatari　伊勢物語

Itō Hirobumi　伊藤博文

Itsumi Kumi　逸見久美

Iwamoto Yoshiharu　巌本善治

Izumi Shikibu　和泉式部

Izumi Shikibu nikki
　和泉式部日記

Jippensha Ikku　十返舎一九

jōcho　情緒

Jogaku zasshi　女学雑誌

jōruri　浄瑠璃

Joshi bundan　女子文壇

Jūjō Genji　十帖源氏

Jun-Daijō Tennō　準太上天皇

Jun'ichirō yaku Genji monoga-
　tari　潤一郎訳源氏物語

jūnihitoe no haregi　十二単衣の
　晴着

kabuki　歌舞伎

Kagamigusa　鏡草

kagamimono　鏡物

(Kagawa) Kageki　香川景樹

Kagerō nikki　蜻蛉日記

Kagurazaka　神楽坂

Kaibara Ekiken　貝原益軒

Kamoko　鴨子

Kamo no Mabuchi　賀茂真淵

Kanao Bun'endō　金尾文淵堂

Kanao Tanejirō　金尾種次郎

Kanda　神田

Kankō　寛弘

Kansai bungaku　関西文学

Kansai Seinen Bungakkai　関西青
　年文学会

Kanso magai mitate gundan　漢楚
　賽擬選軍談

Kanzawa Tami　神沢民

Kanzawa Tokō　神沢杜口

kashihon'ya　貸本屋

Katō Umaki　加藤美樹／宇万伎

Kawai Suimei　河井酔茗

Keichū　契中

keigo　敬語

Keishū Bungakkai　閨秀文学会

Keishū shōsetsuka no kotae
　閨秀小説家の答

Kenshi　妍子

Ken'yūsha　硯友社

Keriko　梟子
kibun　気分
Kimata Osamu　木俣修
Kimura Eiko　木村栄子
Kinki　近畿
Kinoshita Mokutarō
　　木下杢太郎
Kishiya Seizō　岸谷勢蔵
Kitamura Kigin　北村季吟
Kitamura Koshun　北村湖春
Kitayama Keita　北山谿太
Kobayashi Masaharu (Tenmin)
　　小林政治（天眠）
Kobayashi Yūko　小林雄子
Kōda Rohan　幸田露伴
Kōgakukan　皇学館
Koganei Kimi(ko)
　　小金井きみ（子）
Kogetsushō　湖月抄
kōgo　口語
kohanpon　古版本
Koigoromo　恋衣
Koi murasaki　戀むらさき
Kojiki　古事記
Kojikiden　古事記伝
Kōjimachi　麹町
Kōjirin　広辞林
Kokinwakashū　古今和歌集
kokkeibon　滑稽本
Kokoro no hana　心の華
kokubungaku　国文学
kokubungakusha　国文学者

kokugaku　国学
Kokugakuin　国学院
kokugakusha　国学者
kokumin　国民
Kokumin no tomo　國民之友
kokuminsei　国民性
kokutai　国体
Kōmyōji Saburō　光妙寺三郎
Konakamura Kiyonori
　　小中村清矩
Konakamura Yoshikata
　　小中村義象
Kōno Tetsunan　河野鉄南
Koōgi　小扇
Kōshoku ichidai otoko
　　好色一代男
koten　古典
kōten　皇典
Kōten kōkyūsho　皇典講究所
Koten kōshūka　古典講習科
Kotoba no izumi　ことばの泉
Kotoba no tama no o　詞玉緒
kouta　小唄
Kuga Katsunan　陸羯南
kugiri　区切り
Kujō Tanemichi　九条稙通
Kumazawa Banzan　熊沢蕃山
Kume Kunitake　久米邦武
kumikyoku　組曲
Kunikida Doppo　国木田独歩
kusazōshi　草々紙
Kyōbashi　京橋

Kyokutei (Takizawa) Bakin
曲亭（滝沢）馬琴

Kyōto machi bugyō　京都町奉行

Maihime　舞姫

Mainichi shinbun　毎日新聞

Makura no sōshi　枕草紙

Man'yōshū　万葉集

Masamune Atsuo　正宗敦夫

Masamune Hakuchō　正宗白鳥

Masamune Tokusaburō
正宗得三郎

Masatomi Ōyō　正富注洋

Masuda Masako　増田雅子

Masukagami　増鏡

Matsukage nikki　松蔭日記

Matsunaga Teitoku　松永貞徳

Matsuo Bashō　松尾芭蕉

Matsuo Taseko　松尾多勢子

Meigetsuki　明月記

Mesamashigusa　めさまし草

Midaregami　みだれ髪

Midō kanpaku ki　御堂関白記

mikaeshi　見返し

Mikami Sanji　三上参次

Minamoto Tamenori　源為憲

Mina no kawa　女男能加和

Mingō nisso　岷江入楚

minkan　民間

Mitani Kuniaki　三谷邦明

Miyake Kaho　三宅花圃

Miyake Setsurei　三宅雪嶺

Miyako no hana　都の花

Miyako shinbun　都新聞

Mizoguchi Hakuyō　溝口白羊

monogatari　物語

Mori Fujiko　森藤子

Mori Ōgai　森鴎外

Motoori Norinaga　本居宣長

Motoori Ōhira　本居大平

Motoori Uchitō　本居内遠

Mune no omoi　胸の思

Murasaki Shikibu　紫式部

Murasaki Shikibu nikki
紫式部日記

Murasaki Shikibu shinkō
紫式部新考

Murasaki Shikibu shū　紫式部集

Myōjō　明星

Naden　南殿

Nagai Kafū　永井荷風

Nagano　長野

nagi　竹柏

Nagizono　竹柏園

Nagoya　名古屋

Nakae Tōju　中江藤樹

Nakai no jijū　中居ノ侍従

Nakajima Hirotari　中島広足

Nakajima Utako　中島歌子

Nakanoin Michikatsu　中院通勝

Nakazawa Hiromitsu　中沢弘光

Nansō Satomi hakkenden
南総里見八犬伝

nasakenai　情けない

nazukeoya　名付親

Nihonbashi　日本橋

Nihon bungaku zensho
　日本文学全書

Nihongi　日本紀

Nihon koten zenshū
　日本古典全集

nikki　日記

ninjō　人情

ninjōbon　人情本

ninjō shōsetsu　人情小説

Niroku shinpō　二六新報

Nise murasaki inaka Genji
　修紫田舎源氏

Nitobe Inazō　新渡戸稲造

Nonoguchi Ryūho　野々口立圃

Noto no Eikan　能登の永閑

Numata Gabimaru　沼田娥眉丸

Nunami Keion　沼波瓊音

oboshi iraruru　思し入らるる／焦
　らるる

Ochiai Naobumi　落合直文

Ōe no Chisato　大江千里

Ogikubo　荻窪

Ōgimachi Machiko　正親町町子

Ōkagami　大鏡

Oka Kazuo　岡一男

Okinagusa　翁草

Omokage　於母影

Onoe Torako　尾上登良子

Ono no Komachi　小野小町

Ōsaka Mainichi Shinbun
　大阪毎日新聞

Osana Genji　おさな源氏

Ozaki Kōyō　尾崎紅葉

Ozaki Masayoshi　尾崎雅嘉

ren'ai　恋愛

renga　連歌

Rihaku [Li Bo]　季白

rinri　倫理

risō　理想

Ryūsei no michi　流星の道

Ryūtei Tanehiko　柳亭種彦

Saganoya Omuro　嵯峨の屋お室

Sagoromo monogatari　狭衣物語

Saikun　細君

Sakai　堺

Sakai no shigai　堺の市街

Sanbōe　三宝絵

Santō Kyōden　山東京伝

Sarashina nikki　更級日記

Sasakawa Rinpū　笹川臨風

Sasaki Hirotsuna　佐々木弘綱

Sasaki Masako　佐々木昌子

Sasaki Nobutsuna　佐佐木信綱

Sassa Seisetsu　佐々醒雪

satogo　里子

Satō Haruo　佐藤春夫

Satō Kyū　佐藤球

Satomura Jōha　里村紹巴

Seigaiha　青海波

*Seirō hiru no sekai: Nishiki no
　ura*　青楼昼之世界錦之裏

Seiyōken　静養軒

Setagaya　世田谷

shajitsu　写実

shajitsu monogatari　写実物語

shajitsu shōsetsu　写実小説

sharebon　洒落本

Shigarami zōshi　柵草紙

Shiga Shigetaka　志賀重昂

shikishi　色紙

Shikitei Sanba　式亭三馬

Shimada Kashiko
　島田嘉志子

Shimada Utako　下田歌子

Shinchō　新潮

shinchū　新注

Shin'etsu　信越

shingai na/da　心外な／だ

shingeki　新劇

Shin kokin(waka)shu
　新古今(和歌)集

shinpan　新版

Shinpen shishi　新編紫史

Shinsaibashi　心斎橋

Shinseisha　新声社

Shinshaku Genji monogatari
　新釈源氏物語

Shin-shin'yaku Genji monogatari
　新々訳源氏物語

Shinshisha　新詩社

Shinshōjo　新少女

Shinshōsetsu　新小説

shintaishi　新体詩

Shin'yaku Eiga monogatari
　新訳栄華物語

Shin'yaku Genji monogatari
　新訳源氏物語

Shin-zen-bi Nihonjin
　真善美日本人

Shishinden　紫宸殿

Shitaya　下谷

shizenshugi　自然主義

shō　抄

Shōjo no tomo　少女の友

Shōkōshi　小公子

Shomoku jisshu　書目十種

shōsetsu　小説

Shōsetsu shinzui　小説神髄

Shōshi　彰子

Shōyūki　小右記

Shundeishū　春泥集

Shun'ōten　春鶯囀

Shunshoku umegoyomi
　春色梅児誉美

Shunshoshō　春曙抄

sōai　相愛

Sōchō　宗長

Sonpibunmyaku　尊卑分脈

Sōseki　宗碩

sōshiji　草子地

Subaru　昴

Suematsu Kenchō　末松謙澄

Sugawara Takasue no Musume
　菅原孝標女

Surugadai　駿河台

Surugaya　駿河屋

Taiheiki　太平記

Taionki　戴恩記

Taiyō　太陽

Takamura Kōtarō　高村光太郎

Takatsu Kuwasaburō　高津鍬三郎

Taketori monogatari　竹取物語

Takita Choin　滝田樗蔭

Tamakatsuma　玉勝間

Tama no ogushi　玉の小櫛

tamasasa　玉笹

Tamenaga Shunsui　為永春水

Tanabe Tatsuko　田辺龍子

Tanikawa Shuntarō　谷川俊太郎

Tanizaki Jun'ichirō　谷崎潤一郎

tanka　短歌

tanzaku　短冊

Teramoto Naohiko　寺本直彦

Togawa Shūkotsu　戸川秋骨

Tōhaku　冬柏

Tōkaidōchū hizakurige　東海道中膝栗毛

Tokugawa Tsunayoshi　徳川綱吉

tokuhon　読本

Tokutomi Sohō　徳冨蘇峰

Tokyo Joshi Daigaku　東京女子大学

Tōkyō nichinichi shinbun　東京日日新聞

torikoshigurō　取越苦労

Tosa no otodo　土佐ノ大殿

Tsubouchi Shōyō　坪内逍遥

Tsujihara Genpo　辻原元甫

Tsukubakai　筑波会

tsurashi　辛し

Tsurezuregusa　徒然草

Uchida Roan　内田魯庵

Uchino Benko　内野辣子

Ueda Bin　上田敏

Uji　宇治

Ukiyoburo　浮世風呂

uretashi　慨たし

Utsuho monogatari　宇津保物語

wabun　和文

Wada Hidematsu　和田英松

Wakamatsu Shizuko　若松賤子

Waseda bungaku　早稲田文学

Yabu no uguisu　薮の鴬

yakubun　訳文

Yamada Bimyō　山田美妙

Yamada Yoshio　山田孝雄

Yamaji Aizan　山路愛山

Yamakawa Tomiko　山川登美子

Yamato shōgaku　倭小学

Yanagisawa Yoshiyasu　柳沢吉保

Yoda Gakkai　依田学海

yōkan　羊羹

yome-iri dōgu　嫁入り道具

yomihon　読本

Yomiuri shinbun　読売新聞

Yoriki　与力

Yorozu chōhō　万朝報

Bibliography

Unless otherwise noted, the place of publication of Japanese works is Tokyo.

WORKS BY YOSANO AKIKO

With a couple of exceptions, only those works not collected in *Teihon Yosano Akiko zenshū* are cited separately.

Akarumi e. 1916. Reprint, *Sakka no jiden* 3. Nihon Tosha Sentaa, 1994.

Akiko koten kanshō. Yosano Akiko senshū, vol. 4. Edited by Yosano Hikaru and Shinma Shin'ichi. Shunshūsha, 1967.

"Eiga monogatari shōkai." *Myōjō* 8.5 (May 1907): 104–6.

"Genji monogatari." Tsurumi Daigaku Toshokan, MS. (913.365 Y).

"Genji monogatari kaidai." In *Genji monogatari*, ed. Yosano Hiroshi, Masamune Atsuo, and Yosano Akiko. 5 vols. Nihon koten zenshū series. Nihon Katen Zenshū Kankōkai, 1926, 1:1–8.

"Genji monogatari kōyō jo." In Fujita Tokutarō, *Genji monogatari kōyō*, 1–9.

"Genji monogatari raisan." *Myōjō* 2nd ser., 1.3 (1922): 3–8.

Kōgai Genji monogatari. Yokohama: Tsurumi Daigaku, 1993.

"Muikakan (nikki)," *Bunshō sekai* 7.5 (April 1912): 74–79.

Shin-shin'yaku Genji monogatari. 6 vols. Kanao Bun'endō, 1938–39. Reprint, *Nihon bunko*, vols. 20–25. Nihonsha, 1948–49.

"Shin-shin'yaku Genji monogatari atogaki." In *Shin-shin'yaku Genji monogatari*, 6:1–10 at end of volume.

Shin'yaku Genji monogatari. 4 vols. Kanao Bun'endō, 1912–13. Reprint, Shinkōsha, 1935.

"Shin'yaku Genji monogatari no nochi ni." In *Shin'yaku Genji monogatari*, vol. 4, 1–7 at end of volume. Kanao Bun'endō, 1912–13.

"Te no ue no kōri." *Joshi bundan* 4.5 (April 1908): 5–8.

Teihon Yosano Akiko zenshū (TYAZ). 20 vols. Edited by Kimata Osamu. Kōdansha, 1979–81.

Watakushi no oidachi. 1985. Reprint, Kankōsha, 1990.

Yosano Akiko kashū. 1938. Rev. ed., Iwanami Shoten, 1985.

Yosano Hiroshi Akiko shokanshū: Tenmin bunko zō. Edited by Ueda Ayako and Itsumi Kumi. Yagi Shoten, 1983.

Yosano Hiroshi Akiko shokan shūsei. Edited by Itsumi Kumi. 4 vols. Yagi Shoten, 2001–2003.

PRIMARY AND SECONDARY SOURCES

Abe Akio, Akiyama Ken, and Imai Gen'e, eds. *Genji monogatari*. 6 vols. *(NKBZ* 12–17). Shōgakukan, 1970–76.

Abe Tomoji. "Yosano Akiko no omoide." *Nihon no koten geppō*, no. 2 (Kawade Shobō Shinsha, 1971): no page numbers.

Akiyama Ken. "'Utsurikotoba' to iu koto." *Murasaki*, no. 21 (1984): 58–61.

———, ed. *Genji monogatari jiten*. Bessatsu kokubungaku series, no. 36. Gakutōsha, 1989.

Albertson, Nicholas. "Tangled *Kami*: Yosano Akiko's Supernatural Symbolism." *U.S.-Japan Women's Journal*, no. 47 (2014): 28–44.

Arntzen, Sonja and Moriyuki Itō. *The Sarashina Diary: A Woman's Life in Eleventh-Century Japan*. New York: Columbia University Press, 2014.

Aston, W. G. *A History of Japanese Literature*. New York: D. Appleton and Company, 1899.

Atsumi, Ikuko and Graeme Wilson. "The Poetry of Yosano Aldko." *Japan Quarterly* 21.2 (April-June 1974): 181–87.

Ban Kōkei. "Utsushibumi warawa no satoshi" (1794). In *Ban Kōkei shū*, edited by Kazama Seishi. Vol. 7 of *Sōsho Edo bunko*, edited by Takada Mamoru and Hara Michio. Kokusho Kankōkai, 1993.

Beichman, Janine. "Yosano Akiko: Return to the Female." *Japan Quarterly* 36.2 (April–June 1990): 204–28.

Beichman, Janine. "Portrait of a Marriage: The How and Why of Yosano Akiko's Paris Foray," *Transactions of the Asiatic Society of Japan*, 5th series, vol. 8 (2016): 135–55.

———. *Embracing the Firebird: Yosano Akiko and the Birth of the Female Voice in Modern Japanese Poetry*. Honolulu: University of Hawai'i Press, 2002.

———. "Akiko Goes to Paris: The European Poems." *Journal of the Association of Teachers of Japanese* 25.1 (1991): 123–45.

Bowring, Richard. Review of *Paragons of the Ordinary: The Biographical Literature of Mori Ōgai*, by Marvin Marcus. *Journal of Japanese Studies* 20.1 (Winter 1994): 230–34.

———. *Landmarks of World Literature: Murasaki Shikibu: The Tale of Genji*. Cambridge: Cambridge University Press, 1988.

———. *Murasaki Shikibu: Her Diary and Poetic Memoirs*. Princeton: Princeton University Press, 1982.

Brower, Reuben A. *Mirror on Mirror: Translation, Imitation, Parody*. Cambridge: Harvard University Press, 1974.

Brownstein, Michael C. "From *Kokugaku* to *Kokubungaku:* Canon-Formation in the Meiji Period." *Harvard Journal of Asiatic Studies* 47.2 (December 1987): 435–60.

Caddeau, Patrick W. *Appraising Genji: Literary Criticism and Cultural Anxiety in the Age of the Last Samurai*. Albany: State University of New York Press, 2006.

Chō Tsuratsune. *Genji monogatari kōgai*. Shinchōsha, 1906.

Chūō kōron 27.6 (June 1912): 127–44. Special issue "Yosano Akiko Joshi ron."

Clements, Rebekah. "Suematsu Kenchō and the First English Translation of *Genji monogatari*: Translation, Tactics, and the 'Women's Question'." *Japan Forum* 23.1 (2011): 25–47.

———. "Rewriting Murasaki: Vernacular Translation and the Reception of *Genji Monogatari* during the Tokugawa Period." *Monumenta Nipponica* 68.1 (2013): 1–36.

———. "Cross-Dressing as Lady Murasaki: Concepts of Vernacular Translation in Early Modern Japan." *Testo a Fronte*, no. 51 (2014): 29–51.

———. *A Cultural History of Translation in Early Modern Japan*. Cambridge: Cambridge University Press, 2015.

Clements, Rebekah and Niimi Akihiko, ed., *Genji monogatari no kinsei: zokugo-yaku, hon'an, e-iribon de yomu koten*. Bensei Shuppan, 2019.

Copeland, Rebecca L. "The Meiji Woman Writer 'Amidst a Forest of Beards'." *Harvard Journal of Asiatic Studies* 57.2 (1997): 383–418.

Cranston, Edwin A. *The Secret Island and the Enticing Flame: Worlds of Memory, Discovery, and Loss in Japanese Poetry*. Ithaca: Cornell East Asia Series, 2008.

Cranston, Edwin A. "Carmine-Purple: A Translation of 'Enji-Murasaki,' the First Ninety-Eight Poems of Yosano Aldko's *Midaregami*." *Journal of the Association of Teachers of Japanese* 25.1 (April 1991): 91–111.

———. "The Dark Path: Images of Longing in Japanese Love Poetry." *Harvard Journal of Asiatic Studies* 35 (1975): 60–100.

———. "Young Akiko: The Literary Debut of Yosano Akiko." *Literature East and West* 18.1 (1974): 19–43.

Daijinmei jiten. 10 vols. Heibonsha, 1957–58.

Danly, Robert Lyons. *In the Shade of Spring Leaves*. New Haven: Yale University Press, 1981.

Dodane, Claire. *Yosano Akiko: Poète de la passion et figure de proue du féminisme japonais*. Paris: Publications Orientalistes de France, 2000.

Eco, Umberto. *Six Walks in the Fictional Woods*. Cambridge: Harvard University Press, 1994.

———. *Interpretation and overinterpretation*. Edited by Stefan Collini. Cambridge: Cambridge University Press, 1992.

Emmerich, Michael. *The Tale of Genji: Translation, Canonization, and World Literature*. New York: Columbia University Press, 2013.

Fujii Sadafumi. "Kōten kōkyūshō." In *Kokushi daijiten* 5, edited by Kokushi Daijiten Henshū Iinkai. Yoshikawa Kōbunkan, 1985, 459.

Fujita Fukuo. "Shinshisha no patoron Kobayashi Tenmin." *Kokubungaku: kaishaku to kyōzai no kenkyū* 9.15 (December 1964): 135–38.

Fujita Tokutarō. *Genji monogatari kenkyū shomoku yōran*. Rokubunkan, 1932.

———. *Genji monogatari kōyō*. Furōkaku Shobō, 1928.

Fujiwara Teika. *Meigetsuki*. 3 vols. Edited by Hayakawa Junzaburō. Kōbundō, 1911–12.

Fukuda Kazuhiko, ed. *Ehon ukiyoe sen*. Kawade Shobō Shinsha, 1990.

Fukuda Kiyoto and Hamana Hiroko. *Yosano Akiko*. Hito to sakuhin series. Shimizu Shoin, 1968.

Fukunaga Takehiko. "Gendai no *Genji monogatari*." *Asahi shinbun*, 20 December 1964, 18.

Gendai Nihon bungaku zenshū. 99 vols. Chikuma Shobō, 1953–58.

Gluck, Carol. *Japans Modern Myths: Ideology in the Late Meiji Period*. Princeton: Princeton University Press, 1985.

Goldstein, Sanford and Seishi Shinoda. *Tangled Hair: Selected Tanka from Midaregami*. Lafayette, Ind.: Purdue University Studies, 1971. Reprint, Rutland, Vt. & Tokyo: Charles E. Tuttle, 1987.

Haga Noboru. "Bakumatsu henkakki ni okeru kokugakusha no undō to ronri." In *Nihon shisō taikei* 51, edited by Haga Noboru and Matsumoto Sannosuke. Iwanami Shoten, 1971, 662–714.

Haga Tōrn. *Midaregami no keifu*. Bijutsu Kōronsha, 1981.

Hagino Yoshiyuki, Ochiai Naobumi, and Konakamura Yoshikata, eds. *Nihon bungaku zensho*. 24 vols. Hakubunkan, 1890–92.

Hamill, Sam, and Keiko Matsui Gibson, trans. *River of Stars: Selected Poems of Yosano Akiko*. Boston and London: Shambala, 1996.

Harper, T. J. "Noringa on the Translation of *Waka:* His Preface to *A Kokinshū Telescope.*" In *The Distant Isle: Studies and Translations of Japanese Literature in Honor of Robert H. Brower*, edited by Thomas Hare, Robert Borgen, and Sharalyn Orbaugh, 205–30. Michigan Monograph Series in Japanese Studies, no. 15. Ann Arbor: Center for Japanese Studies, The University of Michigan, 1996.

———. "More *Genji* Gossip." *Journal of the Association of Teachers of Japanese* 28.2 (November 1994): 175–82.

———. "*The Tale of Genji* in the Eighteenth Century: Keichū, Mabuchi and Norinaga." In *18th Century Japan: Culture and Society*, edited by C. Andrew Gerstle, 106–23. Sydney: Allen and Unwin, 1989.

———. "Motoori Norinaga's Criticism of the *Genji monogatari:* A Study of the Background and Critical Content of his *Genji monogatari Tama no ogushi*." Ph.D. diss., University of Michigan, 1971.

Harper, Thomas and Haruo Shirane, ed. *Reading The Tale of Genji: Sources From the First Millennium*. New York: Columbia University Press, 2015.

Hidaka Hachirō. "Futatsu no Yosano Genji." *Tosha shinbun*, no. 720 (24 August 1963): 8.

Hinata Kimu. "Akiko-shi no Shin'yaku Genji monogatari o hyō su." *Joshi bundan* 9.11 (November 1913): 81–84; 9.12 (December 1913): 42–43; 10.1 (January 1914): 60–63; 10.2 (February 1914): 34–38.

Hiranuma Megumi and Igarashi Masataka. "*Genji monogatari* gendaigoyaku no nagare—Yosano Akiko kara Hashimoto Osamu made—." *Kokubungaku: kaishaku to kanshō* 59.3 (March 1994): 159–65.

Hiratsuka Raichō. *Genshi, josei wa taiyō de atta*. 2 vols. Ōtsuki Shoten, 1971.

Hisamatsu Sen'ichi. *Nihon bungaku kenkyūshi*. Yamada Shoin, 1957.

Hobsbawm, E.J. *Nations and Nationalism Since 1870: Programme, Myth, Reality*. 2nd ed. Cambridge: Cambridge University Press/Canto, 1992.

Ibuki Kazuko and G. G. Rowley. "'The Tanizaki *Genji*': Inception, Process, and Afterthoughts," with translations by Thomas Harper of Tanizaki Jun'ichirō's "On Translating *The Tale of Genji* into Modern Japanese" (1938) and "Some Malicious Remarks" (1965). In *The Grand Old Man and the Great Tradition: Essays on Tanizaki Jun'ichirō in Honor of Adriana Boscaro*, edited by Luisa Bienati and Bonaventura Ruperti, 25–52. Center for Japanese Studies, The University of Michigan, 2009. Open access edition: https://doi.org/10.3998/mpub.9340226.

Ichijō Kaneyoshi. *Kachō yosei.* Edited by Ii Haruki. *Genji monogatari kochū shūsei,* 1st ser., 1. Ōfūsha, 1978.

Ichikawa Chihiro. *Yosano Akiko to Genji monogatari.* Kokuken sōsho series, vol. 6. Ryūgasaki: Kokuken Shuppan, 1998.

———. "Yosano Akiko no kotenteki eihō ni tsuite." *Namiki no sato,* no. 46 (June 1997): 1–10.

———. "Yosano Akiko to *Genji monogatari*—hyōron, kansōbun ni mieru *Genji monogatari* ishiki—." In *Genji monogatari no shii to hyōgen,* edited by Uesaka Nobuo, 360–88. Shintensha kenkyū sōsho series, vol. 103. Shintensha, 1997.

———. "*Yokohama bōeki shinpō* to Akiko." *Namiki no sato,* no. 42 (June 1995): 35–41.

———. "Yosano Akiko no *Genji monogatari-ei*—kanmei no yomikomareta uta ni tsuite—" *Namiki no sato,* no. 40 (June 1994): 8–16.

———. "Yosano Akiko to koten—Akiko no koten santai—." *Kokubungaku: kaishaku to kanshō* 59.2 (February 1994): 136–40.

———. "Yosano Akiko no koten *sesshu*—*Sarashina nikki, Tsurezuregusa*—." *Namiki no sato,* no. 38 (June 1993): 1–10.

———. "Yosano Akiko to *Genji monogatari*—*sono* gyōseki to 'kako ni asobu' Akiko—." In *Kindai no kyōju ta kaigai to no kōryū,* edited by Imai Takuji et al., 44–55. Genji monogatari kōza series, vol. 9. Benseisha, 1992.

———. "Yosano Akiko to *Genji monogatari*—chimei o megutte—." *Namiki no sato,* no. 35 (December 1991): 80–87.

———. "Akiko-ka ni okeru *Genji monogatari* tōei—yōgo o chūshin ni—." *Heianchō bungaku kenkyū,* n.s., 1.3 (October 1987): 130–38.

———. "Akiko no uta ni miru *Genji monogatari.*" *Heian bungaku kenkyū,* no. 77 (May 1987): 249–61.

———. "Hirano Banri *Akiko shūkasen* ni okeru 'Genjifuri' rokujūnana shu ni tsuite." In *Genji monogatari to sono juyō,* edited by Teramoto Naohiko, 487–506. Yūbun Shoin, 1984.

———. "Yosano Akiko to *Genji monogatari*—*Midaregami* to 'Ukifune' o megutte—." *Heianchō bungaku kenkyū,* n.s., 1.2 (October 1983): 100–12. Translated by G. G. Rowley as "Yosano Akiko and *The Tale of Genji:* Ukifune and *Midaregami,*" *Journal of the Association of Teachers of Japanese* 28.2 (November 1994): 27–43.

Ichikawa Fusae. "Yosano Akiko-shi no omoide." *Teihon Yosano Akiko zenshū geppō,* no. 8 (July 1980): 3–6.

Ii Haruki. *Genji monogatari no densetsu.* Shōwa Shuppan, 1976.

Ikari Akira. *Ken'yūsha no bungaku.* Hanawa Shobō, 1961.

Ikeda Kikan. *Genji monogatari jiten.* 2 vols. Tōkyōdō Shuppan, 1960.

———. *Hana o oru.* Chūō Kōronsha, 1959.

Ikeda Setsuko. "Utsurikotoba." In *Genji monogatari jiten*. Bessatsu kokubungaku series, no. 36, edited by Akiyama Ken, 156–57. Gakutōsha, 1989.

Ikeda Toshio. "Kaisetsu." In *Kōgai Genji monogatari*, by Yosano Akiko. Yokohama: Tsurumi Daigaku, 1993, 1–16 at end of volume.

———. "Yosano Akiko no sōko nidai." *Tsurumi Daigaku kiyō*, no. 21 (February 1984): 131–62.

Inō Kōken. *Inago gusa* (1690). In *Nihon kyōiku bunko* 12, edited by Kurokawa Mamichi and Otaki Jun, 48–50. Dōbunkan, 1911.

Inokuma Natsuki, ed. *Teisei zōchū Genji monogatari Kogetsushō*. 5 vols. Osaka: Tosho Shuppan, 1890–91.

Irie Haruyuki. *Yosano Akiko no bungaku*. Ōfūsha, 1983.

———. "Saikin no Akiko kenkyū ni tsuite." *Tanka kenkyū geppō* no. 20 (November 1981): 4–6.

———. *Yosano Akiko shoshi*. Osaka: Sōgensha, 1957.

Itō Hiroshi. "Genji monogatari to kindai bungaku." *Kokubungaku: kaishaku to kanshō* 48.10 (July 1983): 135–40.

Itō Sei, et al., eds. *Shinchō Nihon bungaku shōjiten*. Shinchōsha, 1968.

Itsumi Kumi. *Maihime zenshaku*. Tanka Shinbunsha, 1999.

———. *Shin Midaregami zenshaku*. Yagi Shoten, 1996.

———. *Yume no hana zenshaku*. Yagi Shoten, 1994.

———. "*Midaregami*—Awatayama teisetsu to Saga no hitoyo—." *Kokubungaku: kaishaku to kanshō* 59.2 (February 1994): 49–52.

———. "Yosano Akiko no *Genji monogatari* kōgoyaku ni tsuite." *Kokugakuin zasshi* 94.1 (January 1993): 14–35.

———. *Koōgi zenshaku*. Yagi Shoten, 1988.

———. "Jisshō no teiji o." *Tanka shinbun*, 10 August 1985, 6.

———. "Hiroshi, Akiko no tegami kara mita Akiko Genji," *Komabano*, no. 33 (Tōkyō-to Kindai Bungaku Hakubutsukan, March 1982): 3–13.

———. *Midaregami zenshaku*. 1978. Rev. ed. Ōfūsha, 1986.

———. *Hyōden Yosano Tekkan Akiko*. Yagi Shoten, 1975.

Izumi Shikibu. *Izumi Shikibu nikki Izumi Shikibu shū*. Edited by Nomura Seiichi. Shinchō Nihon koten shūsei. Shinchōsha, 1981.

Journal of the Association of Teachers of Japanese 25.1 (April 1991). Special Issue "Yosano Akiko (1878–1942)."

Kaibara Ekiken. "Joshi o oshiyuru hō." In *Wazoku dōji kun*, edited by Ishikawa Ken. Iwanami Shoten, 1961.

Kamens, Edward. *The Three Jewels: A Study and Translation of Minamoto Tamenori's Sanbōe*. Michigan Monograph Series in Japanese Studies, no. 2. Ann Arbor: Center for Japanese Studies, The University of Michigan, 1988.

Kanao Tanejirō. "Akiko fujin to *Genji monogatari*." *Dokusho to bunken* 2.8 (August 1942): 7–9.

Kaneko Sachiyo. "Yosano Akiko to Mori Ōgai." *Ōgai to josei—Mori Ōgai ronkyū—*. Daitō Shuppansha, 1992.

Kannotō Akio. "Kaisetsu: *Shin'yaku Genji monogatari* to maboroshi no *Genji monogatari kōgi*." In *Yosano Akiko no Shin'yaku Genji monogatari*, 2 vols., 500–41. Kadokawa Shoten, 2001.

———. "Yosano Akiko *Shin'yaku Genji monogatari* shoshi shūi." *Genji kenkyū*, no. 8 (April 2003): 213–16.

———. "Yosano Akiko no yonda *Genji monogatari*." In *Genji monogatari e Genji monogatari kara*, edited by Nagai Kazuko, 269–302. Kasama Shoin, 2007.

———. "Yosano Akiko no rōdoku shita *Genji monogatari* no tekisuto wa nani ka: *Shin-shin'yaku Genji monogatari* no shūhen." *Heianchō bungaku kenkyū*, 2nd series, no. 16 (March 2008): 39–41.

———. "Yosano Akiko no *Shin-shin'yaku Genji monogatari* no shippitsu, seiritsu no kei'i." In *Genji monogatari no gendaigoyaku to hon'yaku*, edited by Kawazoe Fusae, 165–99. *Kōza Genji monogatari kenkyū* vol. 12. Ōfū, 2008.

———. "Akiko to ōchō jidai." *Kokubungaku: kaishaku to kanshō* 73.9 (September 2008): 38–46.

———. "Yosano Akiko *Shin-shin'yaku Genji monogatari* waka no seikaku: ikyo tekisuto no kaimei wa kanō ka." In *Heian bungaku no kōkyō: kyōju, sesshu, hon'yaku*, edited by Nakano Kōichi, 459–85. Bensei Shuppan, 2012.

———. "Shihatsuki no kindai kokubungaku to Yosano Akiko no *Genji monogatari* yakugyō." *Chūkō bungaku*, no. 92 (November 2013): 1–20. https://doi.org/10.32152/chukobungaku.92.0_1

———. "Yosano Akiko *Shin'yaku Genji monogatari* no seiritsu jijō to honmon no seikaku." *Kokugo to kokubungaku* 91.4 (April 2014): 3–20.

———. "Akiko, Genji, Pari." *Kokubungaku kenkyū*, no. 182 (June 2017): 1–17.

———. "Yosano Akiko ga kakikaeta *Shin'yaku Genji monogatari*: sono shutsugen fukyū to waka hon'yaku o megutte." In *Genji monogatari o kakikaeru: hon'yaku, chūshaku, hon'an*, edited by Terada Sumie, Katō Masayoshi, Hatanaka Chiaki, and Midorikawa Machiko, 157–73. Seikansha, 2018.

Kanzawa Tokō. "Mingō nisso." In *Okinagusa* book 141. *Nihon zuihitsu taisei*, 3rd ser., 13. Nihon Zuihitsu Taisei Kankōkai, 1931.

"Kashū sōmakuri." Review of *Midaregami*, by Yosano Akiko. *Kokoro no hana* 4.9 (September 1901): 77.

Katagiri Yōichi. "Yosano Akiko no koten kenkyū." *Joshidai bungaku: kokubun hen*, no. 43 (Ōsaka Joshi Daigaku Kokubungakka kiyō, March 1992): 18–40.

Kawai Suimei. "Akiko-san no Sakai jidai." *Shomotsu tenbō* 12.7 (July 1942): 72–79; 12.8 (August 1942): 85.

Kawazoe Fusae. *Genji monogatari jikūron*. Tokyo Daigaku Shuppankai, 2005.

"Keishū shōsetsuka no kotae." In *Jogaku zasshi*, no. 204 (15 March 1890): 104; no. 205 (22 March 1890): 127–28; no. 206 (29 March 1890): 158–59; no. 207 (5 April 1890): 187–90; no. 208 (12 April 1890): 216; no. 209 (19 April 1890): 247.

Kerlen, Henri. *De talloze treden naar mijn hart*. Soest: Kairos, 1987.

Kimata Osamu. *Kindai tanka no kanshō to hihyō*. Meiji Shoin, 1964.

Ki no Zankei. *Ise monogatari hirakotoba*. Edited by Imanishi Yūichirō. In *Tsūzoku Ise monogatari*, 2–142. Tōyō Bunko no. 535. Heibonsha, 1991.

Kindaichi Kyōsuke, et al., eds. *Shin-meikai kokugo jiten*. 4th ed. Sanseidō, 1989.

Kitamura Yuika. "*Genji monogatari* no saisei—gendaigoyaku ron." *Bungaku* 3.1 (Winter 1992): 44–53.

Kitayama Keita. *Genji monogatari jiten*. Heibonsha, 1957.

Kobayashi Tenmin. "Akiko *Genji* ni tsuite." *Uzu* 4.2 (February 1956): 1–3.

Koganei Kimi. "Yubi kuitaru onna." In *Kagekusa*, edited by Mori Rintarō [Ōgai], 614–17. Shun'yōdō, 1897.

Koganei Kimiko, "Genji kyōen," *Tōhaku* 10.10 (October 1939): 58.

Kokubungaku Kenkyū Shiryōkan, ed. *Kotenseki sōgō mokuroku*. 3 vols. Iwanami Shoten, 1990.

Kokuritsu Kokkai Toshokan, ed. *Meiji-ki kankō tosho mokuroku: Kokuritsu Kokkai Toshokan shozō*. 6 vols. Kokkai Toshokan, 1971–76.

Kokushi daijiten. 15 vols. Yoshikawa Kōbunkan, 1979–97.

Kokusho sōmokuroku: hoteiban. 8 vols. Iwanami Shoten, 1989–1990.

Kornicki, Peter F. "Unsuitable Books for Women: *Genji Monogatari* and *Ise Monogatari* in Late Seventeenth-Century Japan." *Monumenta Nipponica* 60.2 (2005): 147–93.

Kornicki, Peter F. *The Book in Japan: A Cultural History from the Beginnings to the Nineteenth Century*. Leiden, Boston, Koln: Brill, 1998.

———. *The Reform of Fiction in the Meiji Period*. London: Ithaca Press, 1982.

———. "The Survival of Tokugawa Fiction in the Meiji Period." *Harvard Journal of Asiatic Studies* 41.2 (December 1981): 461–82.

———. "The Novels of Ozaki Kōyō: A Study of Selected Works with Special Reference to the Relationship between the Fiction of the Tokugawa and Early Meiji Periods." D.Phil. diss., University of Oxford, 1979.

———. "*Nishiki no Ura:* An Instance of Censorship and the Structure of a *Sharebon*." *Monumenta Nipponica* 32.2 (Summer 1977): 153–88.

Kōuchi Nobuko. *Yosano Akiko—Shōwa-ki o chūshin ni—*. Domesu Shuppan, 1993.

Kōuchi Nobuko. *Yosano Akiko to shūhen no hitobito*. Sōjusha, 1998.

Kubo Kazuko. "Yosano Akiko: nazo." *Kokubungaku: kaishaku to kyōzai no kenkyū* 31.11 (September 1986): 132–33.

Kugimoto Hisaharu. "Kōgotai undō: Meiji no kokugo kaikaku undō." In *Kindai bungaku kōza*, vol. 1, edited by Nakano Shigeharu, 135–47. Kawade Shobō, 1952.

Kumasaka Atsuko. "Yosano Akiko." *Kokubungaku: kaishaku to kanshō* 37.10 (August 1972): 116–20.

"Kumikyoku *Genji monogatari* no fukikomi." *Fujo shinbun*, no. 1900 (8 November 1936):3.

Kurahashi Yōko. *Koi murasaki: shōsetsu Yosano Akiko*. Kōdansha, 1992.

Kurahashi Yōko and Takahashi Chizuru. *Koi murasaki—Yosano Akiko monogatari—*. 3 vols. Kōdansha, 1991.

Kuwahara Satoshi. "Tanizaki Genji no tokusei." *Heian bungaku kenkyū*, no. 77 (May 1987): 148–56.

Larson, Phyllis Hyland. "Yosano Akiko: The Early Years." Ph.D. diss., University of Minnesota, 1985.

Lewis, C. S. *Studies in Words*. 2nd ed. Cambridge: Cambridge University Press, 1967. Reprint Cambridge: Cambridge University Press/Canto, 1990.

Maeda Ai. *Kindai dokusha no seiritsu*. Yūseidō, 1973.

Maloney, Dennis and Hide Oshiro. *Tangled Hair: Love Poems of Yosano Akiko*. Fredonia, N. Y.: White Pine Press, 1987.

Manguel, Alberto. *A History of Reading*. London: HarperCollins, 1996.

Markus, Andrew L. *The Willow in Autumn: Ryūtei Tanehiko, 1783–1842.* Harvard Yenching Institute Monograph Series, no. 35. Cambridge and London: Council on East Asian Studies, Harvard University, 1992.

———. "Representations of *Genji monogatari* in Edo Period Fiction." Paper presented at the 8th conference on Oriental-Western Literary and Cultural Relations, Indiana University, August 1982.

Maruoka Katsura and Matsushita Daizaburō, eds. *Kokubun taikan.* 10 vols. Itakuraya, 1903–6.

Masamune Hakuchō. "Dokusho zakki (8)." In *Masamune Hakuchō zenshū,* vol. 9, 304–13. Shinchōsha, 1965.

———. "Saikin no shūkaku—Eiyaku *Genji monogatari* sono ta—." In *Masamune Hakuchō zenshū,* vol. 7, 184–88. Shinchōsha, 1967.

Masatomi Ōyō. *Akiko no koi to shi: jissetsu Midaregami.* San'ō Shobō, 1967.

Masubuchi Katsuichi, trans. *Yanagisawa Yoshiyasu sokushitsu no nikki—Matsukage nikki—.* Ryūgasaki: Kokuken Shuppan, 1999.

Masuda Yukinobu. *Shinpen shishi.* 10 vols. Various publishers, 1888–1904.

Matsuda Yoshio. *Midaregami kenkyū.* Isshōdō Shoten, 1952.

Matsumura Hiroji. "Kaisetsu." In *Eiga monogatari,* translated by Yosano Akiko, 418–22. *Koten Nihon bungaku zenshū,* vol. 9. Chikuma Shobō, 1962.

———. "Yosano Akiko no *Eiga monogatari* hihyō." *Heian bungaku kenkyū,* no. 20 (September 1957): 39–46; no. 21 (June 1958): 16–25.

Matsunaga Teitoku. *Taionki.* Edited by Odaka Toshia. *NKBT* 95. Iwanami Shoten, 1964.

May, Katharina. *Die Erneuerung der Tanka–Poesie in der Meiji-Zeit und die Lyrik Yosano Akikos.* Wiesbaden: Otto Harrassowitz, 1975.

McMullen, James. *Idealism, Protest and the Tale of Genji: The Confucianism of Kumazawa Banzan (1619–91).* Oxford: Oxford University Press, Clarendon Press, 1999.

———. *Genji gaiden: The Origins of Kumazawa Banzan's Commentary on The Tale of Genji.* Reading: Ithaca Press, 1991.

McKinney, Meredith, trans. *A Thousand Strands of Black Hair,* by Tanabe Seiko. London: Thames River Press, 2012.

Mehl, Margaret. "Suematsu Kenchō in Britain, 1878–1886." *Japan Forum* 5.2 (October 1993): 173–93.

Meiji bungaku zenshū. 100 vols. Chikuma Shobō, 1966–89.

Midorikawa, Machiko. "Coming to Terms with the Alien: Translations of *Genji Monogatari.*" *Monumenta Nipponica* 58.2 (2003): 193–222.

———. "Shifting Words from *Monogatari* to *Shōsetsu*: The Translation of Internal Speech in Japanese Literature." *Testo a Fronte,* no. 51 (2014): 131–46.

Mikami Sanji and Takatsu Kuwasaburō. *Nihon bungakushi.* 2 vols. Kinkōdō, 1890.

Miller, Roy Andrew. "Levels of Speech *(keigo)* and the Japanese Linguistic Response to Modernization." In *Tradition and Modernization in Japanese Culture,* edited by Donald H. Shively, 601–65. Princeton: Princeton University Press, 1971.

Minamoto Tamenori. *Sanbōe.* Edited by Mabuchi Kazuo and Koizumi Hiroshi. In *Sanbōe, Chūkōsen,* edited by Mabuchi Kazuo, Koizumi Hiroshi, and Konno

Tōru. Vol. 31 of *Shin Nihon koten bungaku taikei,* edited by Satake Akihiro et al. Iwanami Shoten, 1997.

Mitani Kuniaki. "Meiji-ki no *Genji monogatari* kenkyū." *Kokubungaku: kaishaku to kanshō* 48.10 (July 1983): 52–57.

———. "Kaisetsu." In *Genji monogatari I.* Nihon bungaku kenkyū shiryō sōsho series. Yūseidō, 1969.

Mitsutani, Margaret, trans. "A Mirror for Womanhood." *The Magazine* 3.5 (1988): 50–55; 3.6 (1988): 51–54.

Miyakawa Yōko. *Yanagisawa-ke no kotengaku (jō): Matsukage nikki.* Shintensha, 2007.

Miyake Setsurei. "Shin-zen-bi Nihonjin." In *Gendai Nihon bungaku zenshū,* vol. 5. Kaizōsha, 1931.

Miyamoto Masaaki. '"Maboroshi no Akiko Genji' to Tenmin Kobayashi Masaharu." *Ube kokubun kenkyū,* no. 24 (August 1993): 1–28.

Mizoguchi Hakuyō. *Katei shinshi Genji monogatari.* Okamura Shoten, Fukuoka Shoten, 1906.

Mori Fujiko. *Midaregami.* Rukkusha, 1967.

———. "Haha Yosano Akiko." *Fujin kōron* 28.1 (January 1943): 62–68; 28.2 (February 1943): 53–55; 28.4 (April 1943): 58–61; 28.5 (May 1943): 60–63.

Mori Mayumi. *Taishō bijinden: Hayashi Kimuko no shōgai.* Bungei Shunjū, 2000.

Mori Rintarō [Ōgai]. Untitled preface to *Shin'yaku Genji monogatari,* by Yosano Akiko, 1:1–6.

Morris, Ivan. *As I Crossed the Bridge of Dreams.* New York: Dial Press, 1971.

Morris, V Dixon. "The City of Sakai and Urban Autonomy." In *Warlords, Artists, and Commoners: Japan in the Sixteenth Century,* edited by George Elison and Bardwell L. Smith, 23–54. Honolulu: The University Press of Hawaii, 1981.

———. "Sakai: From Shōen to Port City." In *Japan in the Muromachi Age,* edited by John W. Hall and Toyoda Takeshi, 145–58. Berkeley: University of California Press, 1977.

Morton, Leith. "The Canonization of Yosano Akiko's *Midaregami.*" *Japanese Studies* 20.3 (2000): 237–54.

———. *The Alien Within: Representations of the Exotic in Twentieth-Century Japanese Literature.* Honolulu: University of Hawai'i Press, 2009.

Motoori Norinaga. *Motoori Norinaga zenshū.* Edited by Ōno Susumu and Ōkubo Tadashi. 23 vols. Chikuma Shobō, 1968–93.

Motoori Toyokai and Furuya Chishin, eds. *Genji monogatari.* Vols. 7–8 of *Kokumin bunko,* 1st ser. Kokumin Bunko Kankōkai, 1909–11.

Murai Toshihiko. Review of *Yosano Akiko to Genji monogatari* by Ichikawa Chihiro. *Tekkan to Akiko,* no. 5 (October 1999): 143–46.

Murasaki Shikibu. *Murasaki Shikibu nikki Murasaki Shikibu shū.* Edited by Yamamoto Ritatsu. Shinchō Nihon koten shūsei. Shinchōsha, 1980.

Nagahata Michiko. *Yume no kakehashi—Akiko to Takeo yūjō.* Shinhyōron, 1985.

Naito, Satoko, trans. "Seven Essays on Murasaki Shikibu," by Andō Tameakira. In *Reading The Tale of Genji,* edited by Thomas Harper and Haruo Shirane, 392–411. New York: Columbia University Press, 2015.

Nakada Norio, Wada Toshimasa, and Kitahara Yasuo, eds. *Kogo daijiten*. Shōgakukan, 1983.

Nakamura Yukihiko. "Kinsei no dokusha." In *Nakamura Yukihiko chojutsushū*, vol. 14, 38–67. Chūō Kōronsha, 1983.

Nedan-shi nenpyō: Meiji, Taishō, Shōwa. Edited by Shūkan Asahi. Asahi Shinbunsha, 1988.

Nihon kindai bungaku daijiten. 6 vols. Kōdansha, 1977–78.

Nihon kindai bungaku taikei. 60 vols. Kadokawa Shoten, 1970–75.

Nihon kokugo daijiten. 20 vols. Shōgakukan, 1972–76.

Nishio Yoshihito. *Akiko, Tomiko, Meiji no atarashii onna—ai to bungaku—*. Yūhikaku, 1986.

Noguchi Takehiko. *Genji monogatari o Edo kara yomu*. Kōdansha, 1985.

Nomura Seiichi. "Yosano Genji to Tanizaki Genji." In *Genji monogatari no sōzō*. Ōfūsha, 1969.

Nonoguchi Ryūho. *Jūjō Genji*. Vols. 11–12 of *Genji monogatari shiryō eiin shūsei*, edited by Nakano Kōichi. Waseda Daigaku Shuppanbu, 1990.

———. *Osana Genji*. Vol. 10 of *Genji monogatari shiryō eiin shūsei*, edited by Nakano Kōichi. Waseda Daigaku Shuppanbu, 1989–90.

Ochi Haruo. *Kindai bungaku no tanjō*. Kōdansha, 1975.

Oda Sugao and Shikada Genzō, eds. *Genji monogatari Kogetsushō*. Vols. 1–8 of *Kōsei hochū kokubun zensho*. Osaka: Kokubunkan, 1890–91.

Ōgi Motoko. "Yosano Akiko to Taishō jaanarizumu." In *Kindai Nihon ni okeru jaanarizumu no seijiteki kinō*, edited by Tanaka Hiroshi, 155–72. Ochanomizu Shobō, 1982.

Oka Kazuo. *Genji monogatari no kisoteki kenkyū*. Revised edition. Tōkyōdō, 1966.

Oka Kazuo ———. *Genji monogatari jiten*. Shunshūsha, 1964.

Okano Takao. *Kindai Nihon meicho kaidai*. Yūmei Shobō, 1962.

Ōno Susumu and Maruya Saiichi. *Nihongo de ichiban daiji na mono*. Chūō Kōronsha, 1990.

Ōno Susumu, Satake Akihiro, and Maeda Kingorō, eds. *Iwanami kogo jiten*. Rev. ed. Iwanami Shoten, 1990.

Onoe Torako. *Genji monogatari tai'i*. Daidōkan, 1911.

Pyle, Kenneth B. *The New Generation in Meiji Japan: Problems of Cultural Identity, 1885–1895*. Stanford: Stanford University Press, 1969.

Rodd, Laurel Rasplica. "Yosano Akiko on Poetic Inspiration." In *The Distant Isle: Studies and Translations of Japanese Literature in Honor of Robert H. Brower*, edited by Thomas Hare, Robert Borgen, and Sharalyn Orbaugh, 409–25. Michigan Monograph Series in Japanese Studies, no. 15. Ann Arbor: Center for Japanese Studies, The University of Michigan, 1996.

———. "'On Poetry,' by Yosano Akiko, with a Selection of Her Poems." In *New Leaves: Studies and Translations of Japanese Literature in Honor of Edward Seidensticker*, edited by Aileen Gatten and Anthony Hood Chambers, 235–46. Michigan Monograph Series in Japanese Studies, no. 11. Ann Arbor: Center for Japanese Studies, The University of Michigan, 1993.

———. "Yosano Akiko and the Taishō Debate over the 'New Woman'." In *Recreating Japanese Women, 1600–1945*, edited by Gail Lee Bernstein, 175–98. Berkeley and Los Angeles: University of California Press, 1991.

————. "Yosano Akiko and the Bunkagakuin: 'Educating Free Individuals'." *Journal of the Association of Teachers of Japanese* 25.1 (April 1991): 75–89.

Rowley, G. G. "Yosano Akiko's Poems 'In Praise of The Tale of Genji'." *Monumenta Nipponica* 56.4 (2001): 439–86.

Rowley, G. G. trans. "Preface to *A New Exegesis of The Tale of Genji*," by Sassa Seisetsu. In *Reading The Tale of Genji*, edited by Thomas Harper and Haruo Shirane, 550–56. New York: Columbia University Press, 2015.

————. "Jendaa to hon'yaku: Yosano Akiko no baai." In *Genji monogatari o kakikaeru: hon'yaku, chūshaku, hon'an*, edited by Terada Sumie, Katō Masayoshi, Hatanaka Chiaki, and Midorikawa Machiko, 174–78. Seikansha, 2018.

————. *In the Shelter of the Pine: A Memoir of Yanagisawa Yoshiyasu and Tokugawa Japan*. New York: Columbia University Press, 2021.

Rubin, Jay. *Injurious to Public Morals: Writers and the Meiji State*. Seattle and London: University of Washington Press, 1984.

Sakanishi, Shio, trans. *Tangled Hair*. Boston: Marshall Jones, 1935.

Sakurai Yūzō. "Genji monogatari kenkyū bunken mokuroku—zasshi kankei—." *Kokugo to kokubungaku*, no. 390 (October 1956): 164–87.

Sansom, G. B. *The Western World and Japan*. 1930. Reprint, Rutland, Vt. & Tokyo: Charles E. Tuttle, 1977.

Sasaki Nobutsuna. "Kotenka jidai no omoide." *Kokugo to kokubungaku* 11.8 (August 1934): 23–31.

————. "Akiko to Ichiyō to wa Meiji no Sei-shi." *Chūō kōron* 27.6 (June 1912): 141–42.

————, ed. *Nihon kagaku taikei*. 10 vols. Kazama Shobō, 1956–64.

Sassa Seisetsu. "Genji monogatari ni egakareta onna." *Jogaku sekai* 14.3 (February 1914): 11–14.

Sassa Seisetsu. "Jo." In *Shinshaku Genji monogatari*, edited by Sassa Seisetsu et al., 1 :1–11. Shinchōsha, 1911.

Sassa Seisetsu, Fujii Shiei, Nunami Keion, and Sasakawa Rinpū. *Shinshaku Genji monogatari*. 2 vols. Shinchōsha, 1911–14.

Satake Kazuhiko. *Zenshaku Midaregami kenkyū*. Yūhōdō, 1957.

Satō Haruo. *Midaregami o yomu*. Kōdansha, 1959.

Satō Haruo.————. *Akiko mandara*. Kōdansha, 1954.

Satō, Hiroaki and Burton Watson, eds. and trans. *From the Country of Eight Islands: An Anthology of Japanese Poetry*. Garden City, NY: Anchor Press/ Doubleday, 1981.

Satō Kazuo. *Yume no hana kanshō: Akiko to sono isshō*. Sōbunsha, 1988.

————. *Maihime hyōshaku*. Meiji Shain, 1978.

Satō Motoko. "Eiga monogatari to Yosano Akiko—'saiwa' toshite no 'Emaki no tame ni' shūsai tanka—." *Shitennōji Kokusai Bukkyō Daigaku Bungakubu kiyō*, no. 15 (1982): 47–66.

Satō Ryōyū. *Midaregami kō*. 1956. Reprint, *Kindai sakka kenkyū sōsho*, vol. 104. Nihon Tosha Sentaa, 1990.

Seidensticker, Edward G., trans. *The Tale of Genji*. 2 vols. New York: Alfred A. Knopf, 1976.

Seki Reiko. *Ichiyō igo no josei hyōgen: sutairu, media, jendaa*. Kanrin Shobō, 2003.

————. "Uta, monogatari, hon'yaku: Yosano Akiko *Shin'yaku Genji monogatari* ga chokumen shita mono." In *Genji monogatari no gendaigoyaku to hon'yaku,* edited by Kawazoe Fusae, 135–64. *Kōza Genji monogatari kenkyū* vol. 12. Ōfū, 2008.

Shepherd, Geoffrey. Introduction to *An Apology for Poetry,* by Sir Philip Sidney. Manchester: Manchester University Press, 1973.

Shigematsu Nobuhiro. *Shinkō Genji monogatari kenkyūshi.* Kazama Shobō, 1961.

Shikitei Sanba. *Ukiyoburo.* Edited by Nakamura Michio. *NKBT63.* Iwanami Shoten, 1957.

Shimauchi Keiji. *Bungō no kotenryoku: Sōseki, Ōgai wa Genji o yonda ka.* Bungei Shunjū, 2002.

Shimizu Fukuko. "Kaisetsu." In *Shusho Genji monogatari Eawase Matsukaze.* Izumi Shain, 1989.

Shimano Enkō. *Ese Genji.* Keigyōsha, 1892.

Shinma Shin'ichi. *Yosano Akiko.* Ōfūsha, 1981.

————. "Bin to Hiroshi, Akiko." *Teihon Ueda Bin zenshū geppō,* no. 8 (1980): 9–12.

————. "Yosano Akiko to *Genji monogatari.*" In *Genji monogatari to sono eikyō: kenkyū to shiryō—kodai bungaku ronsō dairokushū,* edited by Murasaki Shikibu Gakkai, 249–81. Musashino Shain, 1978.

————. "Hiroshi, Akiko to *Nihon koten zenshū.*" *Nihon kosho tsūshin* 41.10 (October 1976):2–3.

————. "Yosano Akiko shū kaisetsu." In *Nihon kindai bungaku taikei,* vol. 17, edited by Sakamoto Masachika, Moriwaki Kazuo, and Mukawa Chūichi, 8–21. Kadokawa Shoten, 1971.

————. *Kindai tankashi ron.* Yūseidō, 1969.

————. "Akiko to Ōgai, Takuboku." In *Kindai tankashi ron.* Yūseidō, 1969.

————. "Akiko to koten bungaku." In *Akiko koten kanshō,* 194–202.

————. "Yosano Akiko to *Genji monogatari.*" In *Genji monogatari kōza,* vol. 1, edited by Tōkyō Daigaku Bungakubu Genji monogatari kenkyūkai, 183–98. Murasaki no Kokyōsha, 1949. Reprinted in *Shinbungei tokuhon: Yosano Akiko.* Kawade Shobō Shinsha, 1991.

Shin'yaku Eiga monogatari, by Yosano Akiko. Reviews of, in:
  Chūō kōron 29.10 (September 1914): 95.
  Mita bungaku 5.9 (September 1914): 160–61.

Shin'yaku Genji monogatari, by Yosano Akiko. Reviews of, in:
  Shinshōsetsu 18.9 (September 1913): 78.
  Hototogisu 15.7 (April 1912): 22.
  Joshi bundan 8.4 (April 1912): 294.
  Bunshō sekai 7.3 (March 1912): 126.
  Shinchō 16.3 (March 1912): 126.
  [Tōkyō] Nichinichi shinbun, 21 March 1912, 4.
  [Tōkyō] Yomiuri shinbun, 11 March 1912, 1.
  Ōsaka jiji shinpō, no. 1540 (26 February 1912): 3.

Shioda Ryōhei. "Katen to Meiji ikō no bungaku." In vol. 14 of *Iwanami kōza Nihon bungakushi,* edited by Iwanami Yūjirō, 1–39. Iwanami Shoten, 1959.

————, ed. *YosanoAkiko.* Vol. 16 of *Nihon bungaku arubamu.* Chikuma Shobō, 1955.

Shively, Donald H. "The Japanization of the Middle Meiji." In *Tradition and Modernization in Japanese Culture*, edited by Donald H. Shively, 77–119. Princeton: Princeton University Press, 1971.

Sōchō. "Renga hikyō shū." In *Renga ronshū ge*, edited by Ijichi Tetsuo. Iwanami Shoten, 1956.

Sonpibunmyaku. *Shintei zōho Kokushi taikei* edition, edited by Kuroita Katsumi. 4 vols. Yoshikawa Kōbunkan, 1980.

Suematsu Kencho. *Genji Monogatari*. 1882. Reprint. Rutland, Vt. and Tokyo: Charles E. Tuttle, 1974.

Sumi, no. 78 (May–June 1989).

Taguchi Keiko, et al., eds. *Shinbungei tokuhon: Yosano Akiko*. Kawade Shobō Shinsha, 1991.

Takeda, Noriko. *A Flowering Word: The Modernist Expression in Stéphane Mallarmé, T. S. Eliot, and Yosano Akiko*. New York: Peter Lang, 2000.

Tamagami Takuya. *Genji monogatari kenkyū*. Kadokawa Shoten, 1966.

Tamura Sachi. "Yosano Akiko yaku *Genji monogatari* shoshi." *Tsurumi Daigaku kiyō*, no. 32 (March 1995): 157–98.

Tamura Takashi. "Shōhitsu no yakushutsu: Akiko *Genji* no saikentō." *Bunken tankyū*, no. 43 (March 2005): 27–38.

Tanabe Seiko. *Chisuji no kurokami: Waga ai no Yosano Akiko*. Bungei Shunjū, 1972.

Tanikawa Shuntarō. *Meiji no shiika*. Gakken, 1981.

Tanizaki Jun'ichiro. *Shin-shin'yaku Genji monogatari*. IO vols. Chūō Kōronsha, 1964–65.

———. *Shin'yaku Genji monogatari fukyūban*. 6 vols. Chūō Kōronsha, 1956–58.

———. *Jun'ichirō yaku Genji monogatari*. 26 vols. Chūō Kōronsha, 1939–41.

Tawara Machi. *Chokoreeto-go yaku Midaregami*. 2 vols. Kawade Shobō Shinsha, 1998.

Tawara Machi and Nomura Sakiko. *Moeru hada o daku koto mo naku jinsei o kataritsuzukete sabishikunai no*. Kawade Shobo Shinsha, 1998.

Teramoto Naohiko. *Genji monogatari juyōshi ronkō (seihen)*. Kazama Shobō, 1970.

Tōhaku 10.10 (October 1939). Special issue "*Shin-shin'yaku Genji monogatari* shuppan kansei."

Tokutomi Sohō, ed. "Shomoku jisshu." *Kokumin no tomo*, no. 48 (supplement: April 1889): 1–18; no. 49 (May 1889): 30–32; no. 54 July 1889): 28–29.

Tōkyō Daigaku hyakunenshi Henshū Iinkai, ed. *Tōkyō Daigaku hyakunenshi: bukyokushi*. Vol. 1. Tōkyō Daigaku Shuppankai, 1986.

Tōkyō Teikoku Daigaku gojōnenshi. 2 vols. Tōkyō Teikoku Daigaku, 1932.

Trede, Melanie. "Terminology and Ideology: Coming to Terms with 'Classicism' in Japanese Art-Historical Writing." In *Critical Perspectives on Classicism in Japanese Painting, 1600–1700*, edited by Elizabeth Lillehoj, 21–52. Honolulu: University of Hawai'i Press, 2004.

Tsubouchi Shōyō. "Harunoya shujin etsu." Introductory essay to *Yabu no uguisu*, by Tanabe Kaho. Kinkōdō, 1888, unnumbered pages before p. 1.

Tsurumi Daigaku Toshokan, ed. *Geirinshiiha: Tsurumi Daigaku Toshokan shinchiku kichōsho toroku*. Yokohama: Tsurumi Daigaku, 1986.

————, ed. *Tsurumi Daigaku Toshokan zō kichō shoten mokuroku.* Yokohama: Tsurumi Daigaku, 1989.

Twine, Nanette. *Language and the Modern State: The Reform of Written Japanese.* London: Routledge, 1991.

Ueda Ayako and Itsumi Kumi, eds. *Yosano Hiroshi Akiko shokanshil: Tenmin bunko zō.* Yagi Shoten, 1983.

Ueda Bin. Untitled preface to *Shin'yaku Genji monogatari,* by Yosano Akiko, 1:1–10.

————. *Teihon Ueda Bin zenshū.* 11 vols. Edited by Yano Hōjin. Kyōiku Shuppan Sentaa, 1980–85.

Ueda, Makoto. *Modern Japanese Poets and the Nature of Literature.* Stanford: Stanford University Press, 1983.

Ukiyo-e sanbyakunen meisakuten. Nihon Keizai Shinbunsha, 1979.

Vendler, Helen. *The Music of What Happens.* Cambridge: Harvard University Press, 1988.

Wada Hidematsu. "Koten kōshūka jidai." *Kokugo to kokubungaku* 11.8 (August 1934): 32–39.

Wada Hidematsu and Satō Kyū. *Eiga monogatari shōkai.* 17 vols. Meiji Shoin, 1899–1907.

Wakita Haruko, trans. G. G. Rowley. "The Japanese Woman in the Premodern Merchant Household." *Women's History Review* 19.2 (2010): 259–82.

Walthall, Anne. *The Weak Body of a Useless Woman: Matsuo Taseko and the Meiji Revolution.* Chicago: Chicago University Press, 1998.

Watanabe Jun'ichi. *Kimi mo kokuriko ware mo kokuriko—Yosano Tekkan, Akiko fusai no shōgai—.* 2 vols. Bungei Shunjū, 1996.

Watson, Burton. *Early Chinese Literature.* New York: Columbia University Press, 1962.

Woolf, Virginia. "The *Tale of Genji:* The First Volume of Mr. Arthur Waley's Translation of a Great Japanese Novel by the Lady Murasaki." *Vogue* 66.2 (July 1925): 53, 80.

Yamamoto Chie. *Yama no ugoku hi kitaru—hyōden Yosano Akiko.* Ōtsuki Shoten, 1986.

Yamamoto Masahide. "Genbun'itchi." In *Nihon kindai bungaku daijiten,* vol. 4, 140–42. Kōdansha, 1977.

————. "Kindai kōgobuntai no seiritsu to tenkai." In *Kōza Nihon bungaku,* vol. 9, 139–61. Sanseidō, 1969.

Yangu redei 15.5 (8 March 1977).

Yosano Akiko—sono shōgai to sakuhin—. Edited by Sakai Hakubutsukan. Sakai: Sakai Hakubutsukan, 1991.

Yosano Hikaru. *Akiko to Hiroshi no omoide.* Kyoto: Shibunkaku Shuppan, 1991.

Yosano Hiroshi, Masamune Atsuo, and Yosano Akiko. "Nihon koten zenshū kankō shushi." *Myōjō,* 2nd ser., 7.3 (September 1925): 130–31.

Yosano Shigeru. *En naki tokei.* Saika Shobō, 1948.

Yosano Tekkan. "Nihon o saru uta." *Myōjō,* no. 10 (January 1901).

Yosano Uchiko. *Murasakigusa—haha Akiko to satogo no watakushi.* Shintōsha, 1967.

Yuasa Mitsuo. "Akiko *Genji* to Kanao Bun'endō." *Nihon kosho tsūshin* 39.2 (February 1974): 5–6.

Zenshū sōsho sōran: shinteiban. Edited by Shoshi Kenkyū Konwakai. Yagi Shoten, 1983.

Index

Abe Tomoji, 166n.60
Amayo monogatari damikotoba by Katō
  Umaki, 28
Andō Tameakira, 32, 159, 160
Ansei unequal treaties, 67
Arishima Ikuma, 165
Arishima Takeo, 7, 57, 165
Arisugawa, Prince, 64
Asada Sada, 6n.13
Asakasha, 155
Atsumi Ikuko, 10

Bakin. *See* Kyokutei Bakin
Ban Kōkei, 97
Beichman, Janine, 8n.19, 10, 85n.21,
  167n.61
Bowring, Richard, 20n.7–9, 25, 105
Bungakkai, 40, 81, 82, 142, 199
Bungei kurabu, 2, 74
Bunka Gakuin, 83, 146, 147, 154, 166
bushidō, 71–72

canon, 15, 25, 47, 58, 60, 63–66, 75,
  78n.5, 91n.43, 155–156, 168; Akiko's
  place in, 91n.43; of *kokugaku*, 61–62; of
  Nihon koten zenshū, 153–154; *See also*
  classics; *koten*
Chūō kōron, 87, 88, 91, 96n.54,
  99n.6, 149; special issue on Akiko, 91
Chūō Kōronsha, 30n.38, 74n.49,
  163–164, 170n.3, 174n.10, 193n.3
classics, and national identity, 60–62,
  72; custodianship of, 23, 68, 70–71;
  demand for, 25; renewal of interest
  in, 60; translations of, *see* translation.
  See also canon; *koten*

Classics Training Course. *See Koten
  kōshū–ka*
colloquial style. *See genbun'itchi* style
Cranston, Edwin A., 5–6n.10, 8n.19, 11

Daini no Sanmi, 157, 159, 192, 201,
  203, 204

earthquakes, of 1 September 1923, 146
Eco, Umberto, 1

Fujita Tokutarō, 26–27, 57n.2, 97, 119, 156,
  157n.33
Fujiwara no Kintō, 20
Fujiwara no Michinaga, 17n.2, 20,
  21n.12, 156, 158
Fujiwara no Nobutaka, 3
Fujiwara no Yorimichi, 157, 203
Fujiwara Shunzei, 22–23
Fujiwara Teika, 21–22
Fujo no kagami by Kimura
  Akebono, 46
Fujo shinbun, 161

genbun'itchi style, 74–75, 94, 100, 103, 105,
  119, 148, 198; Akiko'swriting in, 75, 94;
  Genji as *genbun'itchi*, 94, 148; style of
  Shin'yaku as, 94, 96, 102, 105; style of
  Shin-shin'yaku as, 200–202
gendaigoyaku. *See* translation
Genji monogatari, and Confucianism,
  22, 30–31; and prostitutes, 28n.34,
  33, 34; as classic, 18, 21–23, 36, 96,
  119, 168–169, 186–187; as cultural
  scripture, 56, 68; as romance,

229

Nagai Kafū, 57
Nakajima Hirotari, 126–127n.3
Nakajima Utako, 44
Nakazawa Hiromitsu, 94, 99, 160, 200n.2, 201
National Learning. *See kokugaku*
National Learning scholars. *See kokugakusha*
National Literature. *See kokubungaku*
National Literature scholars. *See kokubungakusha*
naturalist literature. *See shizenshugi bungaku*
Nerval, Gérard de. *See* Labrunie, Gérard
Nihon bungaku zensho, 58, 64, 65, 66n.30, 143n.7, 154
Nihon koten zenshū, 14, 153–156, 162, 164, 196
ninjō (human emotions), 47, 73
Nise murasaki inaka Genji, 27, 65
Nitobe Inazō, 146
Noguchi Takehiko, 27, 33n.49
Nonoguchi Ryūho, 26
Numata Gabimaru, 33

Ochiai Naobumi, 58n.7, 64, 80n.8, 143n.7, 154–155, 194
Ōgimachi Machiko, 28, 34
Oka Kazuo, 159, 160
Okinagusa by Kanzawa Tokō, 30
Ono no Komachi, 11
Onoe Torako, 58n.8, 100–101
Ozaki Kōyō, 65, 188–189

People's Rights movement, 64
Pitt, William, first earl of Chatham, 1
Po Chü-i, 41, 126n.3
poetry, importance in Meiji period, 88, 155

reading, Edo period, 29, 34
reading, Meiji period, 50
Rodin, Auguste, 77, 86n.25, 200
Rubin, Jay, 74n.49, 90n.42, 91n.44
Russo–Japanese War, 72, 74, 88–89
Ryūtei Tanehiko, 27, 37, 65

Saganoya Omuro, 47
Sakai, 5, 38, 40–42, 52, 55, 80, 130
Sanbōe, 18, 19n.4
Santō Kyōden, 33, 47
Sarashina diarist. *See* Sugawara no Takasue no musume
Sarashina nikki, 22, 77n.1, 204
Sasaki Hirotsuna, 46n.33
Sasaki "Masako," 46, 47
Sasaki Nobutsuna, 46n.33, 48, 61n.18, 78n.4, 87n.30, 88, 156
Sassa Seisetsu, 56, 68–74, 78, 92, 101, 158; *see also Shinshaku Genji monogatari*
Satō Haruo, 8n.19, 9n.20, 41, 122n.1, 165, 166
Satō Kyū, 81, 194
Satomura Jōha, 2n.3
Seirō hiru no sekai: Nishiki no ura by, 33
Santō Kyōden, 33
Seiyōken Restaurant, 165
shajitsu (realism), 73
Shiga Shigetaka, 66
Shigarami zōshi, 39, 46
Shikitei Sanba, 29, 30n.38
Shimada Utako, 49
Shinma Shin'ichi, 7n.15, 38n.4, 40n.12, 42n.19, 84n.19, 88, 90n.39, 99n.5, 149n.14, 154n.25, 156n.31, 157n.35, 185n.16
Shinpen shishi by Masuda Yukinobu, 58n.9, 100
Shinseisha, 154–155
Shinshaku Genji monogatari, 68–69, 92, 101, 187n.17; editors of, 65; language of, 69, 92–94; preface to, 65–68
Shin-shin'yaku Genji monogatari, 94, 161; absence of omissions, 129–130, 153; afterword to, 155, 157, 188–200; Akiko's view of, 161–162; celebrations for, 165; compared with other translations, 116n.2, 130, 153, 159n.3, 174; contemporary views of, 169, 170; edition of *Genji* used, 162n.48;

ABOUT THE AUTHOR

G. G. Rowley teaches English and Japanese literature at Waseda University in Tokyo. She has written and/or translated several biographies of Japanese women, including *An Imperial Concubine's Tale*, Masuda Sayo's *Autobiography of a Geisha*, and Ōgimachi Machiko's *In the Shelter of the Pine*.